THE WAY

A HAWAIIAN STORY OF GROWTH, RELATIONSHIPS, & VOLLEYBALL

CHRISTOPHER AUSTIN

D1468949

Disclaimer: Within this book, "Hawaiians" does not singularly refer to a people of Hawaiian blood/ancestry, as it often does on the island of Hawai'i. In addition, this book uses "Hawaiians" as a label for one particular team from the state of Hawai'i.

Copyright © 2016 by Christopher Austin

All rights reserved. No part of this book may be reproduced, distributed, or transmitted in any form or by any means without the prior written consent of the author, excepting brief quotations used in reviews.

For permission requests or purchasing information visit www. chrispaustin.com

This is a work of creative non-fiction. Information and events retold in this book are based on the author's memory and recollections of interviews, and may not be presented with exact accuracy.

In some cases certain events have been fictionalized in varying degrees to fill in gaps or to provide additional detail. The author and the editor do not assume and hereby disclaim any liability to any party for any loss or damage caused by errors or emissions, or the use or misuse of information contained in this book. Names, place names, brands, and trademarks mentioned in this book are used to aid narration and we recognize they are the property of the trademark holder.

Printed in the United States of America

ISBN 978-0-9976371-0-6 (HC)
ISBN 978-0-9976371-1-3 (PB)
ISBN 978-0-9976371-2-0 (eBook)
ISBN 978-0-9976371-3-7 (Audio)

Praises Of The Way

"Finally, a literary creation that will spread a deeper appreciation of the sport to the general public. This group's revolutionary training style is a MUST-READ! Volleyball is knocking; this book will burst it through the door."

— DOUG BEAL, CEO of USA Volleyball

"Riveting! Austin perfectly blends the growth process of an extraordinary community of young athletes with an intimate look at their cultural and family dynamics. *The Way* makes the close-knit circle of volleyball accessible to the rest of us, as we get the opportunity at a sneak peak into the legendary Ka Ulukoa."

— STEVE JOHNSON, 2X Amazon.com Best Seller & LA Times Best Seller
If You're Not Out Selling You're Being Outsold

"Chris Austin was a trial-blazing Setter and two-time NCAA champion who consistently displayed a knack for making the important play. His compelling work here chronicling a special group of young volleyball players is his latest assist."

— BARRY FAULKNER, LA Times Community News Sportswriter

"A really enjoyable inside look at the next generation's volleyball stars as they developed through the junior ranks. Austin has great insight from the reward of playing top-level competition. His book provides drama, excitement, and the process to creating a championship team."

— LEE FEINSWOG, VolleyballMag.com

For Bonnie, facilitator of what should be impossible

For the person who is told that they can't do it

For the permanent Growth of the Game

BASED ON A TRUE STORY

Contents

Diagram Of A Court

An indoor volleyball court is 900 square feet in total, 30ft X 30ft on each half of the net.

Preface - Water

I hope I never forget the way that I felt the first time I saw them compete. It was like a river flowing full of unmatched cohesion. Poetry in motion wouldn't even be a title that gave it justice. It was like water. It was as if something unfamiliar was injected into my DNA and my eyes would not look away. My eyes could not look away.

January 14, 2011 was the day, and it was a day of firsts for me. I was only 19 years old and I had no idea where the experience would take me. I had an idea of where I wanted to go, but that, I could not imagine. The best part about seeing that team from Hawai'i was that they weren't in direct competition with my team. My group and their group were both teams of 15-year-olds, in high school, but our stories could not have been more separate.

My team was in its first season of organized playing. Many of my athletes were in their first year of trying a sport at all. It was also my first time head coaching a male team. Like I said, my team was not in the same conversation with this group from Hawai'i, yet. I caught myself straying to their court any free moment that I got during the tournament. I was on their court to steal — there to steal knowledge, information, and tendencies. I wanted it all. In the most respectful way possible, I wanted to break them down. There was something so special about that team that it would have me in bed at night during the tournament, writing down my thoughts on a notepad. Unfortunately, that tournament ended two days later and I would not see that group again for a little while. Their mark was imprinted on me, though. Anytime I was in an athletic setting from that point on, their imprint was nearby. In my own observations, and every time that I was asked for a comparison of the best, that team from Hawai'i came to mind.

When I thought about the state of Hawai'i, I remembered the culture that I experienced living there in my first semester of college just one year earlier. Attending the University of Hawai'i at Manoa, I was exposed to the history and the island's everlasting passion for volleyball. Great names from the men's side, like Clay Stanley and Allen Allen, played there at UH. And historical names, like Robin Ah Mow-Santos and Kim Willoughby, played there under Hall Of Fame Coach, Dave Shoji. As my memory bank of the sports world was becoming more complete, I also learned about the memorable players who were from Hawai'i, like Kevin Wong, Stein Metzger, Lindsey Berg, Tony Ching, Kanani Danielson, Sean Scott, and so many more. Spending some time there, it was easy to see how the volleyball culture could be infectious. Along with its

Mainland neighbor, California, Hawai'i was a breeding ground for many of the best who played the game. But, what I witnessed in Anaheim on January 14, 2011 was something different from a good athlete who became a good player growing up surrounded by volleyball.

FAST FORWARD

Four years later, I was in Houston, Texas, just hours away from my birthplace. I knew the scene all too well. In a convention center that was heating up, I had the opportunity to watch Hawai'i in their final playoff match. Call it a rivalry match, if you would like. It was a battle of two extremes and it was worth the price of admission that Tuesday in July. That morning had a routine similar to the mornings before it. It had a build similar to the playoff matches before it. One could only hope for a result that was similar. The result proved itself to be similar, yet not identical. When it was over, the world did not stop rotating, the sun did not stop shining, but the celebration was trailed by a moment of silence for a good match, and a better group of young men.

After the match, I remember sitting in that convention center next to my long time friend, John Xie, in my own moment of silence, thinking about what those guys had provided for me from a distance. I thought about what they'd given me that they may never even realize had been passed on: years of curiosity; they put me through trial and error. For me, the experience was a time capsule of learning from a group that would not have a duplicate. This is their story.

Chapter 1 - `Ohana

Unrelated by blood, these four had a gift to present to the world. They all held their own piece of the islands of Hawaii.

LARRY

On Oahu, in the lovely Kaimuki area of Honolulu, was Larry Masani Tuileta Junior. After being born full Polynesian on September 24th, 1995 at Queens Hospital, he was taken straight to his grandparents' house in Kaimuki, where his mother, Maile Thiim Tuileta, his father, Larry Tuileta Senior, he, and the three oldest of his seven total siblings lived. The house was split into two pieces like a duplex and his extended family occupied the second half. Small living quarters for a large bundle of people created Larry Junior's first family atmosphere.

Growing up in the Tuileta family, Larry Junior spent the majority of his time at Fort Derussy Beach in Honolulu. There wasn't much else to do for an infant outside of being where his family was. His mom did most of the talking, most of the socializing, and most of the shot calling. She was tough on Larry Junior, even in his youngest years of life. Yet, she was always upfront and direct, whether it was in private occasions or in public. More than anything else, she was caring. Compassion was a trait that Larry Junior learned to count on from his father as well. Larry Senior, who was more of the quiet father who chose his moments and his words carefully, never fell short of his role. He was conservative and was not overbearing, and he could find the most opportune timing to deliver his advice and his serious conversations. Larry Junior was raised in a large family with many branches to it. The road to the end destination was never the easiest with so many siblings, so many family members, and so little money to go around.

Larry Senior was working in the construction business while Maile was staying at home. By the time that Larry Junior was beginning preschool at Merry-Go-Round Pre-K, Maile had the added responsibility of parenting two more kids, in addition to Larry Junior's three older siblings, Mabeleen, Kaila, and Kylee. Maile gave birth to a girl, Kiani, and a boy, Larson, two years later.

Every year, since before Larry Junior was born, the family packed up on 4th of July morning and cruised down to Fort Derussy Beach. It was a family tradition not to be missed. Volleyball, too, was tradition in the Tuileta family. Larry Junior was constantly with his dad. So often, local players caught sight of Larry Senior with his son and told the younger Larry grandiose stories of how good his dad was—back in the day. Larry Senior played at the Open-level on the beach, as well as indoor, for over a decade.

The locals said, "Your daddy here, he took over matches with his physicality. And the way his presence consumed the court? Forget about it."

Larry Junior was around so often that he took on the shape of his dad with his curly hair and caramel brown complexion. His physique was rock solid since exiting the womb. It wasn't long before all the locals started calling Larry Junior by his new nickname, Tui.

His large family spent loads of time in parks and outdoors. Tui naturally dabbled in everything athletic, whether it was tossing the baseball, shooting the basketball, bumping the volleyball, throwing the football, or dribbling the soccer ball. There were few sports to which he was not exposed. Larry Senior and Maile were tough.

"Try your hardest, boy! Don't be out here wasting people's time!" they shouted to Tui.

However, playing sports wasn't forced. There wasn't even an emphasis placed on the continuation of sports for Tui. He enrolled in kindergarten at Wai'alae Elementary, an easy transition for him, considering he was accustomed to kids around his household all the time. Tui enjoyed school, but he was sports-minded, and the times he was practicing sports were the best times in his mind.

As part of learning the Hawaiian culture, Tui added another hobby to his list of practices. He learned to dance with fire knives. Fire-knife dancing was introduced in Samoan culture as a tradition representing grace and no fear. The tradition had towels attached to a pair of machete knives that were lit on fire and spun, twisted, and turned for the excitement of spectators. Fire-knife dancing was something that Tui latched onto with purpose because he began to dive into a heap of information on the insides and outsides of Polynesian culture. The gap was not as big as one could imagine from his start, dancing with sticks and towels, to his progression into sharp knives and real flames. What he enjoyed most was that fire-knife dancing allowed him to explore more of the Polynesian culture, and his roots, of which he would seldom hear from his father.

The last of Tui's seven siblings, Larae and Nive, were born. In the 3rd grade, along with his parents and his siblings, Tui moved away from his grandparents' house, just down the road to Metcalf Street. Some things changed. Tui's intrigue for sports didn't. He played often. His dad began to take him down to Fort Derussy on the weekends. For a short while, he'd watch volleyball from the side and play *Pepper* with a partner.

His muscles matured swiftly and while he was short in comparison, his dad felt his body could hold up and invited him, "Hey Tui, you ready? Come on the court and get a game in."

Tui darted on without hesitating. Yet, sports were not viewed as something that could pay the bills for the Tuiletas, until Tui's oldest sister, Keila, received an offer to a small school in Texas called Clarendon College. Larry Senior and Maile saw a new light that had the potential to relieve a financial burden from the family.

Senior said to his wife, "If we go about things the right way, perhaps sports could take the kids into college."

EVAN

He was the oldest of the Enriques boys birthed by Guy and Julie together. The strands of his silky brown hair seemed to sit perfectly atop his head. Residing on the Big Island of Hawaii, with an ocean between his island and the island of Oahu, was Evan Guy Enriques. Born November 2nd, 1995, his first experiences of life happened at his family's house in Kona. His father, Guy, was half-Filipino, one-quarter Chinese, and one-quarter Hawaiian. His mother, Julie, was a tall Norwegian, Irish, and German woman from Gresham. Guy and Julie owned a t-shirt shop right on the sand in Punalu'u, miles down the road from their home in Kona.

Evan's oldest sibling was his half-brother, Cory, from his dad. His younger brother, Emmett, ran around on the beach with Evan near the playpen outside of the t-shirt shop, and snuck away to swim in the ocean every opportunity that came along. Three years from Evan and two years from Emmett were their youngest brothers, twins, Addie and Avery. Evan's mother, who played indoor college volleyball at Oregon State, always wanted to be a part of her kids' lives and was active in all of their activities. From the beginning of her first boy's life, Julie was involved. She had the video camera at every stagnant moment. She woke up every morning to cook breakfast for her sons. She held everything together and polished every mess back to mint condition.

His father attended the University of Hawai'i at Hilo on a full basketball scholarship, before coaching girls' volleyball at Oregon State University on the Mainland. Both locations influenced Guy to appreciate the outdoors. He taught Evan the outdoor lifestyle, like how to swim and how to fish. Evan spent all of his time near the water. Fishing quickly became what Evan latched onto as a boy.

"Guy frequently said to Evan, "Giving something to get in return.""

In 2001, the Enriques family moved to a new residence in Punalu'u. They constantly had guests over to their new home, usually family. Evan's Hawaiian aunties and uncles were regular visitors. His Auntie Myra Samida was his caretaker as a child when his parents weren't home. She provided a motherly care for Evan and his brothers. Myra's husband, Uncle Cyrus Samida, had been the guidance instructor and the disciplinarian for Evan's family every time that he was near.

"Keep screwing around, and that pillow is coming upside your head," he'd say. Or, "You think it's funny? Cross that line again and that Tabasco sauce will be on your tongue."

Discipline was his deal and respect was a mandatory.

Around the time the twins were born, Evan enrolled in Montessori Preschool. Naturally, Guy and Julie relied on Evan to help raise his youngest brothers, just as he did with Emmett.

By the time Evan began Kindergarten at Ka'u Elementary, he'd developed a reputation around the Big Island. From the earliest years of his life he was going out onto the boat with his dad and following Guy around with the fishing bag. Evan was constantly running around the beach with his siblings, and even without the rest of the Enriques crew, he was easily recognized as Guy's son. That was the reputation he developed. Whatever Guy was doing, Evan was doing.

There was an apparent sibling rivalry with the Enriques boys. Let Evan tell the story and he was just a bystander during the trouble. Regardless, there was endless arguing between them, wrestling matches, and a disturbance of peace in the least general sense. Car rides were the worst. Guy would get so fed up that he'd stop the car and tell them all to get out and walk home. It didn't make a difference whether they were a five-minute, or a two-hour walk from home. Although the Big Island of Hawaii was not big enough for a resident to get legitimately lost, Guy would always eventually turn back and pick them up — only for his moment of understanding and sorrow to disappear with the sound of continued arguing from his sons.

The Enriques boys may not have gotten along, but they did spend large amounts of time together and they found new ways to raise the hairs on their parents' necks. All four of Guy and Julie's boys were afraid of the dark. So when they acted up, Guy rounded them up at night and made them go outside to run around the house or down the street and back—that being perhaps one of the few moments when teamwork showed. Emmett, Addie, and Avery all lined up behind Evan and told him that he had to go first, and they'd follow. There were not enough strategies in a lifetime for Guy to use on his *rascal sons. He used the paddle on their butts; they got the *slippah on their rears, and the belt on their backsides. When there was no car to kick them out of, Dad would make them sleep outside on the porch. Eventually he always folded and called them back into the house.

In one of his more popular solutions, Guy broke out the *Rock 'Em Sock 'Em Bopper* gloves.

"You want to fight and argue all the time? Then here, box it out," he said, completely serious.

His sons saw it as a joke and an opportunity to give each other lickings, instead of getting them from Dad. They laughed. Guy got mad. No matter what trials the boys went through together, Evan was happy about having brothers because he had friends to play with and people to talk to. He understood what the picture looked like for those without siblings.

Entering the 1st grade, Evan applied to Kamehameha Schools Hawai'i, and was accepted. That started the trend of an early wake-up at 5am, a quick shower and breakfast, followed by a 20-minute walk to the bus stop, on to an hour and a half ride to school to make the 8am bell. Evan was the illustration of a good student. He did all of his work on time or early. Most notably, he stayed out of trouble. Outside of the classroom, Evan also showed an outgoing side, which made him successful at making friends.

Volleyball started as soon as Evan could stand on his own two feet. He began playing indoors, hacking the volleyball around with the team managers at Kamehameha Hawai'i, where his dad became the head coach of the *varsity team that season. Unless he had plans to be fishing, Evan had no problem being in the gym. He really had no problem being anywhere that his parents asked him to be.

Volleyball was fun right away, and although his parents had a background with the sport, it was not something they forced upon him. In reality, there wasn't much of his time spent practicing. The extent of his athletic training was being at his dad's practices and playing *Pepper* with the team managers, accompanied by the occasional comment from his mom and dad about volleyball. Evan did enjoy watching the game, though. Paying attention to Evan at six or seven years old, anyone who bothered to look could see that he was taking in information from what he was watching. His mind was turning.

He'd ask Guy and Julie, "When does the team play next?" or, "What time is practice today?"

That left a smile on Guy's face, but he thought it better that he didn't push his son towards the sport at all.

SKYLAN

April 9th, 1996 at Queens Medical Center in Honolulu, Arlene and Dave Engleman gave birth to a boy, Skylan Kelly Kulani Engleman. Arlene was from Manila and worked as a medical biller. Dave, from Kalihi Honolulu, also worked as a medical biller. The drive into the west side of town was a long two hours each way. Skylan was taken from the hospital to a small home with a dirt yard, one purebred dog and a pit-bull mix, owned by his grandparents. Only two years later, he moved with his mom, dad, and grandparents into his dad's hometown of Kalihi in Honolulu.

Skylan, Arlene, and Dave shared the new house with their immediate family, as well as extended family. A cousin, older by six years, and another, older by four, were the only-child's primary companions. Until Skylan's younger brother by two years, Seyj, was born, his cousins used their imaginations in antagonizing the only-child, and made him feel like a younger brother. Living inside of a packed house, they found their fun in obscure forms, throwing rocks at each other outside. Although he couldn't count on his fingers and toes the *yellings that he took each week for breaking shelves and glass and expensive China, he was usually able to feel the love from his family.

Skylan's upbringing was not without challenges, though. A burden weighing on Arlene and Dave strained them to a divorce. Then, Arlene Salvador created her own medical billing business, forcing her to work ten-hour days, thus seeing her boys less often.

Preschool began in Kalihi at Early Education for Skylan. Each morning his mom made the time to drive him by the mini-mart for breakfast. Dressed in his oversized pre-k outfit, drowning his tiny brown body, he hopped out of Arlene's car to grab a juice box, a local favorite, *Musubi (a grilled piece of spam on top of a block of rice, wrapped in dried seaweed), and one pastry.

"Please, Mom, it leaves the sweet taste in my mouth," he persuaded her.

Skylan was rascal himself, excusing himself from singing and dancing with the other students at lunchtime. Instead, he got busted for pinching and punching his peers. One night, Skylan woke up in his house and walked from his crowded room. He put on his grandfather's slippahs, opened the front door, and walked off into the night, alone. Dave found his eldest son's empty bed and panicked. He called Arlene.

"Hello?" she answered sleepily.

"Arlene, wake up, it's Dave. Skylan is missing."

Arlene shot out of bed and rushed over to her ex-husband's home. Together they searched for hours, without luck. They found him later, on a curb near a neighborhood party, chewing on grapes.

That was as far as it needed to go. Arlene and Dave, who'd been separated for five years, decided to tie their knot back together. Both Arlene and Dave were street smart and they were a good team in raising their boys. Arlene was the brains and put her emphasis largely on education. Dave was the brawn of their operation and knew the lay of the land in Hawai'i. Skylan took an early notice that the academic path he was on might not have been as successful as he'd hoped.

With Skylan not even scraping satisfactory marks from his teacher, his father told him, "Work ethic now translates to work ethic later in life. You need to get on the right track."

The Englemans had decided to place Skylan into kindergarten at Kapālama Elementary, a blue ribbon school that served as a nice educational upgrade for their son. Skylan fancied himself brighter than his peers, on the lone fact that he could spell *because*. He showed off his organization with new pencils and fresh markers and crisp folders for class. Unfortunately, his teachers discovered a setback. From the 1st grade through the 3rd grade, they required Skylan to enroll in developmental English classes, in order to change his inbred language of Hawaiian *Pidgin to proper American English. He enjoyed his time at school so much because outside of Kapālama Elementary he lacked the feeling of belonging.

Skylan came from a family that enjoyed playing volleyball. Barely exceeding five feet in height, Arlene played all the way up to being eight months pregnant with Skylan. Old videos magnified his memories of running around the gym in diapers when his dad played as an undersized *Middle Blocker at the height of 6'1". When they weren't working as medical billers, his mom and dad constantly cruised to McKinley High School to play weekend tournaments, while Skylan ran around the parking lot outside playing hide-and-seek in the daylight. As he got older, his mom made it mandatory-optional for him to stay in and watch the volleyball. This was the '90s, a time when the level of volleyball competition was peaking in Hawai'i.

"It seems like everyone is into the sport right now," Arlene said to her son, trying to be persuasive.

He was just amazed at how fast the ball went. Yet still, he didn't like volleyball very much. After spending so much time playing at McKinley, the Engleman family found a spot closer to home that they could frequent: Susannah Wesley, a community turn-around center for delinquent youth. There was a gym there, so the Englemans started playing there with the B and A level *(see glossary for rankings)* players on Mondays and Thursdays.

When the family was at Susannah Wesley, Skylan went from being a bored spectator to creating his own action on the side. He learned to *dig, *set, and *spike with his feet on the ground, playing *Pepper* with whomever he could find in between his parents' *points. Regardless of how informal it was, when Skylan began to practice volleyball, he began to feel more accepted by his father. That was an important feeling for him because of the fact that he had no trade of his own. The seeds to the flower of his dad's acceptance being planted were enough reason for Skylan to continue trying to learn volleyball, no matter what his own feelings on the sport were.

His family moved again, just down the street in Kalihi. Susannah Wesley was just as close as before, so Arlene and Dave continued to play there on Mondays and Thursdays. By default, Skylan was taken along. Skylan's first opportunity to step onto the court came in a six-on-six game of volleyball. *This is the best and worst mistake that I have ever made*, he thought to himself. He stepped onto the court and Dave verbally plowed into him.

"You've gotta dig that ball, Knucklehead! You couldn't get that easy ball? Why did I even let you step on the court?" Dave's word dug into Skylan. His mother told Skylan to just leave the court, likely with the intention of sparing him any further hurt feelings. But Dave made him stay there, and play, and take the punishment.

Skylan didn't want to travel to the rec league to play anymore. His dad said, "Suck it up! Get in the car. You are coming."

The transition was hard for Skylan. He went from having nothing to really call his own and feeling a lack of acceptance from those closest to him, to having found something that sparked the interest of his parents and feeling inadequate any time that he didn't perform to the standard of his father. An emotional sacrifice was required — to show up and play and learn through trial and error. To Skylan, the emotional toll was worth the foreign feeling of belonging.

Micah

Born April 16, 1997 in Castle Hospital in Kailua was Micah Ma'a, the only son of Pono Ma'a and Lisa Strand Ma'a. Micah lived in the dorms of Kamehameha Hawai'i's sister school on Oahu, Kamehameha Kapālama. On the island, a fitting synonym for a *rascal* could be Micah Ma'a. His parents ran a tight ship at the house. That was necessary for a family that had their parenting experience from an outgoing and adventurous girl as their eldest child, and expected from a father at the head of the household, like Pono, who came from a family with three girls in it. Micah also had three sisters, Misty, Mehana, and Maluhia.

His father worked at the school as a gym cleaner before becoming a dorm advisor. Born and raised on the island, Pono was taught baseball by his father, Thomas Ma'a. Pono went to the Little League World Series and was a star through high school at Kamehameha Schools Kapālama Campus in baseball, basketball, and volleyball. Micah's Grandpa Thomas made Pono breakfast every morning, until Pono was drafted by the *Saint Louis Cardinals* Major League Baseball organization and made the decision not to go. After that, Grandpa Thomas never made Pono breakfast again.

Pono and Lisa met attending the University of Hawaii at Manoa, where Lisa played on the historical women's volleyball team. The first time Pono saw her at school, he tightened up his black *Kamehameha Warriors* hat, cleaned his pearly white teeth, and approached her. Unfortunately, Lisa didn't go for it. That was until she went to a University of Hawaii Men's Volleyball match and saw that Pono was on the team and was, "an above average kind of cute." Instead of baseball, he chose to pursue volleyball. There he was heavily decorated and went on to play professionally overseas, and with the USA Volleyball Men's National Team.

Lisa was raised on the Mainland in Santa Barbara, California. She made the decision to play volleyball at UH Manoa and came away with two NCAA Championships. After graduating, she joined the Association of Volleyball Professional Beach Tour, better known as the AVP. And after his years spent on the indoor scene, Pono also made the transition to beach on the AVP. Lisa swore that she was the one who taught her husband how to play beach volleyball.

From the youngest years of his life, Micah ran and jumped and played with no regard for the danger that could be involved in his actions. Most decisions were made impulsively. He grew up in the dorms at Kamehameha with his dad, the disciplinarian, his mom, the kind hearted tag-team enforcer, and his older sister, Misty. The Ma'as kept their routines through the birth of Micah's younger sister, Mehana. Every night the family played a card game, Hanafuda. Micah threw a fit if the game turned and things didn't work out in his favor. By the time he found out that his youngest sister, Maluhia, was going to be born a girl, he flipped out. A lamp was broken; loads of books were knocked off the shelves; he ran amuck. It was things like that that earned the young Micah his spankings. He took his *lickings from both mom and dad.

His mom said often, "In this family, Micah, a negative reaction because of something that is affecting just yourself, and not the others around you, is selfish."

Although selfish behavior was unacceptable, Pono and Lisa did understand Micah's predicament. He was a young boy, with no other boys in his family. Reality was that Micah was placed into a situation where most kids would feel lacking in companionship. Pono believed he understood how to fill that void for Micah. Every morning in the car, on the way to wherever they were going, whether it was just Micah or Micah and his sisters, Pono would talk. He would talk about the stories of his life and the stories of their lives. He talked about the structure and strength in the old concepts of Hawaiian culture. Pono would talk about sports and Pono would talk about art. He would just talk. No radio, no games, no phones, only listening. This was Micah's favorite time because he connected with his father through stories.

Talking story was a favorite time for Pono as well, because Micah was quiet and he knew that he wasn't in any trouble. Sports were where Micah took the opportunity to expend his energy. Lisa trained all of her kids in soccer, baseball, and volleyball. She was such an accomplished athlete herself that they had no struggle using her as a coach, even if they did share a dinner table. Being a product of Pono and Lisa's genes, Micah wasted little time becoming a successful athlete. The games came naturally to him. The problem was, for Micah, everything had to be a competition.

Following his father's baseball path, Micah started playing on the tee-ball team. It wasn't long before he could step up to the plate, flick the long uncombed hair out of his face, and use his scrawny arms to launch home runs over the short back fence. Micah found himself bored after excelling at what took his peers so long to master. His creativity led him to start the habit of bunting short at the plate, getting on base, and then playing *pickle until he coaxed the other team into allowing him to score at home plate. It was reminiscent of watching Benny "The Jet" Rodriguez in an old *Sandlot* movie.

Lisa signed her son up for a youth soccer league. The youth league played games on the weekends. Often, before the first half was even complete, Micah would reach the goal limit that an individual was allowed. Therefore, his coach was forced to put him at the net as goalie for the rest of the game. Problem solved. Until Micah started shooting at the opponent's goal from his own. There were no limits and no mercy to his competitiveness as a child.

As Micah finished preschool at Central Union and Hanahauoli, his parents planned to enroll him into elementary. In Hawaii, where children attend even elementary school was an important decision for their future. It was a topic for conversation throughout the island for weeks and sometimes months. Kamehameha was a historic name and a historic academic institution on the island. It was also the most financially successful place anywhere on the Hawaiian Islands. The school required applications for admission, and excellence beyond its necessity for quality grades. A requirement to be accepted was that Hawaiian blood runs through the students' veins. Micah was accepted into Kamehameha Schools Kapālama for kindergarten.

Volleyball began for Micah in the dorm with balloons. Along with being the dorm advisor at Kamehameha Kapālama, Pono began helping with the high school's volleyball team. When Micah was finished with school for the day, his ride home had volleyball practice. So that's where Micah was, alongside his dad, spending more time in the gym. Wherever Pono went, Micah went. That was the male companionship that he had available. Quickly, Micah started getting antsy just watching from the side. So, watching turned into walking onto the court, and walking onto the court became asking to play *Pepper* with the high school guys. Micah got turned down constantly.

Finally, during the warmup for a match, he was behind the *Hitting Lines drill and asked if he could *Pepper*, expecting to be turned down as usual.

The two high school players said, "Okay," and Micah was right in there.

They played and played until Micah got hit in the face with the ball. He burst out in a scream and ran to the bench to hide his cry. His shirt was soaked in tears. But, as Pono looked over at the bench where his son rested with his hands buried in his face, Micah wasn't there. Pono scanned the gym looking for his son.

There he was, back behind the Hitting Lines once again, yelling, "Come on, and hit me again!"

Entry into academics was not a smooth transition for Micah. He constantly found himself in the principal's office for something he wasn't supposed to be doing. He'd come home to his sisters laughing about what his mom listened to on the answering machine, and Micah took lickings. Pono and Lisa knew that spankings were a short-term solution. Behind closed doors the couple pondered what their solution would be for the long-term. They had to, because Micah was still running rascal at school. Passing notes in class and leaving his leftover food inside of the shelved books in the library were the least of his discretions.

While Micah was by no means contained on the athletic field, that seemed to be the place where his energy and attention span were best focused. Pono stepped away from coaching at Kamehameha Kapālama and the Ma'a family began their first move away from the dorms at Kamehameha Kapālama. Micah was approaching eight years old and his family was complete. The time had come for a new chapter in his life.

Da ʻĀina

Hawai'i is an island full of culture. The legends of the land have great stories about the past of Hawai'i and how it developed into the historical place that it is. The sacred spots like Diamond Head on Oahu and The Stairway To Heaven in Kaneohe are a few of the places that are said to have had God lay his hand upon them as a location that could not be tarnished by man. The Kamehameha Schools across Hawai'i emphasize the Hawaiian culture in their teachings. Inside of the curriculum are the lessons of being respectful and having gratitude. The schools teach "Pono," which is Hawaiian for doing the right thing, and "Ha'aha'a" which means to be humble. The culture at school is often just a compound of the cultural teachings that the young boys and young girls have while growing up in their homes. It speaks of how to interact with others, whether older or younger. The culture tells how to treat all people, those with the same ethnic background and those without. It tells what the stance on giving versus taking should be, regardless of what amount is in someone's pocket. The culture is magnificent. More importantly, the culture is marinated, ingrained, and harvested. It is consistent.

The beach is a piece of Hawaiian lifestyle. With their entire island surrounded by water, Hawaiians take advantage of what nature has to offer them. Each of those young boys embodied his own location on Hawai'i. At the same time, they could all be representatives of the same thing. Hawai'i holds a special place in the heart of a true Hawaiian.

CHAPTER 2 - STRANGERS

At eight years old, Skylan told his dad that he would play professional volleyball. Eight years old. Dave's response was turning up the training to a new level. That year, Dave and Arlene entered Skylan into a youth league at Booth District Park for nine-year-olds and abōve. As Skylan grew older, he continued to play on Mondays and Thursdays at Susannah Wesley with the A and B players. His dad decided to start having him go on Tuesday nights as well, when the BB level players had league, to give him more repetitions and more opportunities to play. It was clear that volleyball was the trade that Skylan could practice to be in his dad's good graces, so he continued to play.

Dave took a job coaching the *junior varsity boys at Kamehameha Kapālama's high school. The varsity head coach was Guy Kaniho. Kaniho gave the okay for Skylan to come in with his dad and practice with the junior varsity team. Skylan was in the second half of his 4th-grade year, jumping into drills with these high-school athletes. Dave had Skylan follow along with them everywhere. In the gym, he practiced. In the weight room, he learned to lift. In the scrimmages, he played. Throughout his 4th- and 5th-grade years, Skylan attended school at Kapālama Elementary, practiced and lifted with the Kamehameha Kapālama junior varsity team, while also playing three nights a week in the Susannah Wesley rec leagues.

When 6th grade came around for the eldest Engleman boy, Kaniho told Dave, "We could use Skylan's help with the varsity team." That season, Skylan started working out with the varsity squad. He had a new level to step up to and Dave placed no barriers on his training. Kaniho invited Skylan to his extra training group called *Extreme Fitness Club*, so Skylan began training there. On top of that, Dave started taking Skylan to the beach during the weekends to add onto his developing skill set. Dave was one court away with JV as his son practiced with Kamehameha Kapālama's varsity team. However, once Skylan began at *Extreme Fitness Club*, he ended up in a small group with Kaniho, having volleyballs hammered at him. The desired result, of course, being digs before the ball hit the ground (or their faces). It was Skylan's first time training away from his dad and he felt like it was the time that he could learn even more. He said that he wanted to be a professional player, and that he wanted to play in the Olympics. This time around, it was for Skylan's own individual reasons, his own desire, and his own path.

When his dad was involved, Skylan got ripped on, continuously, and there was no break. Every day after volleyball, he cried. Arlene began doing her best to translate what point Dave was trying to get across to him. Skylan couldn't understand why his father was yelling at him. The training didn't soften. Dave had Skylan doing exercises on the grass and doing plyometric jumps in the garage. Dave hit balls at Skylan, always hard, always with good pace, and if Skylan shanked the ball over the fence then he was the one to chase it back. The time was progressive for the young Skylan. Again, that progression did not come without sacrifice. To compound the mental callusing, within the same year his first dog died and the other ran away from home. Arlene understood the struggle that Skylan was having so the family picked up a new dog, a husky and pit-bull mix. Not long after, they acquired two mini-terrier Chihuahuas and a purebred pit-bull. Those three new dogs were a part of the household. And with Skylan having an undeveloped relationship with his younger brother, Seyj, those dogs were crucial to his peace of mind.

Routines for the Tuiletas didn't face drastic changes after Larry Senior uttered the thought to his wife of sports potentially providing dividends. But, Senior kept things simple; there was no resistance if the kids decided that they wanted to practice their athletics. Tui started playing indoor volleyball on a local club team, Asics, named after their clothing sponsor. That was a brand new experience for him. He had run around at the beach with his dad and had surpassed the ability to count the number of locals with whom he'd played *Pepper*. It was different, though. There was an addition, the idea of team and structure. Most unusually, there were teammates his age. Well, not quite.

In boys' club volleyball there were divisions 12 & Under through 18 & Under. Tui started on his first 12 & Under team with Asics. All of his teammates were older than he. Tui took some time to get his feet wet. He was only eight, but it would be rare for even a 12-year-old to excite the crowd with his physical presence or outstanding court sense. As the season pressed on, it was not as structured as originally projected. The kids would show up once or twice a week and the coaches would roll out the balls for them to bump around for a while. They basically played jungle ball with limited rules or restrictions, until it was time to put the balls in the bag and leave. Tui was satisfied, though. He was a young boy getting the chance to play on a team and learn through experience in an activity that his family supported.

At that time, school was a secondary focus for Larry Junior. He was much more interested in learning more about his background through the fire-knife dancing and playing sports outside with a group or inside with his new club teammates. In early July, there was a massive four-day tournament scheduled to end the season. There was a tournament for boys, and there was a tournament for girls, as well. It was called Junior Olympics.

Tui's Asics 12s team traveled to JOs. That was his first time getting on an airplane and his mom traveled with them to make sure things ran smoothly for her son, who had just turned nine the previous fall. The tournament was long and Tui was mostly a spectator taking in the experience, living and learning through his teammates' opportunities on the court. The team was very raw and had not found its direction. It was a miracle they didn't finish in last place. No, they did not. Instead, they finished second to last.

After returning to Kaimuki, Tui and his family had to decide if that little bit of playing time and expensive bit of money for Asics were going to be worth that feeling of disappointment. He had side conversations with Keila, Mabeleen, and Kylee, about their experiences with volleyball. Kylee looked at him and simply shrugged her shoulders.

Keila and Mabeleen didn't say much other than, "You never know, Tui. It might get better."

In the summer months, Tui revisited the fire-knife dancing competition. He went with his dad down to the beach at Fort Derussy to play pick-up and watch Larry Senior's older friends. More than anything else, Tui enjoyed his break away from school. That meant more time at the beach, more time with his family, more time with his athletics, and no time sitting at a desk.

When the school year began at Wai`alae, Tui shifted toward a new group of friends. Out of the classroom his lifestyle remained. He and his parents tussled with a decision. Would he play club volleyball for a second season, understanding the potential to have similar results as the last? Or would he skip out of club and use his time elsewhere? Tui was in a predicament, because although he'd just turned 10 in September, he did not have the chance to stay and play 12 & Under. The numbers were not available to field a 12 & Under team and his 12s team from the previous season was moving to the 13 & Under Division. They struggled, until Maile said something profound that rattled Tui's mind in a strong way.

"Tui, in this family we don't quit something because it gets hard. We use that chance to rise to the occasion." The decision came in October. Tui would be attending the tryouts at Asics.

Thirteen & Under tryouts began in Klum Gym at the University of Hawaii. Mixed in with the expected returning players, there was just one addition: a young boy, three years older than Tui, whose age was just right for the team. He was skinny, but relatively tall for a 12-year-old turning 13. His bowl-shaped haircut covered his eyebrows, and his bright white flowery Hawaiian shorts hung too big on his waist — no doubt they were a pair of hand-me-downs. Micah Christenson was the name. He was offered a spot to join the team, and along with the previous season's players, that was the Asics 13s group for the season. Once again, all of Tui's teammates were older than he.

A few weeks later, early on into a team practice, a scrawny Hawaiian boy, with hair like he just stepped out of bed and a smile filled with leftovers from the snack in the car ride over, entered Klum Gym with his dad by his side. That scrawny bed-headed boy was Micah Ma'a. Pono brought Micah over to the tryout to get him started in a new team sport. It was worth a try since his dominance in youth tee-ball and youth soccer had worked out so well.

Larry Senior was at that practice. He knew Pono from their volleyball history on the island and said hello at the door. Then Larry Senior called Tui over and told him to be Micah Ma'a's partner for the *ball control. Although it was the boys' first time meeting, it didn't take long for them to chat it up. Micah was outgoing, and Tui had been 10 years old for two weeks, playing with the 13s team. He wasn't going to pass up the opportunity to make a friend who was about to be in the same boat. Being much younger and coming in holding near-to-no development under their belts, it was going be an interesting ride for those two Hawaiians.

Family time was all of the time for Evan, because of how close his siblings were to him in age. In addition to his father having a job at his school, fishing was his passion. But fishing out on the water was an all day affair and could only be done when his dad had the time to separate from work to take him. Evan was the oldest sibling and he was placed into a leadership role over his brothers. He did want to have things that were his own; however, it was never a real emphasis. If his brothers were to follow the choices he made, then that was fine. In the fall of 2006, Guy started a club volleyball program called *Southside Volleyball Club*. On his very first team, in the 12 & Under Division, Guy slotted the 10-year-old Evan. To the same team, he added Emmett, Addie, and Avery. The Enriques boys were going to be starting their first sports team together, as part of their dad's brand new club.

Micah and his family moved often after leaving the dorms of

Kamehameha. Unlike Evan, Micah was still without a brother and was in a rare situation being the youngest boy on his Asics club team. He was searching for his identity. Pono was savvy. Now that he'd stepped away from coaching at Kamehameha Kapālama, Pono saw it as an opportunity to be more involved with Micah. He talked with Alan Rosehill, who head-coached Micah and Tui's team. Pono joined the staff as the assistant coach of the Asics 13s.

In Kalihi, Skylan was beginning his first season of club volleyball. He'd already played in the Booth District youth leagues. He spent enough time in EFC with Kaniho. He had been put through the ringer in tons of open gyms with the adults at Susannah Wesley. Dave and Arlene made the decision to put the little money they had into starting up Skylan in club volleyball. The club was called *Sideout*, and was made up of the local guys he played with at McKinley. From the beginning of 12 & Under with *Sideout*, Skylan was a competitive player, but he had developed selfish tendencies.

He yelled at his teammates when they passed badly and shanked a ball out of bounds, "Move out of the way. I will pass." Any time his team lost in practice, he'd scream and hit the ball against the floor as hard as possible. Winning was all that mattered to him. His coach tried to chime in on his behavior. His teammates played their hands at calming him. Skylan's hunger for winning took no regard for the feelings of those around him. He took lickings from his dad and he took yellings from his mom. There was no change until Arlene began to simply speak. She spoke about the importance of being humble and enjoying the game.

She told Skylan softly, "Never think you're the best. There is always someone out there that is better than you." Arlene's words struck a chord with her boy.

"I want people to know who I am because of my character first, and my volleyball abilities second," he told her.

Skylan's team left in March 2007 for a tournament in Hilo, Hawai'i, called Haili. The Haili Tournament was the biggest volleyball tournament that the islands had to offer. Teams from all over Hawai'i attended every year and there were divisions for both males and females of all skill levels. It ranged from the Youth Division, to the B Division, to A, then AA, up to Open, and finally the Masters' Division for those over 40. The event was massive and Hilo was able to bring in big profits from it each year.

Haili lasted just a weekend. Evan was there too, with his

Southside team. All of the parents were playing in the Civic Center of Hilo, in the Masters' Division. Skylan was walking around the arena and caught himself staring at three boys playing volleyball on the concrete, using a 10-foot pillar as a net. Those three were Emmett, Addie, and Avery Enriques. They called Skylan over to be a fourth player for their game. The Enriques boys introduced themselves and Skylan remembered them from playing with Southside in the Haili Tournament Youth Division.

Skylan went back home to Oahu after the Haili tournament was over. After everyone got settled, post Haili, the teams were playing local scrimmages to get ready for Junior Olympics. There was still no qualification necessary in 13 & Under, so any team that could pull enough pennies together to afford it could go. There weren't enough club teams in Hawai'i to separate 12 and 13 & Under teams into their own divisions for local tournaments. Hawai'i didn't even have consistent boys' tournaments for those age groups. Instead, the local teams on the island would challenge one another other to scrimmages in practice and couple the age divisions in tournaments.

In late May, the Asics 13s team came into relevance and was beating everyone in the local scrimmages. A team called Onipa'a 12s was the only team that even had a chance at giving Asics 13s *hard rubs in a scrimmage. Skylan's coach at Sideout 12s called up Alan Rosehill and set up a scrimmage with Tui and Micah's Asics 13s team. They decided on Farrington High School as the location. The two teams ball controlled and played *Pepper* for warmup. There was no time for more extravagant drills. Skylan stood on his side of the court, observant as could be. Across the net was a bushy-haired Tui, standing there with his chest completely filling out his size-medium shirt. Next to Tui was a light-skinned Micah, skinny as a beanpole, and standing shorter than his dad's waist. They were the back-up players for Asics 13s. Tui and Micah both lined up in the *Outside Hitter positions, to do the majority of the serve reception and hitting for the scrimmage. They took full advantage of any opportunity they had to get on the court and play.

Skylan was heading back to serve the ball and his coach chimed in, "We aren't going to serve number two." Skylan was looking for a challenge, so he disregarded his coach's plan and purposefully served number two. Number two was Larry Tuileta Junior. Tui passed it well, got the set, and crushed it cross-court.

After the match, Pono was talking story with Dave Engleman. Pono called Micah over. Tui walked with him. Dave called Skylan over. Pono and Dave introduced the three boys to one another.

In their first time meeting, all Skylan had to say to Tui was, "Nice hit..."

A week later, Skylan was sitting on the floor playing video games with Seyj when his mom called him into the kitchen.

Dave was waiting there and said, "Your mom and I are letting you know that you'll be switching clubs for the rest of the season."

"But why?" Skylan asked.

Annoyed about being asked for a reason, Dave replied, "It's a family decision."

Skylan yelled bravely, "But —" and before he could finish Arlene jumped in, "Son, it is what is best for you and the rest of us right now."

Skylan had a practice that week with his new team, Onipa'a 12s. During his first drill into training, the coach asked him to step into the right-back, area-one position on the court. He had never set or defended on the right side before, and 20 minutes into his first practice he was now a *Setter. Things were moving uncomfortably fast. The most difficult thing for him was trying to set the *Quick Attack to the Middle Blockers. He was constantly staying back in defense as *freeballs came over the net, instead of running to his setting spot. Skylan never really caught a rhythm. Hell, he didn't even know the names of all of his teammates. Two of Skylan's local friends, Zarin Augustiro and Micah Goshi, who they called Gosh, played at Onipa'a on the 12s. Friends since infancy, those two boys were perhaps the only comforting feeling about all of the rapid change.

The club change was so close to the end of the season, and while he was playing with a team that was better on paper, his game was at a standstill. With three weeks until the team flew out to Junior Olympics, Onipa'a got involved in some local scrimmages. Skylan's team wouldn't be seeing Tui and Micah's team for the remainder of the training block. Asics 13s was off preparing for their age division, so Onipa'a played the local 12 & Under teams in Hawai'i (the whopping two other teams). Skylan's mind was in a constant circle. He'd finished 5th grade and was solely focused on his volleyball. His discomfort stuck with him. The feeling was unshakable, that that was not where he belonged. He avoided sharing his feelings with Zarin and Gosh; yet, anyone who spent a few hours with Skylan was able to sense that something in life was making him uneasy.

More news came as the weeks passed. It was just days away

from Junior Olympics, and Onipa'a was planning to add another player. Skylan's mind would reach overflow if he had even sprinkled in the thought of managing fresh confusion. He put it out of sight and out of mind. As long as the player wasn't coming to replace him, he decided not to bother with it. Though Dave found out quickly, and immediately it was put into Skylan's sight as he was bombarded with questions from his family.

"Who is he? What position does he play?" Dave asked.

"Has the coach talked to you?" Arlene added.

Skylan knew none of it and didn't want to know any of it. He sat in his room. Silence was all that surrounded him.

At practice, the group of boys got word that Evan Enriques would be flying in from the Big Island to Honolulu that same day. Skylan turned his head down in familiarity. That name sounded so familiar, but he couldn't place it. He tapped his middle fingernail on his thumb, hoping the answer would shoot out of his hand. Still nothing came. When Evan walked into the gym the next day, the light bulb illuminated. Skylan recognized him from the time he was in Hilo just three months prior. Evan's mom, Julie, accompanied him into the practice and he didn't hesitate before saying hello to everyone. Julie shook the coach's hand before being invited in to sit down and watch. Evan was making his rounds.

When he settled on Skylan he said, "Oh boy, hold on. You are the one that was playing with my brothers at Haili."

Surprised, Skylan answered back, "Yeah, Brah. Hey. I didn't know you saw me. I'm Skylan."

"I'm Evan."

"It's good to have you," Skylan smiled.

Practice continued as usual. The drills weren't very structured; the expectation wasn't that they should be. The boys were young after all. Yet, they all had positions and Evan was asked to join in with the Outside Hitters, doing the passing and hitting. Skylan was still unable to say that he had gotten comfortable in the Setter position, which was brand new to him. But even if it was just by an ounce, Skylan felt more comfort having one more familiar face around — not to mention that familiar face was now the new kid on the team. Evan and Julie left to a local hotel and booked their stay for two weekends. Two weeks was longer than Evan had been away from his dad and his brothers in the past, but the reality was that Emmett, Addie, and Avery were not developed enough to be a part of a Junior Olympics team at any age level. So, to give Evan the opportunity to play, two weeks would have to be doable.

Onipa'a left on their plane flight for Junior Olympics, along with all of the teams from the club. Skylan sat down in his assigned seat and took in a deep breath. It was his first time flying the long five hours to the edge of the Mainland. One of the older players posted up next to Skylan's aisle seat.

As Skylan pulled his headphones back away from of his ears, the older player said, "This is my seat, rookie."

"This is actually my assigned seat," Skylan replied.

"I don't care what the ticket says. I'm sitting here on this flight. Get up."

Skylan snapped back, "This isn't your seat. I am going to sit here, in my seat," and placed his headphones back over his ears. *Is that the way this works?* The young Engleman boy thought. *I'm not a fan, but I stood my ground. I passed my first test.*

The thought of the experience, as a whole, was intimidating. The plane flights were far, the team was new, the arena was large and full, and the trip was nerve-racking. What Skylan wanted more than anything, was to stand his ground. He only wanted to hold his own weight. The days were passing in the tournament and the team was doing fine. Evan was doing well and blending. Skylan's friends, Zarin and Gosh, were constantly laughing and joking. That made things easier. Even though he wasn't in the starting lineup, Skylan got nervous before each match. Fortunately, that feeling would usually go away by the middle of the *first set. It came again when he got his chance to come onto the court. It died down once a few points passed. As Onipa'a left the playing site on day three, Skylan spotted the Asics 13s sitting near the entrance with their parents. He made eye contact with Micah Ma'a, then Larry Junior. Tui gave Skylan a wave and Skylan nodded back.

The morning on the last day of 12 & Under competition had Onipa'a 12s versus Torrimar 12s, from Puerto Rico. It was the day's first matchup. Torrimar had already won the first set and Onipa'a was tied in set two, 23-23, when Skylan got substituted in as a *defensive specialist. He was standing dead center in middle back area-six, with Evan Enriques on his left and Zarin Augustiro on his right. Skylan grabbed his knees as his legs started to shake and he felt his breath escape him. It was the first time in his life that he felt that sort of pressure. It was weighing heavily on him. As expected, the serve came right at Skylan and the ball shanked off of his arms into the spectators' chairs for an ace.

The scorer's table flipped Torrimar's score to 24 to arrive upon their match point.

Skylan felt his eyes start to water. Torrimar organized for the next serve.

Before the whistle blew for service: *This is it. This is it*, Skylan thought to himself.

Once again it was targeted at Skylan. The serve came short and Skylan saw it late, so he dove. He was aced clean, without a touch. He lay there on the floor feeling as if every eye in the arena just saw him lose the match. His watery eyes turned to a stream of tears. And as he briefly lifted his head, he saw that his teammates were crying. That sight caused him to cry harder. Evan picked him up off of the floor and Skylan's coach rounded up the players.

The coach said to the boys, "You all did the best that you could, and that makes me proud."

Onipa'a slapped hands with Torrimar 12s. At the end of the line, a Puerto Rican player from Torrimar stopped Skylan and asked, "Will you trade jerseys with me, amigo?" Skylan's spirit lifted just a little bit at that moment. The Puerto Rican player didn't laugh at him or thank him for not successfully passing the last two serves of the match. It was the end of the tournament for Onipa'a, and all that the other team had for him was a symbol of respect, in the form of a jersey exchange. The boys exchanged jerseys and the Puerto Rican asked for a picture with Skylan. Onipa'a 12s prepared to leave the gym and head back to their homes. As the boys were walking toward the exit, Skylan spotted Micah and Tui. They made eye contact. Skylan raised his hand and waved. Tui nodded back.

CHAPTER 3 - ELEMENTARY

Skylan thanked all of his coaches and gave goodbye greetings to all of his teammates. He was so disappointed in his finish, and felt like he didn't achieve his goal of holding his own at Junior Olympics. JOs was new to him and he was put in a difficult situation in that final match, but he didn't see that as an excuse. After getting back, it was early July in Honolulu. He grabbed three other friends, including Zarin, and they started playing four-on-four beach volleyball. All he wanted to do was play volleyball. Any chance that he could get a ride down to the sand, he would play. Another boy, Kyle Kekina, had a sand court in his backyard at the North Shore. His house quickly became the spot for a weekend hangout. The thought of his last tournament and avoiding that embarrassing display consumed Skylan's brain. He wasted no time in signing up for new tournaments. He asked his friends to play in the four-man beach events on the island and Skylan started to win some events in his age group.

Tui's dad held indoor clinics over the summer called *Champions Training*. Dave Engleman heard about the clinics and sent Skylan to Kalani High School twice a week to participate. The gym at Kalani was sweltering in the summer time. There were termites everywhere, but it had a working net so it made do. The clinics lasted a while so the parents got together outside, on the trunks and hoods of the cars, and passed out cups for drinks. The younger kids ran around and played games as if it was a parking-lot day care.

Regardless of the gym conditions, Skylan was satisfied that he was getting in volleyball practice instead of being in school everyday. That was short-lived, as the summer was coming to a rapid close. Skylan changed schools once again, this time leaving Kapālama and changing to Kalakaua Middle School. Educational change of scenery was trending.

Tui spent 6th grade at Kaimuki Middle School the previous year, not doing very well in his studies. He was hanging around some punks who influenced him into thinking that being good in school wasn't the cool thing to do. Tui allowed himself to develop that state of mind.

When his mom got his report card, the first order of business for Tui was taking cracks from her. And when his arms returned to their normal color after his mom's slaps, she sat him down.

"Tui, if you want to play volleyball when you get older then you are going to have to get good grades." His parents were whom he respected the most. If his mom or dad ever turned anything from a comment into a seated discussion then he would do his best to change the behavior immediately. He threw his friends' thinking to the wind and applied himself in class. By the year's end, he was awarded *Most Improved* for the second half of school.

That award made him proud. Not proud because of his own personal achievement, but proud that his mom asked him to do something and he responded. It took courage for him to ditch what was popular in his friend group and see the next step to which Maile referred. Being a late-born, having a September birthday, and being a full year younger than everyone in his grade put Tui in a position for such influence. During the last month of the summer his parents decided to have him repeat the 6th grade at a private school, Saint Louis, but not before attending the summer-end Youth Volleyball Camp at Punahou.

Punahou is another storied school in Hawai'i, like Kamehameha. An institution with a K-5 junior school, a 6-8 intermediate school, and a 9-12 high school academy, Punahou was by application and acceptance only. The academic curriculum competed locally and nationally since its establishment on Oahu. All of the sports teams held pedigree and boys' volleyball was no exception. The program fielded its first varsity team in the fall of 1961. Four years later, Punahou won its first state championship and went on to win 19 of the next 26, establishing itself as a national powerhouse of boys' volleyball.

Tui showed up at camp and he marveled at how pretty the gym was. Shiny and polished, Punahou's gym had such a clean look in Tui's eyes. As he looked around at the other kids in the camp, he saw that he didn't blend. The boys were groomed so well and they had on the newest shoes to hit the stores. He noticed another inconsistency when he looked at himself and looked at the others in the camp. His skin wasn't the same. When the drills began in the camp, Tui stood out pretty quickly. He was pretty tall for his age and still maintained that mature body type. What really caught the coaches' eyes was how hard he would hit the ball.

"How old are you?" a camp helper asked.

"I'm 11," Tui replied, nervously.

The helper said, "You are hitting the leather off of the ball."

Tui just giggled; he rotated his eyes once left, once right, and then shrugged his shoulders.

One of the camp helpers was Maddison McKibbin, an upperclassman at Punahou's Academy who went on to play indoors at the University of Southern California, and on the AVP Beach Tour. Maddison talked with the young Tuileta and Tui hung onto his every word. Tui knew who Maddison was and he was really impressed that he took his time out to talk with him and show him some volleyball skills.

On the second day of the summer camp, Tui was taking swings in the Hitting Lines on his court, thundering ball after ball. Most of them made a loud thud as they flew out of bounds and hit the back wall. Rick Tune, the head coach of Punahou's varsity team, walked over to Tui's court. He observed a few swings before stopping Tui.

"You are Larry Tuileta's son, right?" asked Tune.

Tui timidly said, "Yes."

Coach Tune chuckled, "Keep doing what you are doing. And remember, power before accuracy." He winked at Tui and walked away.

When the camp was over, Maile and Larry Senior let Tui know that his family would be returning to his grandparent's house in Kaimuki, another reason why Tui would be repeating 6th grade at a new school. His grandparents' house was much farther away from Punahou than his house on Metcalf. Punahou wasn't a reality for Tui, anyway. Everyday he passed the school and laughed with his friends, teasing that only rich Haole people could go there; he'd never get in. *This is where the wealthy kids go, not kids like me,* he thought to himself.

Tui didn't normally attend Champions Training with his dad. For the last training of the summer, Larry Senior asked his son to come along and help out. Skylan came inside the gym, intrigued to see Tui there.

Skylan said softly, "Tui?"

Tui nodded at him. Skylan walked over and gave him a fist bump.

"Howzit, Hawaiian? What are you doing here?"

Tui said, "We just moved back to my old house and I am changing schools this year, so I'm just here helping out my Dad."

Skylan agreed, "Cool, I'm changing schools this year too, heading to Kalakaua."

"Saint Louis for me," Tui replied.

After training, when Skylan's dad came inside to grab him, Dave walked over to Larry Senior and gave him a fist bump.

"Appreciate you taking care of my boy. How'd it go?"

Larry Senior answered, "Good summer. He worked hard. How's your family?"

"We're all good. I see you brought your boy, Mr. Tui, with you today," Dave said with a smile.

Larry Senior smiled back, "Yeah, we've got a lot going on. Is Skylan going back to play for Onipa'a in the fall?"

Dave paused, "We'll see. He's got to get court time, wherever we have him play. You know?"

"Heard that, Braddah." Larry Senior understood. "Talk with you soon."

A week passed before Dave got a call from Lee Lamb. Lee was a coach at Asics who was preparing to start his own club.

Lee had a conversation with Larry Senior, saying, "Hey, I am starting my club this year. Pono Ma'a is going to come over and coach with us. Micah and Tui guys are almost the same age. You should bring Tui over and they can play again in the 12 & Under age group."

Larry Senior thought for a minute.

"Definitely sounds interesting," he replied. "I will talk with my wife. Who is coaching with Pono Ma'a? You've got to talk with this guy, Dave Engleman, though. He could be a big help if you need coaches, and he has a son."

"I will reach out to him. Having options is a good thing." Lee was excited.

Larry Senior agreed and asked, "What are you calling the club?"

Lee said, "Ka Ulukoa (Kah Ooo-loo-koh-uh)."

So Lee Lamb called Dave Engleman and asked him if he could help out for the season. Dave said he could, but he was still figuring out his son's plan for the year.

Lee said, "We will have to see what happens with your son because we only plan to field one 12 & Under team. We would still like to have you coach, though."

Dave considered, "Let's talk more at the tryout."

Ka Ulukoa held their first open invitation club volleyball tryouts for boys in September of 2007. The University of Hawai'i at Manoa's Klum Gym was the site for the tryouts. Pono Ma'a was the first one to arrive at the gym to meet Lee Lamb, who was opening the doors. Pono came with only a few things. He brought a bag of volleyballs, a brown clipboard with two sheets of paper and a pen... *and* his messy-haired son, Micah. Although he was just 10 years old, Pono wanted Micah to play with his team where he could watch him and have a firm and direct hand in his only-son's development.

Skylan was the next to arrive early. There with his father, Dave, who'd be assistant coaching with Pono, Skylan helped set up the nets in the gym. Ka Ulukoa was having tryouts for all of their age groups that day. Different age groups cycled through during different waves of time. Being the youngest, the players aiming for the 12 & Under group had their tryout first. Kids slowly began to file into Klum Gym. Pono assumed the farthest court over, against the wall, away from the door. He paused for a moment and remembered the smell in the air from the warm and humid gym where he'd played so many epic matches with UH. The gym was warm and humid, but the atmosphere was refreshing for Pono. It was the perfect homecoming.

More boys came through the doors to check in. Larry Tuileta Junior walked through the door behind his mom. Skylan looked over, and as he saw Tui come in, he nodded. Tui nodded back.

Micah jumped up and said, "It's about time you showed up. I thought you were leaving us hanging."

Tui smiled and gave his friend a handshake.

Tui was excited. He would be 12 in a few days and that would be his first time trying out for club volleyball in his age group. Skylan was looking forward to having another year and another chance to prove himself. Micah was just happy that he wasn't sitting in a classroom. Coach Pono rounded up the group of tryouts.

For introductions, "My name is Coach Pono. This is Coach Dave. We will be coaching the 12 & Under team this season." That was all he said.

Each tryout grabbed a ball and a partner and started to bump the ball around. Coach Pono called the boys in and said,

"We are going to play a competition game called *Tennis*. Half of you on this side of the net and half of you go on that side of the net. Here are the rules: everyone stand in a line on your side of the net, behind the end line. Each boy steps on, one at a time, and gets one touch to get the ball over the net and try to score on the other team. The catch is, you can only use your *forearm platform to play the ball, nothing else. Look for the ball to come in from me. After each touch, the next boy in line comes in. We will play first side to 10 points. Here we go!"

The start was rocky. It was clear that few had played organized volleyball before. The boys got water from the fountain and moved on to the next set of drills. For an hour, the tryout consisted of mostly short and sweet partner-drills with the occasional drill over the net. Lee Lamb whispered to the coaches that time would soon be up. Lee called all of the tryouts inside of Klum to the center of the gym.

"Thank you for attending Ka Ulukoa's first open tryout," he

shouted in a kind tone of voice. "Your court coaches will break you into small groups to discuss their plan."

Coach Pono, along with Coach Dave, took his group back to the farthest court in the gym and formed a circle. Coach Pono opened the short meeting with an unusual projection for the future, which caused some of the boys to cut their eyes left and right to see one another's reactions. Then, he thanked them for attending the tryout. He asked them to tell the club if they were trying out anywhere else and said that he would call them at the phone numbers that were written on their tryout sheet.

The gym started to fill with the next age-groups of tryouts. Maile grabbed Tui under her arm. She gave a big smile and waved to the coaches as she left with her son. Skylan walked on the outside of his dad and Micah on the outside of his as the two coaches walked slowly to the parking lot. Coach Pono and Coach Dave gave each other a handshake. Skylan gave Micah a silent wave as the families got in their cars and left.

Micah said to his dad, "I'm hungry."

Pono replied, "You are always hungry. Let's go eat."

Skylan rode in the car a few minutes before asking his dad, "So, what did you think?"

"I thought you did fine," Dave answered.

More curious, his son pressed, "Am I going to play there this season, on your team?"

Dave waited, "The decision is up to Coach Pono who he will take on the team."

Pono went home and talked with his wife about how the day went at the gym. The next day was a Sunday. He spent the night and the next day thinking about his decisions before calling Lee Lamb and Dave Engleman to confirm his choices. Pono called every boy from the tryout on his home phone. The 10 boys who Pono asked to come to the team were his 10-year-old son Micah, Larry Tuileta Junior, Noah Hayashida, Keenan Meyer, Austin Amian, Christopher Wise, Noah Faurrot, Joseph Ka'a'a, Kelsey Yogi, and Skylan Engleman. He told them that the first practice would be at Kalani High School at the end of the month.

All of the boys started their new year in the 6th grade as middle school students, with the exception of Micah who was entering his 5th and final grade of elementary at Kamehameha Kapālama. The beginning of Ka Ulukoa practice drawing near was a frequent topic of conversation at the dinner table. The only household that didn't frequently talk about the start of Ka Ulukoa was the Ma'a household. Micah's oldest sister, Misty, was in the middle of her school season. Micah had just completed summer tee-ball and was starting his first weekend basketball league. He came home confused and amused because two of the other kids brought a soccer ball to the indoor basketball league for shoot-around warmup. Misty and Micah's extracurricular athletics on top of raising two younger girls was a handful for the Ma'a family. In his laughter during family time, and while supporting his oldest girl at her matches, Pono still had thoughts of Ka Ulukoa in the back of his mind. He pondered how he would structure it and how he wanted to be as a leader. Yet, Pono was dealing with a group of 12-year-old boys. He wanted them to have fun.

On the last Friday night of September, Pono spoke with Micah and called each of his other nine players. He confirmed that they were joining the team and told each of them that he understood that throughout the year they would have things come up, and that they should just call in advance if they would not make it to practice. He did stress the importance of everyone attending the first practice. Each of the 10 players agreed. The next morning, on September's last Saturday, the team met at Kalani High School. Coach Pono invited everyone in to grab a spot and sit on the bleachers.

He placed his clipboard on the ground, dropped to one knee, leaned his forearm on his leg and spoke firmly. "I want you all to understand what we are doing here. We will work on your game and we will have some fun as a team. We are going to learn a lot of concepts but we have only a few rules."

He put out his fist into a ball and began to extend the fingers, one at a time. He only needed one hand to complete his list of rules. He extended his first finger. "We always show respect to our family and our teammates." His second finger extended. "From the time we walk into practice to the time we leave, we are focused on getting better. Always focused." His third finger, "If any ball touches the floor around us we always give a dive." He extended his fourth finger. "We treat every play and every point with the same care."

Coach Dave looked over the group. Coach Pono was still on his knee. He paused to look each player in the eyes.

"Agreed?" he asked seriously.

The group of boys nodded their heads, yes.

Coach Pono stood the boys up and asked them to run five laps around the court. In a pack, they started to run.

"Straight line!" Coach Pono shouted.

The boys fixed their running formation.

"Circle up. Tui, lead the *static stretch."

The boys went through their stretch and began chatting.

"Focus," Coach Pono said, "We are focused."

The boys closed their lips and continued to stretch.

The practice was similar to the tryout. Towards the end, Coach Dave asked each of the boys for his shirt size and two options for his jersey number.

Micah jumped in and said, "13!"

"Wait your turn Micah, you're the youngest," Coach Pono said.

"I've got to have 13," Micah pleaded.

"Why is 13 so important?" Coach Dave chimed in, curiously.

"All of my siblings have the initials 'MM' and 'M' is the 13th letter in the alphabet. My dad is one boy with three sisters. I am one boy with three sisters. Thirteen is unlucky, and I want to prove people wrong."

Everyone was still.

Coach Dave looked around before he said, "Anyone object?"

No one objected.

The boys practiced twice a week through the Thanksgiving break. The attendance structure was simple. Simple in that there was not much structure. Most of the boys had other things going on in their lives that prevented them from being at every practice. Most practices had six or seven boys there. The agenda was the same every day. They would always play *Tennis*, and then as they moved into their drills, Coach Pono would direct and make sure things had some sort of organization, while Coach Dave would speak out occasionally with a technical modification. The expectation was not for the boys to be there every single time; they were eleven and twelve years old, after all. The expectation was that they just come when they could. However, when they were in attendance, Coach Pono made sure their ears were open.

In November, Coach Pono took his boys to play in the girls' 12 & Under tournament at the Lanakila District Park Gym. The boys were rather confused when they got the news of whom they would be competing against.

Skylan asked, "Coach, why are we playing in a girls' tournament? Isn't that going backwards? They aren't going to be very good."

Coach Pono said, "Just play hard, Skylan."

The Ka Ulukoa boys won their first match and the next one as well. The female playing-style was so different, though. Girls would *tip the ball even when they got a good set and they received every serve with their arms. In the boys' game, every boy tried to hit the ball as hard as he could anytime it was above the net, and they wanted to receive the serve overhead with their hands as much as they could. The most annoying thing was when the girls would set the ball over the net on the second contact.

"Who the heck does that?" the boys joked.

The boys lost their first set in their final match of the day. The girls celebrated, big time. After the boys returned to win the match in three sets, Coach Pono had words for the team.

"How did that feel to lose to those girls? We have to give them their respect. They are the same age as you, and they beat you. We should learn not to judge a book by its cover. We have to respect every team."

The boys kept their stone faces. Skylan looked down at his shoes, and then slowly nodded in understanding.

Coach Pono had a plan. Playing against the girls was not a mindless move on the chessboard. Every weekend that he could register his team for the girls' tournament, he would. It wasn't long before the boys passed the level of girls' 12 & Under volleyball, so they got booted to the girls' 14 & Under Division. On the weekends that didn't have tournaments, Coach Pono and Coach Dave added early Sunday morning practices at 8am.

The boys began to ask questions about what their responsibilities were. Coach Pono called everyone over to him.

He spoke softly, "I am going to introduce a concept today that will hold us together and take away question for the entire season."

He placed his hands in the shape of an O and said, "Big Circle."

The boys looked up at Coach Pono, confused.

"Big Circle. Every one of us holds our area of the circle and is responsible for no more and no less. Every player does the passing, every player does the setting, everyone does the hitting, and so on. Our only individual responsibility is to always play our role so the team can succeed. There is no ball that is Micah's ball, or Tui's ball, or Austin's ball. Everyone will always be ready to do everything. If things get tough, just put the ball in the Big Circle, and we will take care of each other." Coach Pono raised his hands in the O shape again. "This is where we find our comfort. This is where we always return."

Chapter 4 - The Perfect Child

After the holidays, the next tournament the boys traveled to was the Haili Tournament, to play in the Junior Division. Before the boys left, Coach Pono brought each of them something for the tournament. It was a composition notebook.

He said, "I want you all to take one. We are going to start talking about goal setting. For now, just write down any thoughts that you have during the tournament."

The boys didn't think much of it before taking the notebooks and stuffing them into their backpacks.

Once they arrived in Hilo, the boys settled in at their hotel. Everyone was split up into three hotel rooms. Keenan Meyer's mom, Kim, was the chaperone for the trip. All of the boys congregated in her room and they pulled out the Nintendo Wii video game system. Soon they began whipping the controllers back and forth and yelling out any time someone scored in the video game.

They hadn't even unpacked their bags before the hotel manager charged up the elevator and onto their doorstep to say, "You all are making far too much noise. We have gotten numerous complaints and I am going to have to ask your group to leave this hotel."

Kim had to go and tell Coach Pono what happened.

Coach Pono charged down to the boys' hotel floor, snarling like a pissed-off grizzly bear. His fist hammered on the door and Micah cracked it open slowly. Pono burst through the door, nearly knocking his son on his back, demanding that every boy pack his bag immediately and be downstairs within the next five minutes.

"You all come into someone else's place of business and cause a problem for them? How disrespectful can we be? This is a disgrace to the team and to the club. If I hear a bad word out of another hotel manager for the rest of this season, I will personally see to it that each and every one of you doesn't wear a Ka Ulukoa jersey ever again!"

His players stood in amazement. Unsure of whether it would be safe to change their faces, most of them kept their stupid expressions with their mouths wide open as Coach Pono slammed the door shut behind him.

After he defused on a walk down the hall, Coach Pono met with Coach Dave to try to figure out a solution, or the next hotel they would book. Coach Dave said he'd make a call.

He came back 10 minutes later and said, "I found us a place."

Everyone loaded up the vans. Coach Pono wanted it quiet. They drove for a while, passing through miles of trees and seeing only a few scattered businesses.

Coach Dave's directions took them down a long dirt road. The more time that passed, the more space there was between each house. They came upon a seemingly endless brown fence, which enclosed a massive area of land. A peaceful multitude of green trees towered high and thick in the soil. The place to which Dave pointed appeared distant, hidden, and as small as a single-car garage. The boys ran in a sprint through the trees and pine needles toward the nestled house.

Skylan said, "Dad, we are out in the forest."

"You are lucky that a friend of mine had this available. Now go inside," said Coach Dave forcefully.

Half-jokingly, Coach Pono whispered to Coach Dave, "Do you think we will lose some of the boys out here?"

The living area was quite spacious up close. The boys began to throw their bags down in the front room. Coach Pono had his own room, which lightened his mood. The boys ran into his room and asked if they could go outside to play hide-and-seek. Coach Pono said it was fine. Everyone played. The game lasted longer than usual because of the huge open spaces in the forest. The boys were called in for dinner.

After dinner, Coach Pono asked them all to grab their composition notebooks.

"I want everyone to get a pen or pencil and write down two short-term goals and one long-term goal that you have for this season."

He watched, feeling impressed, as they wrote. Yet, he said nothing. Everyone understood that it was a time for silence and focus. Afterwards, he sent them all to bed with this:

"Let's go to sleep, now. It's best that we learn early how important sleep is to our success. Every extra hour that you stay up minimizes our chance of winning. That is not only taking away from yourself. That would be taking away from your teammates."

In the morning, the boys awoke in the front room where they all slept. The houseful was excited for their first competition together against boys. The group was surprised to finish the day with an unblemished record of 3-0 in *pool-play matches. Coach Pono told his team that they did well and it was time to leave.

Micah chimed in, "I'm hungry."

His dad replied, "You are always hungry. Let's go eat."

When the boys were fed, showered, and rested, the coaches took them to the lava rocks in Hilo. Playing on the volcano was fascinating to them. Suddenly, little Kelsey fell off the rocks and into the water. Coach Pono turned his head and started sprinting across the lava rocks toward him. He jumped into the water to grab Kelsey, hoping he hadn't knocked his head on the rocks. Coach Pono pulled him out. Kelsey was still spitting water out of his mouth, unable to catch his breath, but he was safe. Relieved of their momentary fear, all of the boys started a loud, synchronized clap.

They arrived back at the house. Through the entire dinner, every boy was talking about what happened out on the lava rocks.

Coach Pono said, "Make sure we all thank Coach Dave for finding this house for us to stay in."

Together, all the boys shouted their praises.

Skylan said, "Yeah, thanks Dad. I like the house better than the hotel anyway."

The group seconded Skylan's thoughts. Kim cleaned up and Coach Pono asked all of the boys to grab their composition books.

"Tonight, I want you each to write down how you think you can transfer what you do in a game to a real world situation. For Kelsey, maybe that could be writing about how having a frightening moment of falling into the lava rocks transfers to being in a tough and unexpected situation in a match and having to rebound from it. For those of you with siblings," Coach Pono surveyed the boys' eyes, "it could be writing about how taking care of your siblings relates to taking care of your teammates, here."

Silently, the boys thought and pushed their pens into their paper.

On the second day of Haili, Coach Pono's group was into the semifinals. They won rather easily, and were excited when it was time to go on break—until Coach Pono came over and said that they would be refereeing the match for third place.

Micah said, "But Dad, the losing team has to ref. Even I know that."

"Yeah, Dad," Skylan said, speaking to his own father.

Coach Pono cut off their questioning quickly, "That doesn't matter, boys. The other team is not here and we are. It's good community service."

The team conceded and handled its randomly appointed refereeing duties with no more fuss.

Ka Ulukoa was called onto the court for the tournament finals. They had no idea whom they would match up with. Skylan's eyebrows rose when he saw Evan Enriques and his three brothers warming up on the other side of the net. Evan's father, Guy, was coaching his sons.

Coach Dave approached Guy Enriques to shake his hand.

He asked, "Why does Evan have a cast on his arm?"

Guy said back, "He broke his wrist in pool play yesterday. We took him to the hospital to get him a hard cast."

The boys had cruised through the tournament to that point, and they figured it would be the same playing a crippled Evan Enriques and his little brothers, even if it was at their home of the Big Island. Austin Amian was the *Libero. His job was to play back row the whole match for both Middle Blockers, Noah Hayashida and Keenan Meyer. Micah and Skylan lined up in a *6-2 offense with both of them setting in the back row and hitting as an *Opposite, on the right side, when they rotated to the front row. Neither of them were much of an offensive threat. That didn't matter, though. The team had Tui hitting on the left as the Outside Hitter, who was the primary option from anywhere at anytime. He was the main reason that the team was booted from the girls' 12 & Under tournaments, and he was the reason that kids were consistently turning their heads during the tournament when he would hit the ball near them.

Although Ka Ulukoa still won, the match was not as simple as they first believed it could be. Coach Pono's group proved to be a little older and a little stronger but Evan Enriques was something to watch. Even with a hard cast on, he still passed every serve smoothly up to the net, and every time it seemed like he ran out of options on offense, he'd hit off the block out of bounds or deliver a stealthily disguised tip, over the block and to the floor. In truth, the Ka Ulukoa boys were jealous of how easy he made it look to score on them. Guy Enriques came over to Coach Dave and Coach Pono after the match and they talked story for a few minutes. Kim came over and reminded the coaches of their plane flight time. So, they wrapped up their conversation and Coach Pono turned to the boys, "We *Pau! All done."

Micah ran up and tapped his dad on the shoulder, "Guess what?"

Coach Pono hesitated, "What son?"

"I'm hungry," said a smirking Micah.

Coach Pono ran his fingers through his hair and said, "Get your butt in the van, Clown."

Training resumed on Oahu. The boys started bringing their composition books to every practice. The routine didn't change. Coach Pono made sure there was order in training and he added on pieces as they went. A week had gone by since Haili, and Pono was lying in bed with his wife.

He said, "Lisa, I think the boy we played against at Haili could help us."

Lisa replied smoothly, "Maybe he could, but there isn't much that you can do about it. Don't let it build up."

Pono placed his head back on the pillow, "Maybe there is."

In the morning, he finished his breakfast at the table and picked up the phone. Three rings later, Julie Enriques answered the phone. Pono greeted her kindly and asked to speak with Guy.

"Guy, here," he said as he came to the phone.

Pono paused briefly, and then sighed, "Hey Guy, Pono Ma'a here. I will cut straight to it. I am not sure what you guys have planned for Evan this summer but he could help our team at JOs."

Guy rubbed his hand against his chin. "Thanks for calling, Pono. I will talk with my wife and give you a call back."

"Okay, *shoots," Pono said.

The boys talked more about the Haili Tournament at practice. Coach Pono stopped his team during the *Pepper* drill.

"Attention here," he said. "Listen boys, I am glad you are all happy that we had success at Haili. I am glad that we were able to put it together. But don't make a mistake. Riding high on what we did yesterday will put us in a bad mind for what we want to do tomorrow. When we complete a task, we can only spend a little bit of time celebrating before we move on to the next one. That is the way we progress. The next day and the next play."

Pepper continued.

Pono came home to a message on his answering machine. It was from Guy Enriques.

The message said, "Pono, we appreciate the offer, but we will have to decline. Julie and I discussed it. The travel back and forth will be too much. It is best that Evan doesn't impose on the team you already have set up, and we are trying to find a situation where Evan can play with his brothers. *Mahalo."

Pono couldn't deny being disappointed. Again, he lay himself down in bed.

He told Lisa what he heard in the message and added, "I've got to call him back tomorrow."

Lisa said to Pono, "When you call back, it won't hurt to give it another try. Tell them that Evan can stay with us."

Pono looked at his wife and smiled, "We must respect their wishes. Goodnight, sweetheart."

First thing in the morning, Pono sat down at his kitchen table.

He picked up the phone to return Guy Enriques' call.

Guy answered, and Pono said, "I got your message. I understand what you are saying."

Guy cut in, "Hey Pono, I was about to call you again. Julie and I talked with Evan and he begged us to join your team, so we are giving it a second thought. The problem is the travel back and forth. Evan played with Onipa'a for JOs last season, and it wouldn't be fair to the team for Evan to be there with you part of the time."

Pono asked, "What if Evan stays with us? It's cool with my wife. Actually, it was her idea. We can take him while he is here."

Guy asked Julie to get on the phone.

"Julie, Pono says that they can take Evan if he goes up and plays with those guys for Junior Olympics."

Julie said softly, "Hi there, Pono. Okay. If Evan wants to go then I am happy to let him go."

A satisfied Pono replied, "Awesome, let's talk more this week and make a plan to get him up here."

All of the boys got out of school and it was the third week in May when Evan got on a plane for the first time without his family. He was alone. When he landed, Pono and Micah were there to pick him up from the baggage claim. They didn't say much.

Pono asked how the flight was and Evan just replied, "Good. Easy."

They drove in silence back toward the Ma'a home in Kaneohe. Before they arrived, Pono pulled over to buy a *lei from the store. The boys were by themselves now.

Micah turned awkwardly and looked at Evan before saying, "You gave us rubs with that cast on, Brah."

Evan slowly turned and said, "No Braddah, you smacked our whole team, easy."

"We should make it a rematch sometime," Micah said, feeling less awkward. "Hey, if you want to see my dad get frustrated when he comes back, tell him we are hungry."

They were five minutes into speaking and the two boys laughed as if they'd been friends for years.

Pono came back to the car and said, "Nice to see that you two are getting along."

The boys pulled up to the Ma'a residence with Pono leading the way. A long driveway led up to the two-story Kaneohe abode. With each step, Evan's eyes locked onto a new piece of Ma'a family history, with all of the pictures that covered the walls, photos from Pono and Lisa's days at the University of Hawai'i, and pictures of Micah and each of his siblings in their youngest years. As Evan turned his head to observe the repetitive thump of feet coming down the stairs, he was introduced to Micah's three sisters, who were all very fond of Evan right away.

"You have pretty hair," Misty said to Evan.

Micah's second sister, Mehana, chimed in, "And look at his skin!"

Evan just smiled brightly and said, "Pleasure to meet you all. Thank you for having me."

Micah pulled Evan's arm toward the sliding glass door in the back of the house, and Evan's jaw dropped. In the backyard was a canopy over the top of a barbecue grill, a regulation-sized sand court surrounded by grass, without a single brown patch, and green palm trees that seemed to stretch into the mountains of Kaneohe.

"Is that where we can have the rematch?" Evan said, pointing to the sand court.

Micah shouted, "Yes! Anytime, Brah!"

At the next practice, the team had already received the news, so everyone showed up early, anxious about Evan's arrival. Evan entered the gym and the boys were all smiles.

"Good to see you again," Skylan said, taking the lead.

Keenan followed, "Look at that hair! I'm Keenan."

Micah joked, "Now we have another kid who can hit the ball down over the net without it hitting the tape first."

Coach Pono called his group in and everyone introduced themselves.

"You are new with us, Evan, but you are a part of our team now. There is no grace period or initiation. Boys, make sure we show Evan the way we do things here. Hands in here."

All of the boys and the coaches touched their fists together and said firmly, "Koa!"

Tui came over to the Ma'a house after Sunday practice. He was talking with Micah on the couch while Evan took a shower.

"It seems like Evan is going to be pretty good, huh?" Micah asked Tui.

Tui replied, "Yeah. Hopefully he can take some of Coach Pono's yellings away from us."

"Yeah right! You never get busted for anything, because you never do anything fun."

"Ha!" Tui chuckled. "Speaking of which, I've got these water balloons in my backpack."

Micah's face lit up, "Now you are talking. Let's hit Evan with them!"

When Evan came out of the shower and downstairs to the patio, Tui and Micah unloaded all of the balloons they had filled, onto Evan's fresh set of clothes. Evan stood on the patio, soaked — even his hair. It was the first time Tui and Micah had seen it not looking like he stepped off of a movie set.

"Oh, I'm gonna get you guys!" Evan shouted.

The two perpetrators laughed uncontrollably until Pono came bolting outside and yelled, "What the frick are you knuckleheads doing? He just put on those clothes."

They just stared at Pono as he continued.

"Just get inside for dinner."

Evan, Tui, Micah, and the rest of the Ma'a family said a prayer for grace.

After dinner, Micah jumped up and said, "Time to go play Ping-Pong."

Lisa stopped him, "Wait, why don't you try putting your dishes in the sink first, or maybe washing them. You see Evan washing his dishes, don't you?"

Pono added, "Wash your plate, Micah. Our guest shouldn't even be washing his dish. You should be."

The girls laughed.

Micah said, "He always washes his dishes, and always makes his bed, and brushes his teeth like five times a day, and calls his mom every night. He's like the perfect child."

Lisa rolled her eyes, "Boy, just go wash your dishes."

Every morning, Micah and Evan set alarms to wake up early and play Ping-Pong in the garage. They played so often that they made rules to change the style in which they held the paddle each day. They played Ping-Pong all morning until breakfast. Tui would come over and they would play all night until Tui had to go home. Games became so intense, that whenever there was a dispute on a point, Micah and Evan ran upstairs, pushing and shoving, to get the final ruling from Micah's sisters, who weren't even watching them play. They sided with Evan every time, of course.

"First you expose me to my parents by being the perfect child, and now my sisters are siding with you." Micah smiled and asked sarcastically, "What has the world come to?"

Chapter 5 - Chicken Dinner

Evan and Micah began to develop a unique bond. They rode bikes everywhere, until they got the idea to leave them unlocked outside of the mall one day while they went inside. Needless to say, the bikes were nowhere to be found once they returned outside for them. Evan called Tui laughing while Micah cried all the way home, thinking about the lickings that he would take for getting his sister's bike stolen. At the movie theater, Evan would buy a ticket and go inside, then come back outside to pass the stub off to Micah so that he could get in for free. It worked out well, until the managers started to recognize the pair. They raked their neighbors' leaves for pocket money, 20 dollars a yard. The two once raked a lawn that filled six full-sized trash bags, and the old lady who owned the house asked how much for raking the whole lawn, and to take the trash bags to the dumpster — which was a half-mile away.

Micah replied nervously, "Five dollars."

Evan just about pushed him on his butt into the pile of bags. So... the lawn raking side job ended as well. Regardless of how many new adventures those two created and banished together, they always found something new to keep them entertained.

Ka Ulukoa practice was about learning and practicing the skills, and Evan was learning the style under which Ka Ulukoa operated. The boys didn't scrimmage or play six-versus-six games in their training. The opportunities for them to actually compete were the girls' tournaments. Playing against the girls on Oahu was brand new for Evan, but all he had ever played was Big Island volleyball. The highest level of volleyball there was not even up to par with the average skill level on Oahu, so he thought it best to just follow what the team was doing and be open.

Another 14 & Under girls' tournament passed and Tui's powerful swings were hitting girls in the face too often, so the tournament director kicked the boys out of the 14 & Under and pushed them up into the girls' 16 & Under Division. Pono talked more and more in practice about the worth of defense. He told them how important it was to keep the ball in play and snapped at them if they were moving or leaning while the ball was being hit at them. He wanted their feet stopped all the time on defense, and he did not let up.

If a ball hit the floor, he'd yell, "Dive!" If they touched the ball, but made an error, he yelled, "Next!" If he saw their attention start to stray he would say, "Focus."

The team prepared to leave the last week in June. At Junior Olympics, the 18 & Under always played first, followed by the 12 & Under on the next day, then 13 & Under, and so on, all the way up to 17 & Under rounding out the tournament. For two weeks the best boys' teams from around all of North America and England filled a convention center with each age group playing a four-day championship. All of the 12 & Under teams played in one division together, as did the 13 & Under teams. From 14 & Under to 18 & Under, teams were required to qualify for a spot in the Open Division of their age group. The teams that did not qualify had the option to play in the Club Division. The 2008 Junior Olympics were hosted in Sandy, Utah. Throughout the season, Kelsey Yogi's mom had expressed concerns about Pono's coaching philosophy. By mid-May, and after some back and forth, it was decided that Kelsey wouldn't make the trip. With the addition of Evan Enriques, that gave Ka Ulukoa 10 boys.

The boys enjoyed their experience at Haili, staying in a house, and the coaches decided that it didn't create any unwanted problems, so they searched for the same in Sandy. The team flew together and booked a beautiful house at the ski resort in nearby, Salt Lake City. It was the start of summer, so Utah was hot and dry. The house was three stories and made of dark-brown wood, with a massive yard in the back for the boys to play hide-and-seek. The second floor hosted the living room, a kitchen, and one room that Kim occupied. The boys were divided up by positions. On the top floor, the Middles, Keenan Meyer and Noah Hayashida, roomed together. The Libero, Austin Amian, roomed with the defensive specialist, Christopher Wise, along with Noah Faurrot and Joseph Ka'a', the other two defensive specialists. Coach Pono and Coach Dave held down the final room on the top floor. The Outside Hitters, Tui and Evan, roomed together in the first bedroom on the bottom floor. Micah and Skylan, both Setters, filled the last bedroom on the bottom floor.

Once the bags were down and the beds were claimed, it was straight out back. Everyone was having a great time in the backyard. The only one missing was Coach Pono, who was upstairs in his room. He was designing a plan. He thought back to his time with the USA Volleyball Men's National Team and how things were structured there: what time they had to go to sleep, and what time they had to wake up. Coach Pono had a desire for his boys to learn to understand schedules and to develop the right mindset. *This is not a vacation. This is work*, he thought.

Arriving at the convention center in Sandy was a memorable

experience for the boys. No one was more impacted by the team's first arrival than Evan Enriques. It was his first multi-day tournament with Ka Ulukoa and he caught sight of something he had never seen before. Borinquen Coqui was completing its hitting warmup on a side court toward the center of the enormous convention center. Their flashy Setter, Fernando Dias, used his lightning-quick hands to deliver balls to his teammates that seemed to hang on top of the net and say, *come hit me.* Borinquen Coqui also had two attackers named Ricardo Pidilla and Danny Rivera, who caught the eye of any onlooker within the first 10 seconds of watching them jump and swing at the ball.

"Man, I hope we can do that in a couple years," Evan said to the group.

Coach Dave replied, "They are in our division, Evan."

Evan swallowed spit and didn't say anything more. As the boys finished the walk to their court, they were back to their joking ways, until Coach Pono brought them together.

"Work starts now," he said. "Run and stretch."

The first day of round-robin pool play wasn't too stressful for Ka Ulukoa. They were pleased with how well their ability to serve the ball in consistently was working for them. They were more pleased to learn that it was tradition at Junior Olympics, after the match, to give a small gift from your part of the world to each team that you played. Some teams brought small pins from their hometown, a handful brought cookies or nuts, a few, unaware of the tradition, didn't bring anything. The pool ended in a three-matches-to-none sweep of their opponents.

Austin Amian brought a GameCube, and the entire team crowded around a 16-inch television on the second floor of the ski house to take turns battling one another in Super Smash Bros. Coach Dave came downstairs and took a spot off to the side at the dinner table, to teach the boys who were waiting how to play chess.

Day two turned out to be more of the same, as the boys came into the crossover match with relaxed minds and no real expectations. They used their ability to serve the ball in consistently and reset for the next serve to keep themselves in the Gold Bracket on day three. After lunch, the first thing on the boys' minds was getting back to the house.

After the players huddled around the small screen for an hour, Coach Dave came down and said that Coach Pono wanted them off the video game and onto something else.

Micah said, "I have an idea. Stack up the pillows in the middle of the room."

They did. Micah grabbed a mini volleyball, which he got as a gift from an opponent earlier that day, from his bag.

"Five of you over there and the other five over here."

Mini-ball was invented. The boys in the front, near the pillows, sat on their butts and the boys behind were allowed to be on their knees, as if they were back row players. They played. It was like volleyball on the court, but much faster and much more intense. The games started to become too intense, to such a great degree that the coaches had to come down and tell the boys to knock it off. They stopped, until after dinner, when someone started to toss the little ball around the room and before long it became another game of Mini-ball. The coaches snapped at them again, so they began to modify the rules so that only two people could play on each team at a time.

Coach Pono came down the stairs and said, "It's time to sleep. Remember why we are here."

On the third day, Ka Ulukoa came in as the 2nd seed of their three-team pool. Torrimar 12s, of Puerto Rico, was their first taste of real pressure in the tournament. The Puerto Ricans were just so much more physically developed in their pre-teen years. They jumped higher, they moved faster, and they hit with more strength. A few of them were sporting mustaches at 12 years old. Ka Ulukoa struggled early. Coach Pono placed his hands over his head in the shape of an O. His boys responded by digging Torrimar's tough swings to the middle of the court. Occasionally, Torrimar would hit out of bounds and the Hawaiians would accept their error, gladly. Ka Ulukoa kept the games close, and it was their serving that allowed them to walk away with the win. They could all serve in, time and time again, after the score matured beyond 20 points. Torrimar couldn't. Ka Ulukoa won their other pool-play match in the same consistent serving fashion and left the gym with Torrimar's 3rd overall seed in the tournament, as well as a spot in the 12 & Under semifinals on day four. Every night, back at the house, Coach Pono took each one of the boys, individually, and met with them about their trip and how they thought they'd played up to that point. Afterwards, they put their thoughts on paper in their composition books.

On the morning of the fourth day, Evan wore his headphones in the van.

"What are you listening to?" Skylan asked him.

Evan replied, "John Mayer."

"I said what, not who," Skylan said sarcastically.

Micah jumped in, "Yeah, we need to get some Reggae jams going in this van. You are on it, right Keenan?"

"Why don't you do it F-F-Micah?" Evan questioned.

"What the frick? What is F-F-Micah?" asked Micah, confused.

"Ficus," Evan grinned. "Your name reminds me of Ficus, so I am going to call you Ficus."

Micah jumped toward the back seat to wrestle with Evan. Keenan started singing playfully.

"Why can't we be friends? Why can't we be friends?"

The mood was light as the boys walked through the door of the Sandy Convention Center. The players weren't even sure whom they were playing for the semifinals, until they arrived onto the court. Fusion 12s from Guaynabo, Puerto Rico was their opponent. The team was similar to Torrimar 12s, who was set to play in the other semifinal. An explosive group of boys, without as much height as Torrimar, gathered across the net to battle Ka Ulukoa for a place in the tournament finals. The Hawaiians prevailed 25-20 and 25-19, on a solid hitting performance from Tui and Evan. The other semifinal ended shortly after, and the boys received the news of whom they would play against for the Gold Medal.

Evan sat in the hallway with his team after the semifinal. As he bit into his Subway sandwich he felt a pause, a subconscious comparison of his visual experience at Junior Olympics with Ka Ulukoa to the experience of his first time seeing Ka Ulukoa play against him at Haili. The feeling of appreciation came over him. Coach Dave came through the doors and said it was time to go. The boys walked slowly through the convention center, weaving through the brightly colored courts. They settled onto their bench chairs and said nothing. Ka Ulukoa began their warmup. By the time they returned to begin their ball control and *Pepper* drill, their challengers were already into their arm-swing warm-up. Borinquen Coqui 12s was the opponent.

"They looked smaller from a distance," Evan said to Tui, as Ka Ulukoa assumed the court for their four minutes of hitting and serving, alone.

The Ka Ulukoa boys hit one at a time. Most of the swings hit the tape at the top of the net as they made their way somewhere near the deep corners. They definitely weren't the flashiest warm-up team in the division. Borinquen Coqui took the court for their four minutes. The first swing that Ricardo Pidilla took, bounced cross-court on the *10-

foot line and over the spectator chairs near the sideline. Danny Rivera followed with an attack down the line, which bounced in front of the 10-foot line and over the chairs behind the end line. The Puerto Rican crowd screamed with each swing that came, getting louder and louder, to egg on a competition of which Puerto Rican boy would bounce the ball the hardest off of the floor. Tui did his best to look unimpressed. The rest of the Ka Ulukoa boys looked at one another, unable to hide the hint of fear in their eyes.

The teams crossed paths at the net, Ka Ulukoa looking up at the 6'2" Ricardo Pidilla, and the 6'4" Danny Rivera. Not a single smile appeared on the face of a Borinquen Coqui player as the two teams slapped hands at the net.

Skylan spoke in the huddle, "Micah, will you say a prayer?"

The boys bowed their heads and closed their eyes under the lights in Sandy Convention Center. Micah finished the prayer and looked up to realize that no one heard him finish over the chants of the Puerto Rican families, friends, and teams that had already lost in the tournament, forming a posse of supporters. Micah tapped his teammates' chests and they broke out into their areas on the court.

The first whistle blew and Ka Ulukoa received the serve. Micah set Tui in the back row and it was like Borinquen knew it was coming a week ago. Six hands crossed the net on a three-person block, and Tui's hit went straight down on his own side of the net. The Puerto Rican fans erupted in chants and waved their flags back and forth behind chairs.

Coach Pono's voice cut through, "Next! Next!" as he circled his index finger.

Every ball that Fernando Dias set to his waiting attackers was bounced straight down over the net as if Ka Ulukoa wasn't even blocking. The boys looked over at Coach Pono, confused and scared.

Coach Pono raised his arms above his head in the shape of an O, "Big Circle! Big Circle!" until Ka Ulukoa reset to receive the serve.

Micah and Skylan learned quickly that sharing the ball was not going to be an option. After Ka Ulukoa went down by five points in the first set to Borinquen, every ball that was passed and every ball that was dug all went to Tui. Whether he was on the left side in the front row, or in the middle of the back row, he took every set that Skylan and Micah could put in the air. Ka Ulukoa felt a moment of confidence as they crept back into the game by digging a few balls to the middle of the court and transitioning them for points. That was, until Danny Rivera elevated on a high and tight set to the left side and crushed a ball down on the 10-

foot line that bounced up and hit Skylan between his legs. Skylan rolled around on the ground for a while as the referee stopped the game. He finally stood up and limped up to the net for the next serve. On the very next play, Evan passed the serve and Skylan set Tui, who softly rolled the ball over the block to the middle of the court and down.

Coach Pono yelled out from the sideline, "It's the same! One point! One point!"

Borinquen Coqui finished the set in stylish fashion, when their Libero dug Tui's hit up with his foot and Fernando jumped in sideways to setup Ricardo for an inside set that he hammered to the floor untouched. The Puerto Rican whistles and bells were as loud as they had been all match. Coach Pono sat his boys down on the bench and told them to drink water.

"That is why we don't watch warmups. They take these swings straight down and play for the crowd. They beat us 23-25 and we played humble and efficient. One play at a time, now."

The boys took the court for the second set. The Hawaiians couldn't deny that the size and the volume of the crowd were stunning. It added a type of pressure that they had never before faced. Skylan looked through the net at Fernando Dias and he felt a connection with his game.

He thought, *I have everything that he has. He is the Puerto Rican version of me. I just have to do it better. Remember why we are here.*

Ka Ulukoa was able to make just enough digs to keep the set even. Borinquen continued to bounce the ball but Ka Ulukoa started to understand that points were worth the same amount, regardless of how they were scored. Tui took the majority of the sets, and when Borinquen began to close a two- or three-person block on him, he started to hit the ball hard off the top of their hands and out.

After a few successful kills, high off the hands, he thought to himself, *maybe this is why Rick Tune said 'Power before accuracy' at camp.*

The Puerto Rican fans' cheers turned to yelling as their boys started to miss their hitting spots and couldn't score and *sideout on Ka Ulukoa's serve. Ka Ulukoa took the second set 25-20 on a hard cross-court hit by Ricardo, that Austin Amian watched sail out of bounds.

Coach Pono walked his boys to the bench before the third set tiebreak.

When Tui returned from the coin flip and sat down, Coach Pono said, "Nice work boys. Nothing changes. Let these guys try to go harder and harder while we stick to our game. One play at a time, now."

Skylan set Keenan a slow ball in the middle. As he tipped it over, his body maneuvered into a 360, and the ball hit the floor. Borinquen argued over who should take the ball, while Keenan smiled at Skylan on his way back to serve. The convention center was filled with the noise from the Puerto Rican faithful and the Borinquen players fed off of it. Harder and harder they hit the ball as if they were punishing it for being in the air.

"Next! Next!" Coach Pono yelled as he circled his finger.

His boys looked at him and reset quickly, as if they were obeying the order of a video game, trying to achieve the next level. More players and more parents came over and surrounded the court in this battle of North American 12-year-olds.

Micah walked back to serve, and Coach Pono raised his arms as he yelled to his defense, "Big Circle! Big Circle!"

The match swayed point for point. Fernando Dias saw the pass and peeked across the net before he tapped the ball over on the second contact. Micah jumped out with both arms and dug it right on top of the net. Skylan jumped and set it, with only four fingers, just high enough for Keenan to touch it with two fingers, and the ball trickled over the net for a kill. Micah threw his hands in the air and gave a high-five to Keenan as the Borinquen coach called a timeout. Ka Ulukoa served for match point, ahead 14-12 in a third set race to 15.

Evan served a high cross-court ball that Ricardo Pidilla passed uncomfortably. Fernando gave a set to Danny Rivera, which was too wide of the *antenna, and Danny was forced to tip it over. Micah ran in to dig it and Skylan set the left side for Tui — 'crack!' The ball hit the floor and the entire bench ran out and dog piled in the middle of the court. Austin Amian jumped up, and then dropped to his knees and slapped his palms onto the court. The coaches smiled and the Puerto Rican players hung their heads in disbelief.

The announcer called all of the 12 & Under teams to the podium. They called Fusion 12s, they called Borinquen Coqui 12s, and then the announcer paused.

"Your 2008 Boys' Junior Olympic Gold Medalists: Ka Ulukoa 12-Mizuno."

The boys looked at Coach Pono and he raised his arms in the air. The boys copied.

Skylan said, "I feel like we won the World Championship!"

Kim Meyer said, "Let's go to dinner and celebrate."

The boys stayed up all night long at the ski house and that was fine with Coach Pono; they had achieved something special. In the morning, Evan was awake first, sitting alone on the second floor. Tui realized he was alone in his room.

He walked upstairs, "Why are you up so early, Evan?"

"Just thinking," Evan sounded sad.

"We just won the tournament and now you are sad? What's up man?"

"I won't be seeing anyone after we leave today... not until next year, if there is a next year." Evan looked up slowly.

Tui reassured him, "Just try and enjoy it while it lasts. Playing together was cool."

The families made it to the Salt Lake Airport and said their farewells.

"I almost forgot," said Coach Pono. "Lee Lamb is inviting all the families over for a luau, July 16th. Have a good trip home."

Coach Pono left toward his gate. On his walk with Micah, his cell phone rang. It was Doug Beal, the CEO of USA Volleyball.

Doug Beal spoke, "I want you to know that we are very proud of you, Pono. The Puerto Ricans have never been beaten in the 12 & Under Division, ever. Your team was the first and you all did it with a ton of class. Congratulations."

Pono had no idea. After he hung up, he put his arm around his son.

Micah said, "It's crazy that we came here with a bunch of kids who aren't from volleyball families and won. We all looked at you weird in that first meeting at tryouts for saying you think we are going to win the national championship. Now we are like you, with your championships, Dad."

Coach Pono slowed his walk and released his arm from his son's shoulder. "Micah, anyone who was not prepared to achieve that level was not up to par with our goals. There is a reason that I said nothing more than my name at the tryout. Our team had to develop its own identity. You and the boys had to learn your own paths by deciding what level was acceptable. This is yours and your teammates', son. You own it.

CHAPTER 6 - INTERMEDIATE

"May I speak to Tui, please?" Skylan Engleman asked, calling his teammate to ask about playing in a local beach volleyball tournament. The boys heard the news that they were the first American team to beat the Puerto Ricans in the history of Junior Olympics and they took it with them into the summer proudly. The local players on the island congratulated the boys whenever they ran into them at the beach. The victory and the Gold Medal were bigger than their team and their club. They were a representation of the Island of Hawai'i. Pono asked his two long-time friends, Mike Among and Charlie Jenkins, over to the house. Mike played with Pono at the University of Hawai'i. They became close friends after Pono graduated and spent some time coaching together at Kamehameha Kapālama.

That always surprised Mike, who vividly remembers missing the very first morning workout of his freshman year at UH and running into Pono, a senior captain, wagging his finger in Mike's face and saying, "Don't you ever miss another frickin' workout again!"

Charlie Jenkins also had some history coaching with Pono, while Charlie's two sons were at Kamehameha. Mike and Charlie were in Sandy, Utah with their Outrigger 18s team and had the chance to watch Pono's 12s after their 18s lost in the Open Division Quarterfinals.

Mike headed home from the Ma'a's place, and Pono said to Charlie, "I could use your help this season."

Charlie said, "I decided to be done coaching, about two weeks ago. Besides, you've got Dave Engleman and Larry Tuileta helping you, right?"

Pono replied hurriedly, "Yes, and they were good. I want you to come help me out this season, though."

"Sure, I will come by when I can," said Charlie, half-heartedly, as he stood up to head out to the driveway.

Tui submitted his applications for where he would attend intermediate school in 7th grade. He applied to `Iolani Intermediate, Kamehameha Kapālama Intermediate, and Punahou Intermediate. In public, he made it clear to anyone that Kamehameha was his desired choice. The Hawaiian culture was strong there and he was of Hawaiian blood. In truth, Tui was jealous of the lifestyle that he envisioned the Punahou students having, and internally, he wished to experience what those kids experienced. Applications came back and Tui was accepted to Kamehameha, accepted to `Iolani, and waitlisted at Punahou.

Micah, who was enrolling in his first year of intermediate school as a 6th grader at Kamehameha, got a call from Tui.

"Micah, Brah, I have news. I'm coming to Kamehameha with you this year."

Micah didn't contain his excitement. "No way! Nice! I'm gonna show you how we do it over there. Shoots!" Micah prepared himself to return to Kamehameha Kapālama, where his dad had recently taken a job in admissions, and his favorite teacher, Andy Chung, would be teaching two of his 6th-grade classes.

Tui called Micah again in August, "Hey man, I got off the waitlist at Punahou."

"Yeah. And?" Micah asked, searching for relevance.

In almost a whisper, Tui said quietly, "I got accepted, so I am going there this fall."

Micah shouted, "What?! I can't even talk to you right now." He hung up the phone.

Tui was bummed to tell his friend that he was backing out on their school year together, but he felt better after telling him with his own voice. Micah would have to rely on his other reasons to be excited about starting school. That list was short.

Pono invited the boys from the team over to the house to watch the 2008 Olympic Men's Volleyball Gold Medal match. A few boys from the team slowly trickled into the house. Micah would not say a word to Tui as the boys gathered in the garage to play Ping-Pong.

It wasn't until the USA men beat Brazil in the second set that Micah finally shouted, "Yes!" and took a high-five from Tui.

When the school year started, Tui was uncomfortable with the atmosphere. It felt conceited, even privileged. Enrolling at Punahou made him hope that his perception of the school's culture was exaggerated. His first day made him feel like his perception was spot on.

Tui had always played football and baseball, growing up with football in the fall, and baseball in the spring. That year, 2008, was the first year that intermediate volleyball was moved from the fall to the spring. Tui had to make a decision. He chose to play football in the fall and volleyball in the spring, and since he didn't have any friends at his new school, he decided that it was best to get out to the football field as soon as he could. Intermediate football started at Punahou and Tui caught himself in a conversation on the field with Davis Miyashiro, an average-sized Asian-Hawaiian boy with floppy shoes. Tui drifted toward him naturally because Davis was *Da Kine, or a real Polynesian Hawaiian.

Tui struggled in school at Punahou. The curriculum was intense and he wasn't motivated to approach his teachers. He ran into Maddison McKibbin on campus. As a 12th grader in the academy, Maddison still remembered Tui from Punahou Summer Camp the previous year. He asked Tui how his transfer was going, thus far.

Tui was honest, "It's been hard. I feel a little out of place."

Maddison said, "That can happen if you just use your eyes, but all the students here are approachable. Ask your teachers for help. Most of them are from around here too, so they want to help the local kids. I've got class now, but tell me if you need anything. I'm around."

Nothing changed in a day. Running into Maddison did make him feel better, though. It was cool that a 12th grader would talk with someone from the 7th grade. He didn't expect anyone at his school to really understand.

Ka Ulukoa had tryouts in late September at Klum Gym. Lee Lamb introduced himself and sat all of the tryouts down in a circle.

"I see some old faces and some new faces in the gym. In our second season as a club, we would like to continue in our path of preparing you all for the next level of competition and life. Make sure to let us know if you are trying out elsewhere, and do your best."

Lee placed his hands together and turned as the coaches led their groups away to their courts. Coach Dave knew that Skylan was in good hands and moved on to coach the 14 & Under boys' team at Ka Ulukoa. Larry Tuileta Senior helped organize the boys during JOs in Sandy, but had gone back to work his day job, so Maile Tuileta brought Tui to the tryout. Coach Pono ran his tryout alone.

Skylan scanned his eyes around the gym as they walked to the furthest court in Klum Gym.

"Where are Christopher, Joseph, and Noah Faurrot? Is Kelsey coming back?"

Coach Pono sighed and answered Skylan.

"They moved on to play elsewhere." He switched the hand of his clipboard. "For those who are new, I am Coach Pono. I will be coaching the 13 & Under team this season." That was all that he said.

"Let's jog!" said Micah, as he led the group of tryouts around the court.

When the time ran out, Lee Lamb asked everyone to the center of the gym.

"I want to thank you all again for attending the second Ka Ulukoa open tryout. To aid in implementing our club's mission, this season, all of our athletes will be required to maintain a 2.75 minimum Grade Point Average, in order to participate in practice and compete in tournaments."

Tui placed his hands in his face, remembering how he had already started his academic year at Punahou.

Pono made his calls that night. He called Micah, Skylan, Tui, Keenan, Noah Hayashida, Austin Amian, a 5'5" soft-spoken, skinny boy named Taylor Weins, and a 5'7" Hawaiian boy named Kaehu Ka'a'a, who came to tryouts on Skylan's convincing. Pono offered them all spots, and they all accepted. Evan would be spending the season playing on the Big Island beside his brothers at Southside, with his dad as the coach.

Pono leaned on the counter and talked with Lisa after dinner.

"It's nice to be done with callbacks so soon this year. I still have to get an assistant and a team parent, though. Kim was on the bench all of JOs rubbing Keenan's back and following her boy around. That doesn't help us grow."

Lisa ran her fingers through her long blonde hair as she dried the dishes.

"Maybe ask Maile Tuileta. At the luau, she said she would be interested in being more involved this season."

"Good to know," Pono said, as he kissed his wife on the cheek and left the room.

The new team met at 10am in the gym at Susannah Wesley for the first training. Coach Pono called the boys the night before and stressed the importance of attending the first training. He jumped right in, on readdressing the standard on attendance.

"Call when something comes up and be honest. Come when you can come. When you do come, be focused when you are in the gym."

After spending a season with Coach Pono, the returners understood that he was not referring to focus in the sense that a 13-year-old would commonly take it. The focus that Coach Pono was talking about was different. It had the qualities of a laser beam.

"Sit down on the bench, boys," Coach Pono said as he took a knee. "The man standing behind me is a long-time friend of mine. He has been beside me in the past and we will have him around as much as we can get him. This is Coach Charlie."

Charlie Jenkins stepped forward. He was rather small, with dark brown skin, and a full mustache. He wore his baseball cap draped over his forehead, touching just the edge of his eyebrows. He interlaced his fingers together in front of his chest as he spoke.

"Like Pono said, I am Charlie Jenkins. I've known Pono for a long time, since back when my two sons played at Kamehameha, 1998-2006. I coached with Dave Shoji over at Outrigger from 1999-2007. I saw some of you play in the finals in Utah, this past summer. I am glad to be here helping out Coach Pono."

"Warm up," Coach Pono said, as he picked up his clipboard and arose from his knee.

Skylan led the jog around the court. Kaehu Ka'a'a pulled up beside him on the jog and started chatting.

Skylan said, "Hold on," and waved his hand backwards, to signal his friend to stay in an orderly line. Once they stopped jogging and formed a circle to begin stretching, Skylan whispered, "We don't really have extra talking in practice. Try and focus. We can talk after."

Kaehu looked confused. He took Skylan's message harshly. The warmup was done. The boys separated sides for *Tennis*, and Coach Pono explained the drill.

As it had been the previous season, *Tennis* was rough. The touches weren't clean. Boys who were new to the drill tried using contacts other than their forearm platform. Some kids stood up, watching the ball land in on their side of the court, then looked at Coach Pono as if he was just going to enter the next ball. Coach Pono asked them all to go sit down on the bench. Again he dropped to a knee. Coach Charlie stood behind Coach Pono with his arm folded and said nothing.

"It is a good time to go over the rules. We have very few, but all of them are expected to be followed. We always give respect to our family and our teammates. Respect goes beyond what we say. Respect is shown in what we do. In the gym, we are always focused on getting better. That means every play must be treated as an opportunity to get better. Every play is treated the same. If any ball touches the floor around us, we give a dive."

The boys could see the intensity in his face, like he was holding back some frustration. They nervously shook their heads in agreement.

Coach Pono stood up, "Okay, *Partner Setting*! Five and five."

Each of the boys grabbed a ball and a partner then stood across from each other.

Coach Pono gave the instructions, "Partner one, underhand toss to your partner with both hands. Partner two, set back to the forehead of partner one. Partner one, catches in the setting position, above his forehead. Five each and switch."

Coach Charlie walked around, stopping just about every player. "Have your feet even, and shoulder width apart. Lift your arms and shape the ball with your hands. Your hands go one direction when you set. Get it on his forehead."

The boys struggled. Everything seemed unpolished, all of a sudden, if Coach Charlie was watching.

Coach Pono instructed again, "Okay, *Partner Passing*! Same thing. Pass with arms now and catch in the setting position, five and five."

Taylor Weins and Kaehu tried to set with their hands again.

"Okay, everybody stop," Coach Charlie jumped in. "We partner pass with our forearms. Everyone should toss well to his partner. A little shuffle and pass the ball with your arms, to your partner's forehead. Get the ball on his forehead. Pass by using your arms, no legs."

The boys continued. Their passes were sloppy and off target. Coach Charlie stood with his arms folded and shook his head.

He leaned to his left and said, "Pono, they need work."

"Let's go, *Freeball Passing*! Platform first," Coach Pono shouted.

Skylan, Micah, Tui, Austin, Keenan, and Noah led the newcomers to one side of the net and stood in a two-person formation on the court. Coach Pono tossed underhand freeballs over the net as the boys passed with their platforms to the target, just right of the middle of the net, about two or three feet away from the net. Two boys were on the court at a time, and a new one rotated in after each pass. The pace was slow. Coach Charlie occasionally plucked out a boy and gave him simple words on how he could pass better. Sometimes he used his words out loud for the entire group.

"No legs! Strong platform! Hold your platform! Get it to the forehead!"

For 25 minutes, they passed high and lofty freeballs to the target with their arms. Taylor and Kaehu got excited when they heard Coach Pono open his mouth for the first time in 25 minutes. That excitement faded quickly once they heard the words.

"Okay, more *Freeball Passing*! This time with hands."

For another 20 minutes the boys passed freeballs in the same formation, with the same pace.

Coach Charlie continued his additions, "Feet shoulder width!

Strong hands! Finish with your arms! Keep the same height! Pass high! Get it to the forehead!"

"Water break," said Coach Pono after 50 straight minutes of *Freeball Passing*.

The boys walked over toward the bench.

Kaehu started to say, "Man, that was —"

Skylan stopped him, "Remember. Focus."

Kaehu shrugged his shoulders and lifted his hands, "Brah, it's a water break."

Coach Pono shouted out, "*Shoulders*, let's go. Throwing first, five each."

The boys took their spots with a partner, inside of the court, near the sidelines, and faced each other.

"Step and throw to your partner's knees. Finish *left pocket, and then open up. Partner catch between your knees."

"Coach Pono, what do you mean open up?" Kaehu asked.

"Like this", Coach Pono said as he pivoted to face Kaehu with his knees bent and his arms spread just outside of his knees, "Palms up."

They all threw back and forth.

"Catch between your knees!" Coach Pono shouted as some boys stood up to catch and some dropped the ball. "After five, go into strokes. Toss over your hitting shoulder. Drive the ball to your partner with one bounce — then open up — five strokes, each."

Few tossed accurately and few made good hand contact. Coach Pono looked across the gym at Coach Charlie.

Coach Charlie said, "Hold on, guys. You have to toss well. Focus on the toss right now, just the toss. The rest will come."

Not much changed in the results. Coach Charlie may have felt like his eyes were burning from the sloppy display in front of him, but he was temporarily satisfied with seeing that their attention had shifted, primarily, to the toss.

Coach Pono spoke up, "We will introduce *One-Contact* today. This drill is challenging. Doing basic things the right way can be a challenge. All you boys, grab a partner. Tui and Skylan, come out in front for a demo, please. Coach Charlie will instruct."

Tui and Skylan stepped out from the group and onto the court. The two of them faced each other, Tui five feet from the net and Skylan five feet from the back line. Coach Charlie walked beyond the demo boys and turned around toward the group. "*One-Contact* is a rehearsal of live play. It has evolved into what would be the usual sequence of contacts. The attacker is your opponent," Coach Charlie gestured his open palm toward Tui as the attacker, "until he makes contact, and then he turns into a teammate on the court." Looking at Skylan, Coach Charlie said, "The defensive player is totally engaged with the attacker," his eyes shifted to Tui, "gaining information from the toss location, arm motion, and hand contact." Skylan earned the return of his coach's gaze as Coach Charlie added, "The defensive player then executes whatever is necessary to get the ball up to his partner." There was a pause in the instruction, while Coach Charlie scanned to confirm that his words were being followed.

"After attacking, Tui will assume 'the ready' position, gaining information from the digger's (Skylan) body position and platform location, and now executes the set assist toward the partner's (Tui) hitting shoulder. Each of you here are right-handed," he said while pausing again to confirm comprehension. "Skylan, the digger, who is now the attacker, approaches the set assist trying to get the ball into the slot above the hitting shoulder and catches the ball. Five each and switch."

After watching 10 seconds of balls being hit into the ground or digs being shanked into the wall, Coach Pono said, "One thing at a time. Today, attackers just hit and open up in the ready position, diggers dig, and attackers catch in the hitting slot."

Five minutes later, Coach Pono said, "It's 11:30, time's up. Balls in the bag."

Pono walked outside with his team. The boys thanked Charlie for helping them and went home.

Pono turned to Tui, "Ask your mom to call me."

Walking into the parking lot, Kaehu asked Skylan sarcastically, "Can I talk now?"

Skylan replied, equally as sarcastic, "Now you can talk."

Pono took his family to see Misty's high school volleyball match. On his way home, he was thinking about practice with the Ka Ulukoa boys. He decided to call Charlie later that night.

"So what did you think of the guys?" he asked Charlie.

Charlie's reply was delayed by his chuckle, "I think they need work."

Pono told his friend, "We could use your help. I want you to coach with me this season."

"I told you I would be there," Charlie said, luring Pono in for a deeper meaning.

Pono bit on Charlie's lure, "I want you with us, full time."

"I can't say no," Charlie confessed.

At the next practice, Coach Pono said nothing about Coach Charlie's new status. He just told the boys to warm up. They ran their laps and stretched in a circle.

"*Partner Setting*," he said in a conversational volume.

The boys didn't ask why they weren't playing *Tennis*; they just arranged for setting.

"*Partner Passing*, five each," was the next order.

"*Freeball Passing*, platform first." That lasted 20 minutes.

"Now, hands." That lasted another 20 minutes.

Coach Charlie chimed in as they went, intentionally slowing the pace.

Coach Pono maintained his volume, "*Shoulders*, let's go."

The boys moved into throwing and strokes, five for each boy.

Coach Charlie reminded them, "Just the toss for now."

Although their strokes were all over the place, the tosses showed signs of consistency.

Coach Pono progressed, "*One-Contact*, now. You boys separate into partners. Tui and Skylan, come over on this side," he said, pointing to the opposite half of the court on the other side of the net. "For review, Skylan's arms should be out in the ready — always in the ready. Tui is gonna toss and hit directly to Skylan's knees. After Tui hits, he'll open up and get down in the ready, so that he is prepared to set the dug ball. Skylan will dig the ball back to the Tui's forehead. Tui'll set Skylan's hitting shoulder and open up to the ready. Instead of catching in his hitting slot, Skylan will stroke the ball, with one bounce, back to Tui. And Tui will catch. Stroke to the knees, dig to the forehead, set to the hitting slot, stroke into the floor, and catch. Five and switch."

It was far from clean, but the coaches let them learn.

"No more than five, guys. Only five each," Coach Pono said, as he picked up his clipboard to scribble some notes. "Next we'll do *Three-Man Pepper*. Get in groups. Dig, set, hit back and forth. Person in the middle sets. Setters, set the hitting shoulder and open up, turn quick to the digger."

Five minutes went by.

"Move on," Coach Pono said, "**Quick Hitter Timing*. Everyone hit two balls. Shag for the person hitting after you."

"Shag?" Taylor asked.

"Shag means pick up the balls," Coach Pono rephrased. "Micah set first. Tui, Taylor, Kaehu, Skylan, and Austin, you are hitting. Keenan and Noah, Middles are with Coach Charlie. Kaehu, you set after Micah."

Skylan looked confused and walked slowly toward the sideline with the other hitters. He trained his hitting in practice at 12 & Under, but since he started playing organized, he had always been a Setter. Why was Kaehu setting after Micah that day? He brushed it off and continued.

Tui hit first in the drill. His first two swings were smooth and deep. Kaehu and Taylor hit the next four balls, two each. After Kaehu's two attacks sailed from his hand to the back wall, and Taylor's two were mistimed and flubbed into the middle of the net, Coach Charlie looked over and stepped in.

"Stop."

He moved two low boxes, about three feet by three feet, into the deep corners on the opposite side of the net.

"No wild hitting, the same as strokes." He pointed to the two boxes, "And we hit only the area-one box and the area-five box. If you can't hit one of those then tip the ball in down the line."

Keenan and Noah looked over from behind the other hitters, where Coach Charlie was detailing their footwork. Other than the sound of the ball, the gym was silent as the drill continued. Tui made solid contact on the ball as he recalled what Micah's sets were like, and aggressively located his swings near the boxes. Austin, Skylan, Kaehu, and Taylor tentatively tipped the ball over the net to avoid being called out.

After five minutes, Coach Pono said, "Get water and come back."

The boys piled over near Coach Pono.

"Alright, *Partner Serving*. Get a partner."

They started on the 10-foot line for five serves. The pace was slow. Some moved back to mid-court, but Coach Pono kept Kaehu and Taylor at the 10-foot line. Coach Charlie told the boys to serve in a straight line to their partner. A few moved back to the service line, others stayed at 10 and 20 feet away from the net.

"Now we are going to play *back row Three-on-Three*. You can only hit from behind the 10-foot line and each side only gets two contacts to get the ball over. Cooperative first." Coach Pono entered balls, and they played for a while. The rallies ended quickly and the ball hit the floor often, but the returners made sure that the newcomers always knew to give a dive. The fourth player waiting exchanged with someone every time the ball crossed the net.

After five minutes Coach Pono added in, "Same drill, three contacts now."

Only two contacts, digging then hitting the ball over, was much more difficult than having all three contacts. Now, though, the boys were much more aggressive with the third contact hit and made more hitting errors.

"Keep it cooperative and rally", Coach Pono said, before tossing another ball in.

A few minutes passed, and then Coach Pono changed, "Competitive now."

Coach Pono watched a few decent plays and watched a few errors before he spoke.

"To be clear, guys, our mindset doesn't change between cooperative and competitive. The mindset doesn't go from *have* control to *lose* control. We always have control. It's the same game. In cooperative, we dig, then set, and then hit the ball to a teammate. In competitive, we dig, then set, and then hit the ball where a teammate isn't. But we want to keep the ball in play whether the set is good or not. Get water and come back."

Coach Pono always picked a player or two to pass *float serves during the water break.

When they returned, he said, "Let's go over rotations and how we line up, and then time's up."

By the third practice, the boys began to understand the plan and how practice was designed to flow.

In November, Coach Pono entered the team into its first girls' 16 & Under Tournament of the new season. As the tournament went on, it quickly became apparent that the girls were falling further away from being able to keep up with the boys, primarily because the girls were getting further from keeping up with the pace of Tui, alone. The boys won that local Hawai'i tournament, but not everyone left with great feelings about it. Skylan felt uneasy about his new position, which had now been confirmed by tournament play. He had won the Gold Medal at JOs as one of the starting Setters for Ka Ulukoa in the 12 & Under Division. Now he wasn't even in the starting lineup, watching his friend Kaehu take over half of the 6-2 offense setting duties, and playing as a defensive substitute behind the Libero, Austin Amian. Arlene Engleman took it even harder. She watched that tournament, and another the following weekend. While she did her best, externally, to support the team, inside she felt like her world was turning upside down. Skylan came home to her crying in the kitchen. Tears weren't something he was accustomed to seeing from his mom.

"What's wrong, Mom? Are you hurt?" Skylan asked as he closed the door and approached her.

Her head was down. She turned away to hide her tears.

"I'm alright, Skylan. Today has been hard."

"Come on, Mom. Tell me what's up," he said, placing his arm on her shoulder.

"It is hard for me to watch you not setting. I always see you as a Setter. You did so well at Junior Olympics and your team won. I don't understand why you aren't setting."

She looked up at him and her tears became a stream down her cheeks.

Skylan's heart sunk a bit, seeing his mom emotional. "I know, Mom. It is hard for me, too. You don't have to cry."

She asked, "Do you want us to find you another team? We can find somewhere for you to set and play on the court. It's not too late."

Skylan couldn't deny that he thought. He paused to ponder the situation he was in and answer his hurting mother.

"No. No. I trust Coach Pono and Coach Charlie to do what's best. After what we did at 12s, I am attached to this team. Playing a new position is hard, but I can work at it to get on the court."

Arlene sniffed up her running nose and spoke aggressively, "No, I think we should find you a new team. You should be playing, and we didn't do all this work last year and this summer for nothing."

Skylan replied, "It's really okay, Mom. Don't worry."

She could sense the hesitation in his voice, but she said nothing more. At the next practice, Coach Pono rounded up the boys near the bench. The boys prepared to jog as a visitor walked through the door. Someone they would never forget.

Chapter 7 - The Guru

Through the doors of the gym walked a tall, Polynesian man with blue jeans, a faded grey shirt, and a pair of white Reebok shoes that looked as if they had been used for construction work all 90 days of summer.

He shouted to Coach Pono, "Sorry we're late, Braddah."

Beside him stood his son. He had brown skin, darker than any of the boys in the gym. The top of his head was flat and his ears had the shape of a perfect circle. His name was Adrian. Adrian's dad shook Coach Pono's hand.

"Hey. Yeah, Larry told me you would be heading over today." Coach Pono turned to the boy, "Are you Adrian? Go ahead and jump in."

"Thanks for giving him a tryout," said Adrian's dad.

"No problem. We'll check him out. What's your last name?" Coach Pono asked.

"Faitalia."

The boys ran through practice as they normally would, only replacing *Tennis* with foot-speed line drills after stretching. Adrian was rather quiet. The coaches expected very little from him, as it was his first day and he was with boys he didn't know. Micah partnered with Adrian as a guide to how the drills were run: *Partner Setting*, *Partner Passing*, *Freeball Passing*. The practiced progressed and Adrian was sloppy, as the others were when they began. Coach Charlie instructed him with short-worded changes along the way. The team worked into the throwing portion of *Shoulders*. Adrian's throws were inaccurate, but they were getting to Micah's lap fast — very fast. The boys moved into strokes.

"Woah," said Coach Pono quietly as Adrian's first hit bounced straight down near his own feet and 20 feet into the air.

Coach Charlie looked over at Coach Pono and raised his eyebrow.

Coach Pono approached Adrian. "Drive through the ball to Micah's knees. Don't bounce it."

The next stroke hit the floor two more feet out in front of him, but landed nowhere near Micah's knees.

Coach Pono encouraged him, "Keep trying. One at a time."

Coach Charlie stood back with his arms folded. He always seemed to give the boys a little more time to observe themselves.

Adrian couldn't have been ready for *Three-Man Pepper*, but the coaches put him in a group with Micah and Kaehu anyway. A ball hit the floor near Adrian.

"Dive," said Coach Pono in his most patient volume.

Adrian's eyes pointed up at Coach Pono with a look of confusion. He fell to the ground, one limb at a time as if he were a pile of leaves having an encounter with the wind. Another ball hit the floor near him.

"Dive," Coach Pono maintained his volume.

Again, Adrian crumbled like an uncooled cake out of the oven that had been poked with a finger. It was clear to everyone that he had not been asked to dive before.

Coach Pono said, "Adrian, any time that a ball lands on the floor near us we give a dive. Out of respect for our teammates' hard work."

By the time the team made it to *back row Three-on-Three*, Adrian hadn't hit the floor on his own once. As expected, the first ball to hit the ground in the drill fell near him. Adrian looked at it then shifted his eyes to Coach Pono for the next entry.

"Dive!" Coach Pono raised his volume in frustration.

Three plays later, "Dive!" Coach Pono had moved into a full shout by this point.

Coach Charlie stood behind the court with his arms folded, occasionally releasing one hand to adjust the hair on his mustache and hide his smirk.

Coach Pono was on a rant the entire ride home. "Micah, you better not ever go to someone's practice and perform like that. That is why I grabbed you and your sisters up so early. Gosh, that kid was so lazy!"

Micah just sat and listened. In his mind he wanted to bust up laughing, but he feared his dad's head might explode. Once he made it to the house, Pono called Charlie on the phone.

"That kid was so lazy! That's not going to work for the team. He will rub off on the other boys."

Charlie could hear the frustration in Pono's voice.

"And on top of that, they were late and — Man, how can he be that lazy?"

Charlie entered the one-way conversation slowly, "We have to give him time, Pono. It was his first day. I like him. He is raw and we'll be good if we can make players out of boys who aren't good already. Give it time."

The practice for the next week was at Klum Gym. Adrian's dad brought his son and in his left hand he brought the same steel chair on which he always sat.

Tui asked Adrian, "Does your dad bring his own chair everywhere you go?"

"Just about," Adrian replied in a quiet tone.

The practice started on its normal schedule. After completing *Partner Setting* and *Partner Passing*, the boys prepared to move onto *Freeball Passing*.

Coach Pono said, "We are introducing a new technique today. Everyone get in a line behind the service line." He pulled the cart of balls over to the net. "We are going to learn *One-Arm Digging*. Step out into the ready, palms up, and use the big part of your forearm to dig. Hold it after you dig. Each player gets two balls."

"Haha! Cool," the group of boys said behind Tui as he stepped out first.

'Pop!' Coach Pono hit the first ball to the right of Tui and he shanked it into the wall.

Coach Pono said, "No swinging. Get your arm in front of the ball and hold." Coach Pono swung again. 'Pop!' The ball was hit to the left of Tui.

Tui extended his left arm with the biggest part of his forearm facing Coach Pono. He held his arm out after the contact, but the ball still fell straight to the floor after hitting his arm.

Coach Pono critiqued. "Angle the ball up. Let's go, Skylan."

Skylan stepped in for his turn at the new challenge. His teammates looked on with smiles on their faces as if they were next in line for the new rollercoaster at Disneyland. 'Pop!' Coach Pono hit to Skylan's left side. He swung his arm and missed the ball as he fell the opposite way of where the ball was headed.

"Stop," shouted Coach Charlie as he approached the court. "We won't lean-dig and we won't swing. Watch."

Coach Charlie stepped into Coach Pono's line of attack. All of the boys were silent and locked in on what was about to happen. They had only seen Coach Charlie stand on the side with his arms folded and speak, or occasionally place his hand on top of their heads to keep their bodies low to the ground. All eyes were opened wide as if a single blink would ruin their day. 'Pop!' Coach Pono hit and Coach Charlie stepped quickly, and then extended his left arm. The ball bounced off of his forearm and hung in the air for a moment before landing back in Coach Pono's hands.

Some boys gasped. Some let out a "Woah!" in amazement at the execution and accuracy of this foreign technique that they'd just learned.

Each boy couldn't wait to get his turn at two attacks from Coach Pono. They barreled in one at a time, shanking and spraying balls all over the place, though they tried their best to imitate what they saw from Coach Charlie. Coach Pono continued to give critique. Coach Charlie reassumed his spot off to the side and folded his arms.

Ten minutes was long enough and the drill was completed.

Coach Pono started to progress the boys onto *Freeball Passing* when Coach Charlie stepped in again. "We don't use the one-arm for a goofy game. We don't use it just because. We want one move for an efficient dig. So if we can't step-dig between our knees with a platform or overhead with hands making one move, then we use the one-arm outside of our body."

The boys' faces turned from playful and silly to intense and serious, like when a boy gets called from class to the principal's office. They nodded to show that they understood Coach Charlie's message, clearly.

After the team played *back row Three-on-Three*, the coaches added *Primary Passing to the end of practice. For the first few minutes, the *serve receivers would just pass. The next few minutes would have receivers passing, a Setter setting, and Middles hitting Quick Attacks. After a few more minutes there was passing, setting, Quick Attacks, Outside Hitters hitting the *Go-attack on the left side, and Opposite Hitters hitting the *Red-attack on the right side. Coach Pono finished the practice with the starting six in serve receive against live serves from the other players, with another freeball for a second transition attack. It was during this last portion of practice that everyone could see just how hard Adrian hit the ball. His attacks didn't have a hint of consistency in their direction, but he was hitting the ball even harder than Tui.

The boys entered the weekend girls' 16 & Under tournament with Adrian as a part of their new roster. Adrian didn't play; he had not put in enough time with the training yet. He did have an impact on the tournament, though. The local coaches heard from their girls, frequently, how unfair it was that Tui was hitting against them. Those complaints didn't change with this new tournament, but the tournament director decided to step in and make a change when Adrian was attacking on the right side during *Quick Hitter Timing* and hit a ball so hard out of bounds that it took a bounce and broke a porcelain sink on the wall. That was the last 16 & Under girls' tournament that Ka Ulukoa would play.

Pono got a call from Guy Enriques in January.

"Hey Pono, Guy Enriques here. Did your holidays go well? I'm calling to figure out the situation with Evan for this summer. Just heard from USAV where they'll host Junior Olympics."

"Holidays were all good here, Guy," Pono replied. "We got that email too. Evan is coming back with us right? We would like to have him back and he can stay with us again, same setup as last year."

Guy never liked losing his boy for a long period of time but it was what Evan wanted, so he allowed it.

"Yeah, yeah, we will send Evan up there with you when he is out of school. Is Micah around? Evan wanted to talk to him."

"Micah, come to the phone. Evan wants to talk with you."

"Evan!" Micah said, as he sprinted over to the phone. "Howzit? Been a long time since I heard from you, Brah."

Evan was excited to hear from Micah, too.

"Hey, it's not like you called me, either. You hear about Junior Olympics?"

"Yep! Atlanta, Georgia this year. Gonna be super fun. Are you coming with us?" Micah waited impatiently.

Evan stalled out Micah. Then he said, "My dad said I can come stay with you when I get done with school."

"Shoots!" Micah said with a huge grin.

"*Rajah! See you in summer, Braddah." Evan hung up.

Pono got a call from the office at Kamehameha Kapālama that Micah was causing trouble at school. He wasn't allowed to go on any field trips because he was acting out in class. He couldn't attend D.A.R.E. or assemblies, either. He had to sit in the counselor's office and do paperwork during every event. Pono had been consistently working late shifts and wasn't getting home until after 10pm. The night he came home to the message on his answering machine, he walked upstairs and snatched Micah out of bed.

"Get downstairs," he said. Micah knew the discussion would not be pleasant. "If I get another call about you acting rascal at school then there won't be sports for you. You won't so much as touch a Ping-Pong paddle if I hear from the school again this year. Lead by example, Micah. No one will follow a knucklehead. Get upstairs and go to sleep."

Micah didn't say a word as he walked up to his room and closed the door.

The next day, Micah walked into Mr. Chung's class with his chin in his chest and his eyes on the thong of his flip-flops.

"You feeling down, Micah?" Mr. Chung asked, offering half of his attention.

"Eh, just got yellings from my dad last night for school stuff." Micah said faltering, until his voice became sarcastic, "I swear you are the only one that gets me Mr. Chung!"

Mr. Chung laughed and joked with Micah to lighten his mood. "Maybe you should transfer to Punahou. Get yourself in less trouble there."

Skylan's school didn't have intermediate volleyball, so he spent his springtime practicing with his dad's Ka Ulukoa 14 & Under team, in hopes of regaining a spot in his own team's starting lineup. Meanwhile, Tui was in intermediate volleyball at Punahou and he hoped it would be a better experience than he had with his intermediate football team, which achieved a zero-wins-to-six-losses record that fall. The University of Hawai'i at Manoa got a new men's volleyball coach, Charlie Wade, for the 2009-2010 season. Maile took Tui to a spring season match in the Stan Sheriff Center. He was delighted and surprised to find out that his mom, who was never shy, would introduce him to Charlie Wade. After watching that match, and then having a talk with the head coach, Tui's eyes were opened to what the next level of volleyball looked like.

He said to his mom, "I want to make sure I do volleyball the right way so that I can try to play here. Make sure I don't take the easy way out."

She replied laughing, "Easy way? Boy, I wouldn't let you take the easy way to something even if it was written in the law. Let's go."

Evan had his bags packed for a full week before school had finally let out on the Big Island. He boarded a plane the next morning. That next day, Ka Ulukoa was back in the gym. Evan thought he'd be familiar with the practice plan. He was excited to break from Big Island volleyball and experience Coach Pono's high expectation once again. Evan was meeting Coach Charlie Jenkins for the first time, and was curious about Coach Charlie's lack of interference with the drills. He was so used to Coach Pono and Coach Dave being on the team with every repetition that was taken. Coach Charlie stood behind the drills with his arms folded and observed. The gym was silent enough to hear a pin drop. Evan could feel that the level of focus had risen with his new team. He was intrigued upon his introduction of the *One-Arm Digging* technique. Like the others when they got their first glimpse, Evan had never heard of such a thing being practiced. He remembered his role and fell into line with the training.

The team moved through practice and Evan was adding some

new things that the system didn't have at 12 & Under. The players stood face-to-face, in partners, and tossed high, easy, freeballs for each other to pass with their forearm-platform. Then they tossed high freeballs for each other to set with their hands back to their partner's forehead.

Evan asked Tui, "Is this all we do in practice, pass freeballs?"

Tui giggled, "Yep."

The team moved through *Freeball Passing* into *Shoulders.* They snapped their wrists over and over, hitting the ball against the floor and having it land in their partner's lap after one bounce. Evan began to hit his strokes.

Since he stood up straight following his strokes, Coach Charlie spoke up. "Hand to the left pocket and open up to the ready, Evan."

After *One-Contact, Three-Man Pepper* began.

"Turn quick to the digger, Evan. Be ready to set again." Coach Charlie kept his eye on the young Enriques.

Next was *Quick Hitter Timing.* When they *did* get the chance to attack the ball and hit it over the net, it was to one of two places: one deep corner or the other.

Coach Charlie stayed near Evan. "Only the area-one box and area-five box, Evan. Hit the spots." Coach Charlie's constant critiques made Evan question if he was really that sloppy.

Serving was very meticulous. The boys stood in partners across the net from each other and served short distances, one 10-foot line to the other. They would only move back to 20 feet once they could serve to each other consistently standing at 10 feet. Then they'd do the same work-up from 20 feet to full-distance serves at the end line, 30 feet away — but not until they could serve consistently standing 20 feet away from the net.

Coach Pono repeatedly barked, "There is no reason to miss your serve! Your serve is the one thing in volleyball that you have full control over."

Coach Charlie stood behind, stoic, as they served.

Finally, the team got through *Partner Serving* and onto *back row Three-on-Three.* Evan saw this as his time to show his new coach how hard he would work. A ball was hit hard to Evan's right and he jumped out with both arms, swinging his arms through the ball and popping it up, and landed on his chest. Evan felt a smile coming across his face.

Coach Charlie did have a comment. "Stop. Evan, use your one-arm if you can't step-dig inside your bodyline. No swinging the arms. Less is best."

Evan felt like Coach Charlie had just taken his lunch money. He said nothing, though. He chose to follow and listen.

Since the summer began, Tui had been having trouble with his knees from taking so many jumps and swings for the team. Coach Pono considered pulling the team out of their first girls' 18 & Under tournament, but Evan coming into town gave Tui the opportunity to rest for the tournament. It was also an opportunity for the coaches to see what Adrian could do in his new position of Opposite. The team held a Sunday practice after the Saturday tournament.

Coach Charlie said, "We are going to end practice early today because I want to read you all a story." He walked to his backpack and pulled out a book, no longer and no wider than his palm and fingers. "This book is called, *The Precious Present.*"

Coach Charlie read slowly, taking a glance up after each page that he finished. The boys watched him and listened intuitively. After 20 minutes, he closed the book and placed it back in his bag. He placed each of his thumbs and index fingers together in a 90-degree angle, creating the shape of a rectangle with his hands.

He said, "This is *The Precious Present.* Remember this anytime you lose your way."

CHAPTER 8 - GRASSHOPPER

Maile Tuileta took over the team mom duties, and Coach Pono put her in charge of finding the house that the team would stay in for Junior Olympics. Maile was also in charge of getting the boys organized in Georgia, because Coach Charlie was coming in on a separate flight later that day, all while Coach Pono's arrival was stalled one day to watch Misty in Miami, Florida. The team flew into Atlanta three days before 13 & Under competition started so that they could have two full practices in the convention center. It proved to be a keen idea to arrive early when Tui's mom took the boys off track, trying to pick up Coach Charlie from the airport.

"Auntie Maile, we've almost been driving for two hours. Do you know when we... Wait, does that sign say *Welcome To Nashville*?" Micah asked.

Auntie Maile squinted her eyes and giggled to herself. "I guess we drove a little out of the way."

They stopped at the nearest gas station to ask for directions and picked up food to make sandwiches in the car. It was a long drive back to Atlanta. Coach Charlie decided to room alone in a hotel close to the playing site, so when the team pulled up to the house, they were surprised to find Coach Charlie sitting outside in a chair.

"Oh my gosh! I am so sorry that we were late to pick you up. How did you even get to the house?" asked Auntie Maile.

Coach Charlie gave her a thumbs up, "I took the shuttle."

The house they pulled up to was a beautiful three-story cabin on the outskirts of Atlanta, equipped with a billiard table and flat screen television in the basement, and a swimming pool out back. The Ka Ulukoa 17s, coached by Lee Lamb, also had their stay in the Atlanta cabin.

The 17s took the bottom floor in the basement, the adults stayed on the second floor, and the 13s roomed at the top. Auntie Maile collected the five cups of rice and one can of spam that she requested for each one of her 13 & Under boys to bring. Once they got settled, it was straight to the basement for billiards.

When Coach Pono arrived the next afternoon, he took the team over to the convention center. After checking in for the tournament and receiving their passes, the boys took a long walk through the halls and settled at the doors of the arena. Coach Pono led the group. Everyone had his bag in hand for practice.

"Coach Pono, our practice court is the other way," Skylan said as he stopped walking.

Coach Pono kept his head forward and continued on. He finally stopped on one of the few courts that were empty inside of the massive room filled with 17- and 18-year-old boys.

"Boys, this is Court 1."

Coach Pono said nothing more. The boys turned their heads and looked at the red tiles on the court, surrounded by a blue outline of tiles that led into the 30-foot-tall grandstands. The design was magnificent for a volleyball match. Before the boys turned back to Coach Pono in search of a purpose, he had already begun making his way in the opposite direction. The boys followed to the practice court. The practice didn't last long. A nice jog and stretch followed by some ball control and serves was good enough. The sooner they got home and ate, the sooner they could forget volleyball and play games.

The night before the first day of 13 & Under competition, Coach Pono's team was on the third floor, talking story.

All of a sudden, they heard Lee Lamb yell out from the basement, "What in the world? Hey, 17s, get down here!"

Lee's 17 & Under team was just walking in from its third day of competition. The 13s all poked their heads out to look down the stairs. Lee had found a sleeping bag full of candy and wrappers sprawled out across the basement couches.

His voice got louder, "What the heck is this? We are on a clean eating program. Where did you get this garbage from?"

The 17s stared at their coach with straight faces. The 13s looked at each other and covered their mouths to muffle their laughter.

The candy belonged to them, and the health-conscious coach was railing the 17s for it. Lee banned his team from the television and billiards, as no one would step up. As for the 13s, it was their running joke all night.

The next morning was day one. Auntie Maile made the boys a breakfast dish that she called, "The Breakfast of Champions." The dish was spam and eggs, with rice and furikake. It was tasty more than it was healthy, so the boys had no complaints.

Kaehu rubbed his stomach and said, "I'm still going to feel this after we win the finals."

"Woah! Woah!" Evan snapped at him quickly. "Don't talk about the future. We only talk about today."

Auntie Maile inserted herself back in, "Anyone — want more?"

It wasn't until day three, after playing their fifth match against a Spanish-speaking team, that the team realized they were playing a tournament filled with Puerto Ricans. They played Fusion 13s in the match to make the eight-team Gold Bracket for day four and lock themselves into a minimum of a fifth-place finish.

Tui tightened up in the first set. He used his heavy arm-swing to hit early on, but it was of no benefit to Ka Ulukoa. He got stuff-blocked on five swings in a row. Fusion's momentum pulled it ahead by nine points and Tui's head dropped into his lap. His confidence had faded. Fusion took the set and switched sides of the net.

Coach Charlie told Tui, "Don't try and bounce on these boys. Choose the guarantee over the glory."

Tui walked with his team back onto the court and hoped to establish what he thought was the strongest part of his game. That was a tall task with his confidence deserting him. Tui's struggles continued in the second set. He resorted to tipping and rolling softly in bad situations. Fusion inched ahead to a five-point lead and Coach Pono itched to call a timeout. Coach Charlie insisted that he didn't.

"Let him learn," Coach Charlie said, referring to Ka Ulukoa's flailing star Outside Hitter.

As the only Setter in his *5-1 offense, Micah searched around for an alternative option. Tui had always been his automatic. He finally made it to the back row and had three options with Kaehu rotating into the front row at Opposite. Tui served next, after Micah, and Pono's boy was finally able to find his target. He went to Evan, who had just rotated into the front row and drove a pinpoint swing cross-court into the area-five corner, right on top of where Coach Charlie's area-five box would be. The next play in transition, Micah found Evan again for an in-system attack down the line to the area-one corner for a kill, exactly where Coach Charlie's area-one box would be. Fusion still led, but must have felt the pressure as their coach used the first of his two timeouts. Evan's play showed that he had an easier time understanding what Coach Charlie meant by, "Choose the guarantee over the glory." Evan wasn't as tall as Tui, as strong as Tui, or as athletic, but the consistent directions from Coach Charlie over the past few weeks were ingrained in him. He imagined the five-box and the one-box, and he hit those, and nothing else. He didn't see that it would guarantee him a kill. He saw that if he didn't get a kill, it would guarantee that the other 13-year-old team couldn't counterattack strongly. Tui watched his teammate be unwavering and aggressive in his attack of the Guaynabo, Puerto Ricans, and Micah gave him the green light. Evan led them back to a two-sets-to-one victory and it was a clinic of Coach Charlie's offensive tactics. After the match, Tui walked over to his dad on the sideline chairs.

Larry Senior gave his son a fist bump. "That was a close one. Way to pull it out."

Tui responded with his head down, "Man, I sucked. Evan saved us."

Larry Senior squeezed Tui's shoulder. "Look at me, Tui. You can never be afraid to hit the ball and help your team score. They don't rely on you to kill it every time. They rely on you to be aggressive. That's your game."

Tui nodded to his dad and gave him another fist bump before joining his team to leave the arena.

Back at the cabin, the boys set up a game of Mini-ball. Adrian learned fast, and in two days' time, had already become the scariest boy to play against, because of his hard hit. Austin Amian had become Adrian's best friend on the team. Although they were polar opposites in every physical category imaginable, their personalities clicked.

Austin got brave. "I'll play against Adrian. Who's with me?"

No one spoke up.

Austin pulled on Taylor Weins and said sarcastically, "Get in here, since you are always talking junk."

Skylan jumped on the other side of the pillows. "Okay, you two versus Adrian and me."

"Me and Evan ref then we got next," said Kaehu, as he took his refereeing post at the line of the pillows.

Coach Pono was pulling boys into his room for individual meetings one by one. He called for Skylan next, so Skylan left his turn in Mini-ball and walked down the stairs to Coach Pono's room.

"Grab a seat, Skylan. How are you doing so far this tournament?" Coach Pono leaned in and looked his player in the eye.

Skylan paused before he answered. "It's going pretty good. I am just trying to do my part and do my role... I mean, play my role."

Coach Pono sensed he was holding back. "I can see it has been tough on you not being in the Setter position this year. Going from all six rotations to digging for two or three in the back row is a change. I appreciate you being there for the team. Tell me though, is something on your mind?"

Skylan paused again. "Well, it has been uncomfortable in the arena the past few days. Whenever we walk through the doors, I feel like every team stares at us like we are aliens, and they whisper and say stuff under their breath."

Coach Pono leaned away and sat back in his chair, still holding his eye contact.

"They want a piece of you, Skylan. They want a piece of us. They know that we have something special. Listen, sleep well tonight. We are going to need everyone tomorrow."

"Okay, Coach Pono." Skylan stayed sitting for a moment, awkwardly looking around before he stood up and left.

All of the boys met Auntie Maile at the breakfast table. It was clear that she had little sleep the night before.

She said, "You guys sit down and eat up. Be ready to do well today." She slapped her son's hand as he reached for his fork. "Say grace before you eat! You know better."

Micah laughed at Tui being warned by his mom.

"What are you laughing at, Ficus?" said Evan, who was looking directly at Micah.

Micah cut his eyes at Evan quickly. "Ficus? Not this again. What does that even mean?"

Evan just smiled and bowed his head for grace.

After breakfast, Auntie Maile said, "You boys grab your bags and lunches. I got them all packed up."

"Hold on," said Micah. "Are those red jerseys in there? We have to ditch those for sure."

Skylan seconded that, "Yeah, we lose every time we put those on."

"What do you mean? You haven't lost any games." Auntie Maile misunderstood.

Austin chimed in, "Knock on wood."

Micah clarified, "We lost the first set to Fusion yesterday, and we lost the first set to Borinquen last year."

Auntie Maile giggled, "Oh, you boys."

Coach Pono's boys arrived to the arena and the scene was familiar. Winning their pool on the third day gave Ka Ulukoa a bye into the semifinals. The boys appeared to be relaxed. Only one spent the night thinking about much volleyball: Tui. He rolled around in his bed and thought about the way that he let his team down. That's the way he saw it. If he didn't come to play on the fourth day, then he would be to blame. He was the leader. If he didn't play better, his team wouldn't win.

Coach Charlie was already at the court waiting for the boys. He sat in the second chair on the bench with his ankle on top of his knee like he was reading a newspaper, and his head was down under his baseball cap. He looked as if he was sleeping. He picked his head up and looked at the tiptoeing Micah, who was just about to touch Coach Charlie's hat.

"Right on time," Coach Charlie said as Micah backed away, smiling.

Vaqueros of Corozal, Puerto Rico was Ka Ulukoa's semifinal opponent. Before the match started, Larry Senior arrived to the spectator sidelines from getting his morning coffee. He didn't say anything as Tui glanced at him. He simply gave his son a thumbs-up and smiled. Tui bounced back nicely in the semifinals. He attacked aggressively and reestablished himself as the player to whom Micah could set. He led his team to a favorable victory over the smaller, less controlled Vaqueros. Ka Ulukoa was unsure whom they would draw in the tournament finals, but after walking to the hallway to have their lunch, they heard a loud thump of a volleyball and a crowd roar that filled up the arena. They didn't turn their heads to look back, but they recognized that sound.

The finals were set for 12, noon. The boys entered the arena at 11:15am to start their warmup. Court 3, where the 13 & Under finals would be played, began to fill with Puerto Rican fans. The boys were accustomed to the sound of the Spanish language by then. A familiar foe walked to the opposing bench to put on brightly-colored shoes of blue, orange, and neon green. Borinquen Coqui returned to the finals, representing the dominant country of Puerto Rico and seeking revenge on the Hawaiians who stole the Gold Medal away just one year before Tui was back in good form. Early on, Borinquen pushed Ka Ulukoa hard. It wouldn't be enough. Ka Ulukoa was one year more polished, while Borinquen seemed to play the same game that they were playing a year prior. Their flashy play style and consistent attempts to bounce the ball didn't faze Ka Ulukoa this time around, not even when Danny repeated his bounce from the previous finals, off the floor and up between Skylan's legs. After Skylan walked it off and his team took their laugh, the Puerto Rican crowd could see the momentum right back in Ka Ulukoa's favor. They knew they could win, and they did: 25-16, 25-19. Ka Ulukoa raised their arms in the air — back-to-back Gold Medalists.

The victory was satisfying. The year was full of new additions, but after coming off of the medal stand the boys realized quickly that the most pressure they had felt all season had come in practice. Tui hugged his family after the match.

He made his way toward the coaches and he said, "Coach Charlie, did you not get a medal?"

There was nothing around his neck.

Coach Charlie replied confidently, "I got one," as if there were obvious evidence.

"Where — Why aren't you wearing it?" Tui asked politely.

Coach Charlie didn't hesitate. "The medal is in my bag. It's wonderful that we won and it's a big accomplishment, but this season is over, Tui. My focus is onto next season."

Chapter 9 - Rascal Activity

An early finals match allowed for enough time in the afternoon for Coach Pono to take his boys to a water park to celebrate. It was refreshing for the boys, raised near the waters of Hawai'i, who weren't allowed to use the pool at their cabin until after the tournament. Auntie Maile arranged for the team to stay one extra night on the Mainland before heading home. Skylan stayed an extra day to leave with his dad and the 14s. Evan stayed the night then left with his dad, who would take him and his brothers to Oregon for Guy's annual girls' high school camps. Evan knew it was the last night he would spend with the team for a long while, so that last night was cherished.

There was an unexpected ring at the doorbell. Everyone was surprised to see Coach Charlie, with two big grocery bags in his hands. The boys rushed over to the front door to surround him, and to see what he had in the bags.

Coach Charlie stepped through the crowd of boys and into the kitchen.

"I'm making you all steaks for dinner. You all did well."

The boys all cheered and crowded around Coach Charlie again, showering him with hugs.

Auntie Maile pushed through the crowd to help Coach Charlie. "Okay, okay, let the man breathe."

The 17s had finished a day prior, so the 13s had the house to themselves. Evan was playing billiards with Micah and Tui down in the basement. The witty Enriques turned the slim margin that he was beating the other two by, into a big margin. Evan looked up and smirked after sinking another billiard ball.

Tui scratched his head and laughed. "This freakin' guy."

Micah had a different response; also laughing, he grabbed his stick.

He shouted, "This is blasphemy!" and he chucked his stick like a javelin.

'Bam!' The stick made a loud sound as it hit the wall. The boys all dropped their jaws with their mouths wide open as they approached. A hole the size of a *tennis* ball appeared in the wall and the stick just hung there inside of it.

Evan said, "Oooooo, your dad is gonna crack you."

Tui chortled at Evan's claim, predicting some truth to it. Micah grabbed the stick out of the wall and looked around in a panic. He stashed it inside the dirt of a tall decorative plant that sat in in the corner.

"See, that's why we call you Ficus," Evan said.

"What the heck is a Ficus?" Micah asked, his voice still in a panic.

The boys heard Coach Pono's footsteps thumping down the stairs to see what the racket was. All three boys jumped on the couch and did their best to look inconspicuous.

It only took one turn of Coach Pono's neck.

"Who did that?"

No one said anything.

"I'll ask one more time. Who…"

Before his dad could finish, Micah started tearing.

Coach Pono took in a deep, calming breath. "Get upstairs, now!"

In the summertime, the team spent three days together preparing for the Ka Ulukoa Luau. The luau was always designed as a fundraiser for the club. The families of the athletes could pay a small entrance fee to come eat a ton and watch the performances that each boys and girls team put together. Coach Pono's team was coming off of back-to-back Gold Medal seasons, so they earned the pleasure of going last. They came onto the stage and the room exploded in laughter and clapping when they saw Noah, Keenan, Austin, Skylan, Micah, and Tui turn around to the start of the music and perform their ballerina routine. The whole event was a fun time, and it was exciting because it was a chance for the teams to collaborate on something outside of the gym.

Tui started summer training for intermediate football. He wasn't excited about returning to his private school, which provided him few friends. However, there was a highlight to the start of the school year. Tui walked passed the admissions office of Punahou on his way to class. He stopped and did a double take.

"Ho Brah, what are you doing here?" Tui stood behind Micah Ma'a, who was sitting in a chair waiting for his turn in the office.

Micah turned around and jumped up. "Tui! Howzit? I might be transferring in — to Punahou this year."

Tui's eyebrows rose. "What? No way. How'd that happen? I thought you were going back to Kamehameha."

Micah whispered so his mom couldn't hear from the admissions desk, "Causing too much trouble over there." His voice returned to normal, "Plus, I know you missed me so I'm doing you a favor. Now you can see my face everyday."

"Oh, joy," Tui said sarcastically.

Micah made his transfer to Punahou. Pono was still an employee of Kamehameha, so he took some heat in the community for the decision, but he figured it would be a good move for his son. Tui enjoyed football, but he wasn't particularly excited about the potential of another defeated season with his team. Micah decided that he would play fall football, which made Tui optimistic that his team could have a better season. No such luck. His team finished zero and six for the second season in a row. Time showed that Tui and Micah wouldn't see each other very often, at school. Tui was in his 8th-grade year at Punahou, while Micah was starting his 7th.

Skylan spent his summer playing two-man volleyball on the beach. That was where he felt freedom. Out there, Skylan could play every position, and he wanted to be involved during every play. He made his third school switch and enrolled for 8th grade at the Word of Life Academy in Kaka'ako to allow himself a one-year preparation for the coming high school curriculum. Dave took a job coaching the girls' Varsity team at Maryknoll High School. As it was the previous year with his dad's 14s, when Skylan wasn't at school that fall, he was practicing with Dave's girls.

The boys arrived to Ka Ulukoa tryouts to learn that Kaehu had moved to the Big Island and Taylor Weins wouldn't return. The number of tryout athletes had shrunk substantially. That was unexpected, after the success that the team returned to the island with from the past two Junior Olympics. Coach Charlie attended tryouts for the first time and he was happy to see that Adrian had returned after not playing so often. Adrian was the only returning boy with whom Coach Charlie initiated a hello greeting. That made the other boys jealous. To the boys, hearing words come out of Coach Charlie's mouth happened about as often as a solar eclipse. Coach Pono led his boys to the furthest court in Klum Gym and picked up his clipboard.

Coach Pono's decisions for the team were no challenge. After calling the Enriques family and the Ka'a'a family to confirm that Evan and Kaehu would return, Coach Pono extended offers to all of his returners. Micah, Adrian, Tui, Keenan, Noah, Skylan, and Austin all accepted. The number of boys on Oahu was down to seven and just under half were playing intermediate sports for their schools. Coach Pono held the same expectation for attendance that he impressed upon the boys in the past. He knew that the practice numbers would be low consistently. The system remained. Coach Pono instructed the four or five boys who populated the fall practices through each drill and they asked few questions. The practice atmosphere was quiet. It was ideal for Coach Charlie. He enjoyed the quiet.

He said to the boys, "With less, we can do more. Less is more."

He was literal in his message. Coach Charlie treated the small group practices like they were private lessons. With every drill and every technical movement, he was on his boys.

He stood behind the court during *One-Arm Digging*.

"No swing, Adrian. Quiet body, Austin. Do we have to put a strait jacket on you, Keenan? One move, nothing more."

He stood over Adrian during strokes.

"Drive through, don't bounce. Finish left pocket to ready. Every time, left pocket to ready."

He critiqued Noah during serving. "Stay straight, no lean, serve in one line."

During back row Two-on-Two, he stood with his arms still folded.

"No, no, stop. Always dig with quality; there is nothing else. The ball comes up before you switch jobs."

The boys poured sweat during training. The tempo wasn't extreme, but there were few players and there were no plays taken off. Coach Pono and Coach Charlie watched like hawks.

Whenever Micah was there, he set the *Quick Hitter Timing*. If Micah had an intermediate football game, then Skylan would take the setting reps, while Kaehu was still on the Big Island. Every player practiced every thing. Middle Blockers learned to pass and set. Liberos learned to hit and block.

When the hour and a half came to a close, Coach Charlie would leave the boys with this, "Less is best. No unnecessary motion. We got so much more out of being simpler."

Coach Charlie preferred the small group practices. Coach Pono saw the benefit, but he considered how they would fair in competition.

Micah despised the feeling of losing, more than any boy he knew. So, after playing an entire season with the intermediate football team and not winning a game, the decision for him to redeem himself with another sport was immediate. As the primary sport for the upcoming winter season, he chose intermediate basketball at Punahou. Coach Pono took the end of the football season as an opportunity to sign the Ka Ulukoa team up for their first tournament of the season. They picked up where they left off, registering for the girls' 18 & Under Division in Hawai'i. The boys were in decent form as Tui and Micah flowed right into the system they had left. The real highlight of the tournament was the offensive performance of Adrian, who was starting at Opposite for the first time. He took full advantage of Kaehu being away and put on an array of hard-hitting front row attacks, most of them landing in bounds. Skylan subbed into the back row for Adrian. Austin assumed a white t-shirt for his Libero position. It seemed the girls' teams had formed an alliance against the only boys' team that played in their tournaments. The off-teams, with no refereeing duties, were exposing the serving zone signals that Coach Charlie was flashing his team behind his back. Keenan tapped Coach Charlie on the shoulder and pointed to the girls, exposing his signs. Coach Charlie shook his head. He turned back to the match and extended his arm so the entire gym could see his fingers spread wide, signaling to serve at the area-five passer. He continued to deliver his speechless message for the rest of the tournament. It didn't matter what the other team knew, they were going to have trouble stopping it.

Coach Pono told his boys after the tournament, "Really nice, boys. Good volleyball today." Despite missing teammates and having no six-versus-six competitions under their belts for the season, the boys performed well. He didn't say so out loud, but he was impressed.

The boys were happy with their progression through the fall. They were making a good situation out of one that others would turn away from. Coach Pono brought the news to the next practice that Evan would be flying into Oahu for two weeks over the Christmas holiday to prepare for the Southern California Volleyball Association's Junior Invitational in January. California hosted the closest qualifying tournament for the summer Junior Olympics. The boys would have to make the wintertime trek to California if they wanted to have a chance to defend their Junior Olympic Championship.

Micah greeted Evan with a big hug as he walked through the door of the baggage claim.

"How you been, Ficus?" Evan asked Micah smirking.

Micah rolled his eyes, "Ugh, whatever. I have so much to tell you, man."

When they pulled up to Micah's house in Kaneohe, Evan dropped his duffle bag and the boys ran straight to the garage for Ping-Pong. Coach Charlie had spent the last six weeks pulling the Middles out of the drills and working on their transition footwork so that the team could have a strong Quick Attack on second and third chances. Coach Pono saw Evan's return as a good time to add on to the system.

They practiced at Hongwanji Mission School, a small gym with a low ceiling in Honolulu. He huddled the boys after *Shoulders*.

"Today, during *Quick Hitter Timing*, we are going to add in the back row *Pipe-attack for the Outside Hitters. Outsides take two swings each. Setters set the ball high to the center, a few feet in front of the 10-foot line."

The boys all separated into their areas. The Outside Hitters started attacking on the left, Tui first. Micah set the Go for Tui. 'Bam!' Five-box. Transition, another Go-set, 'Bam,' one-box. Evan followed in the same pattern. The Middles were next. Micah set the *Front-1 for Keenan, two feet above his forehead. 'Bam!' Wrist-away to his right. Keenan took three fast steps away from the net and back in for his second attack. 'Bam!' Across his body to the left. Noah copied. Adrian prepared on the right side. Opposites traditionally started to approach from on or outside of the sideline. Coach Charlie had his right-handers start inside of the court and approach in the shape of a backwards C, so that the sets would always stay over their hitting shoulders. Adrian took the first Red-set from over Micah's head. 'Bam!' He hit it hard near the middle of the court.

Coach Charlie paused from tossing balls to Micah during Adrian's transition.

"One-box. Five-box. Control."

Adrian took his second swing. This time he took some speed off and stroked it. It wasn't on target, but it was closer. The boys repeated the full sequence again.

Then, Coach Pono said, "Now, Pipe-attacks, Outsides."

Tui and Evan lined up in middle-back, area-six. Tui saw Coach Charlie's toss and started his approach. Tui stopped and set the ball over. Micah's set flew a few feet behind the 10-foot line.

Coach Pono critiqued, "Five feet closer, Micah."

Tui transitioned back and approached again. He jumped to his left and tipped the ball short over the net.

"Better, Micah, but put it in the center of the court." Micah nodded to his dad.

Evan stepped in for his first swing. 'Bam!' He had to jump to his right a few feet, but he made good contact on the ball. Coach Pono didn't say what he was thinking; he let Micah figure it out. Evan transitioned and took his second approach. 'Bam!' One-box, right on target.

Coach Pono stepped onto the court. "That's the set, right there. Did everyone get a look at that? We all have to be able to set this if we dig Big Circle. It gives us another option."

Being back with the Ka Ulukoa team was refreshing for Evan. He was glad to cut the 11-month-long wait in half.

Tui went with Evan and Micah back to the Ma'as' house. They

decided to take a bike ride to the mall. It took Micah some time to convince Mehana and Maluhia to let him borrow their bikes after what happened the last time that he and Evan took Misty's bike to the mall.

Mehana finally agreed, "Okay fine, Ficus, but only if Evan rides my bike."

Micah opened his mouth in shock at the name that his sister called him. He quickly cut his eyes at Evan and drug out the word, "You-u-u."

Evan just grinned back at Micah, "Let's go, we'll be late."

The three of them rode off to the mall and came up on a wooden fence. Micah slammed on his brakes.

"Hey, Evan, I bet you I can jump this fence."

Tui cut in, "Brah, that fence is like four feet high."

Micah snapped at Tui, "So!" He turned, "Bet me, Evan, 50 dollars."

Evan held in his laughter, trying to keep a straight face long enough for Micah to actually try it. "For sure, let's see it."

Micah reversed on his bike. He took a long lead up and approached the fence. His bike lifted three inches off the ground and his bike, with his body on top, plowed into the fence and gifted the fence a gaping hole. Evan and Tui fell off their bikes and busted up laughing.

"You've really done it this time, Ficus," Evan said, as he tried to catch his breath.

"Hush up," said Micah; pulling himself out, trying to avoid splinters. "Give me a ramp and I've got that.

"For sure you do." Evan joked some more with his friend.

The boys arrived back at Micah's house. Maile was waiting in the driveway with Lisa. Maile stood up as soon as she saw the boys pull up on the bikes.

"Boys, Adrian was shot on his way home from practice."

"What?" Micah said, hoping that he didn't hear Tui's mom clearly.

Evan spoke nervously, "Auntie Maile, is he okay?

"Yeah, he isn't dead is he?" Tui asked.

Maile said, "He isn't dead. We don't know much — only that he was shot while driving home in his parents' car. Make sure you say a prayer for him. Let's go, Tui."

Chapter 10 - Low Net High Ceiling

Evan spent Christmas with the Ma'as. As always, he called his mom every night and gave an update. The boys returned for practice two days later. Everyone had been calling around about Adrian and none of the boys had heard anything. At training, Adrian walked through the door with his dad, steel chair in hand. He was bombarded with questions before he could sit to put on his shoes.

"Oh my gosh, you're alive."

"Brah, what the heck happened?"

"You got shot? Did it hurt?"

Adrian waited until the questions slowed. "Yeah, yeah, I'm all good."

Micah repeated his question, "Did it hurt?"

Adrian said, "Not too bad. It just grazed my arm. Bullet is still in there until we get back from Cali."

"Woah. Gnarly."

The boys had more questions.

Coach Pono shut it down, "Alright, let's get going. Glad to see you're okay, Adrian."

Auntie Maile came to practice to get the jersey sizes handled.

"Mizuno is going to sponsor us again this season. Try these shirts on. I'm ordering each boy one red and one black."

Micah shouted, "What? No! Did you forget, Auntie Maile?"

Tui backed him up, "Mom, no red jerseys. The curse."

"Yeah, Liberos can wear red jerseys but not us," Keenan added.

Auntie Maile giggled, "Curse... right. So what? You all want two black jerseys?"

"Yeah!" The boys shouted unanimously.

Auntie Maile looked over at Coach Pono.

He shrugged his shoulders, "Fine with me."

"Yeah!" The boys obnoxiously celebrated Coach Pono's approval.

Auntie Maile's next responsibility was setting up the travel and the house for the SCVA Junior Invitational. The boys were going to California.

Two days before the tournament, the team arrived in Anaheim, California. Auntie Maile drove one van of boys to the house and Coach Pono drove the other. Coach Charlie stayed by himself at a separate hotel. Keenan collected two songs from each boy and made a mix-CD for each van to listen to during the drive. Evan insisted that John Mayer lead off the playlist. Coach Pono took the boys over to the American Sports Center in Anaheim, the tournament site for the Invitational. They walked through the doors of the ASC to a volleyball heaven. There were 36 courts with wood floors lined up in columns of four, all lettered vertically and numbered horizontally. The American Flag hung over the gym with a banner of congratulations to the 2008 USA Volleyball Men's Olympic Gold Medal Team. The group turned their attention to Skylan, who was a few yards ahead, staring through a glass window.

"What is it?" Evan asked.

Skylan replied, "Brah, come check this out."

It was the USA National Team's weight room, with Rich Lambourne, the starting Libero from the Gold Medal Team, squatting weight from the rack. Clay Stanley, the Most Valuable Player of the 2008 Olympics, walked through the boys' view and waved.

"Come on inside," said Coach Pono.

Doug Beal was waiting for them around the corner, flashing a big smile as if he'd just closed a big business deal. Wearing a dark blue USA Volleyball polo on his long frame, he shook Coach Pono's hand and introduced the boys to Rich and Clay. Doug Beal toured them around the Sports Center. Once they made it back around, Clay grabbed a jersey from Doug's office, signed it and gave it to the team. The experience was unreal.

The next morning they met Coach Charlie at the ASC for practice. Walking through the door was like passing through a wind tunnel; the gym was an icebox. The boys started their warmup and the coach of a girls' team, three courts over, came to ask Coach Charlie if they would scrimmage.

Coach Charlie responded politely, "No, thanks."

The man got upset, "Why not? You guys aren't doing anything over here, anyway, just throwing balls around. Come on, we'll give you some competition."

Coach Charlie turned toward the man again, "No. Thanks."

The boys finished siding-out off of some serves.

"Okay, we pau," Coach Pono said. "Time to go."

"Thank the Lord," Keenan rubbed his hands together. "It's freezing in here."

Tui slowed his walk, "One second, I've got to buy some socks from the pro shop."

"You didn't bring socks?" Adrian asked.

"Come on," Austin elbowed Adrian softly. "You know this guy is superstitious, like the way he keeps all of his fortune cookie messages."

"Hey! Those things are real," Tui said with an indignant expression.

Auntie Maile hurried her son, "Hurry up. We've gotta go to the store for waters."

The boys woke up to the smell of Auntie Maile's cooking. She had collected her standard five cups of rice and a can of spam from each boy to make her Breakfast of Champions, spam and egg dish. Auntie Maile had all their bags lined up on the floor in number order, with an initialed one-liter jug of water in front of each bag. They each gave her a kiss on the cheek as they walked outside and loaded the vans.

The parking lot at the ASC was a zoo of cars. The closest parking under 20 dollars was a 30-minute walk from the door, at minimum. Auntie Maile pulled into the main lot of the building.

She asked the parking attendant, "We can park here all day for 20 dollars?"

"Yes," the lady replied with a smile.

Micah rolled down the back window. "Aloha!" He reached out and exposed a package of macadamia nuts from Hawai'i. "If we bring you a pack of these everyday, will you reserve our spot?"

"You are adorable. Are they good?" the lady asked, teasing Micah.

"I guarantee you can't find better anywhere else. I got what you need." Micah poured on his 12-year-old charm.

Auntie Maile cut him off. "Boy, roll up that window and quit playing." She thanked the attendant and parked.

The scene inside of the ASC was frantic. The gym was full of boys 14 to 18 years old, coaches, referees, family members, friends, and fans. It was similar to JOs, when a few age groups were all playing at the same time, but the gym in Anaheim was much more compact. The 18s took up the A, B, and C columns with four teams per court. That allowed 48 teams to play at the ASC, which wasn't enough for the 63 teams that were in the 18 & Under Division. The bottom half had to play at other local sites. The 17s filled up the D and E rows with 32 teams inside of the ASC, 40 total in their division. The 16s were placed in F and G with 32 teams at the ASC, and 51 in total. The 15s were assigned the H column for 16 of their 21 total teams. Finally, the 14s took the wall on the I column, the ASC hosting 16 of their 31 registered team. The Mainland teams typically started their involvement with volleyball at the 14 & Under level, so the divisions were much more full than Ka

Ulukoa was accustomed to seeing. In 2008, the 12 & Under Division at JOs had 10 teams. In 2009, 13 & Under had just nine. Being a defending Junior Olympics National Champion didn't hold much weight in SCVA. Ka Ulukoa was seeded 15th in the tournament of 31. They *just* made the cut to even be at the ASC with the highly-seeded teams. Court 14, in the furthest corner from the entrance, was their home for the day.

Coach Pono's team was seeded 2nd in their pool, so they played the second match of the day against the 4th seed with a 9am start. The boys took their jog to prepare, holding their arms and shivering, wearing only shoes, socks, shorts, and their short-sleeved jerseys. The boys paid very little attention to their surroundings. When they got into *Quick Hitter Timing*, each player took his turn for two attacks. Tui hit his first two swings on point, both landing right on top of where the five-box would be. Evan took his first swing and paused. He bent down and held his hand, which was throbbing from hitting the ice-cold ball. He got another set from Micah and tipped it over the net to avoid a second round of pain. Noah tried out his attack and ran into the same problem. He also followed with a tip. By the second round of attacks, every boy, with the exception of Tui, was tipping and rolling all of his warm-up hits. Micah put his hands in his shorts between every setting rep. All of the boys looked at Tui sideways with each swing that he took.

"That doesn't hurt your hand?" they asked, hoping to feel less wimpy.

He joked, hiding the redness that developed on his hand. "Because it's cold? You guys are babies."

"My hands feel like rocks," Micah said, as the boys finished their turns.

"Okay, serve. Then, we are off." Coach Pono walked to the bench from tossing balls. "Oh yeah, Skylan, you are in the Libero shirt."

Skylan's eyes shot up quickly, making sure that he'd heard his coach right. He didn't want to ask Coach Pono to repeat himself, in fear that he may have a change of heart, so he rushed to his bag and changed into the red jersey that only he and Austin Amian had.

Ka Ulukoa breezed through their first day of pool play, hardly having a single one of their standing-float-serves returned. That didn't stop Coach Pono from yelling after every other play with his arms above his head.

"Big Circle! Every ball, Big Circle!"

Coach Charlie stood with his arms folded, barking a technical correction on occasion. After the third match finished, Coach Pono grabbed the boys and took them outside.

He said, "Time to go," and walked across the parking lot to get the van.

"Dad, let's go get *grindz," Micah shouted across the parking lot with his empty stomach in mind.

Auntie Maile followed the boys out to get her van.

She said, "Let's take you boys to get some food. Hopefully we don't have to stop and buy Tui any more socks."

Tui smiled to the team. "New pair every tournament day."

Skylan lunged for his seat in the van, "Auntie Maile, we for sure gotta get some hand warmers, though. My fingers were going to fall off in there."

The next morning, Skylan was the first to wake up. Auntie Maile was already in the kitchen at 5am, packing the boys' lunches.

"Why are you up, Skylan? Something wrong?" she asked.

Skylan said, "I don't know. I just woke up. My stomach doesn't feel good, though."

Auntie Maile turned toward her duffle bag. "Let me see if I can find you some medicine."

Before she turned back, Skylan was running to the bathroom When he came back out, Auntie Maile was waiting close to the door.

"Were you throwing up in there?" She asked as comfortably as she could.

Skylan paused, "Umm —"

Auntie Maile raised her eyebrows, waiting for a response.

"Okay, yes I did, but don't tell Coach Pono," he said miserably.

Auntie Maile said, "Skylan, if you are sick, we have to tell Coach Pono."

Skylan was nervous. "I'm okay, really, I feel better now."

Auntie Maile wasn't buying it, but she just walked back toward the kitchen. Skylan still felt discomfort in his stomach, but he had just started playing the Libero position. He didn't want to let a little stomach bug send him back to playing only a few rotations, or worse, no rotations. At breakfast, he did his best to hide his worsening stomachache. By the time the team got to the ASC and Skylan handed out the hand warmers to his teammates, they could see that something was up.

"Are you okay, Skylan?"

"Yeah, Brah, you feeling alright?"

Skylan just nodded his head yes. He thought that opening his mouth to speak could trigger another episode.

The tournament was re-seeded after the first day and all of the teams that finished in the top half of the pools moved up to courts closer to the entrance. Ka Ulukoa was fortunate to take over the 4th overall seed in the tournament. That drew a lot of attention to them from the teams in their division. They resumed their second pool of the tournament on Court E4. Skylan could hear boys passing by and making fun of Ka Ulukoa's slow and tedious warm-up routine.

"What are those guys doing?"

"Did they start playing volleyball yesterday?"

"This isn't a baseball diamond."

They were one spot behind the talk of the tournament. The 3rd-overall-ranked Baja 14s, from Mexico, showed up on the California volleyball scene for the first time. Primarily made up of the Mexican Boys' Select National Team, Baja sported a playing style similar to that of Puerto Rico's best teams, but Baja wasn't permitted in the USA Volleyball Junior Olympics, so the SCVA was their time to shine as a club team. By the middle of the day, the competition improved from day one, but the Hawaiians still hadn't faced anyone who could return their serve in a pass, set, and attack sequence more than twice in a row. During the team's break time, Tui headed outside on a walk to get a snack from his mom's cooler. He made the mistake of stopping at Court E3 for more than a glance.

That was the pool of the Baja 14s. His walk stopped abruptly when he turned his head to Baja's star Outside Hitter, Enrique Ugalde, who was taking a set from his Select National Team teammate, Sebastian Castro. The ball bounced well in front of the 10-foot line and over the 30-foot-high black net that separated the courts of the ASC. Tui rooted to his position and watched another play. To develop momentum for his arms, Micah held the ball when he set, because his 12-year-old wrists weren't strong enough to push it alone. But this Sebastian Castro really held onto the ball, for a while. The difference was that when Castro's setting motion started to go forward, the ball came out quick and got to its location in a hurry. Tui saw his mom at the entrance and started walking. He thought it had to be a mistake that the Mexican team he'd just witnessed was in the same row of courts as his team. There was no way that that group of boys was playing on a 7'4" net.

Coach Pono wanted his boys' eyes roaming around the gym as little as possible. The techniques that he and Coach Charlie were trying to implement were so foreign and so simple to what young boys were doing; he didn't want his boys to watch bad volleyball or flashy techniques and get hooked. That was why he always took the boys straight out of the gym after they played. This time, Coach Pono was off talking to Auntie Maile about Skylan, who was in the bathroom again, throwing up. He had a stomach flu and it was getting worse. Coach Pono was waiting on Skylan at the door of the bathroom when he stumbled out weakly. Skylan shuddered, knowing that his attempt at masking his sickness had been uncovered. He started to ramble, hoping to present a plausible case.

Coach Pono interrupted him, "Look, if you feel that you can play, then give it a shot. If it starts to get worse, then Austin will step in."

Skylan was guzzling through water. He finished his entire liter before the third match of the day. The boys played that third and final match of the pool. Skylan was physically struggling. He left toward the bathroom every time the Beach Cities 14s coach called a timeout. He told Coach Pono that he was going to get more water. There was truth to that, because he did take a sip of water from the fountain near the door, but each time it was followed by a trip to the trash can to vomit. He wanted to be completely honest, but he felt that this was his opportunity. He hadn't played six rotations for the team since they were 12 & Under. He wasn't going to lose his newly-earned spot without fighting his body's resistance.

Coach Pono's boys made it through and into an afternoon crossover match against the number-one-seeded team in the tournament, High Line Volleyball Club. The winner moved onto the semifinals on day three. High Line 14-Black was dominating the Southern California volleyball tournaments. They weren't explosive, yet from the start of the match they were clearly the best ball-control team that Ka Ulukoa had seen. The rallies extended long, and the match dragged on longer than any other of the top 16 teams left in the Gold. Ironically, it was Skylan who played the biggest role for the Hawaiians. He was served the most balls in serve receive and played fantastic area-five defense to give Micah the chance to use Noah and Keenan consistently on the transition Quick Attack. Coach Pono's team won the challenging match in straight sets and could finally end the longest day of volleyball that they had ever played.

The boys got into a game of Mini-ball at their Anaheim house. Auntie Maile stayed with Skylan while he was struggling to get rid of his stomach bug. The rest of the team was happy to be playing well enough to move up in the tournament. Coach Pono told his group that they had done what they had come to do; by beating High Line in the Crossover match, they had qualified for 2010 Junior Olympics Open Division. Coach Pono accepted and signed the bid before leaving the ASC. Auntie

Maile gave Skylan some medicine that would settle his stomach and help him sleep, so Tui became the only boy to have trouble falling asleep that night. His teammates were unaware, but he knew that the previously number-one-seeded team in the tournament was not going to be their biggest roadblock.

As Ka Ulukoa navigated its way through the tournament, the buzz began to spread about their team. The crowds grew larger and larger with each new match that they played. Young boys watched the unassuming warm-up drills and stood by their parents, puzzled by how this team kept winning, while their own team was ousted from the tournament. Ka Ulukoa beating High Line was the last straw for many of the doubters, who chose not to believe that a small, undermanned team from Hawai'i, tossing warm-up balls back and forth, was a tournament title contender. By the time the 11am semifinals came around on day three, the entire Southern California 14 & Under community of athletes and families had gathered around Court E1 to watch Ka Ulukoa 14-Mizuno square off against the Baja 14s.

Baja won the coin flip and chose to receive. They started with their Setter, Sebastian Castro, at left front so that after they sided-out, the Outside Hitter, Enrique Ugalde, would have three full rotations in the front row. That worked out to the benefit of Ka Ulukoa. Micah used his short float-serve to take Enrique out of the Pipe-attack, forcing them to set overhead. Tui stuff blocked the Mexican Opposite and gave Ka Ulukoa the 1-0 lead. After Baja sided-out on a repeat set to their Opposite, their blockers were able to get hands in the face of Ka Ulukoa's attack and set Enrique on three straight transition balls to take the lead 1-4. Tui sided-out for his team and headed for the back row, but missed his *topspin-jump-serve from the service line. Toward the middle of the set, Adrian shuffled out and made a big stuff-block on Baja's second Outside Hitter (OH2).

Auntie Maile shouted from the sideline, "Every time, Adrian! Every time!"

That was the spark to shift the momentum and Ka Ulukoa won the next three points to bring the score back level on the springy team from Mexico. Baja called for time.

Austin Amian subbed in for Adrian to serve and play defense. His deep, *standing-float-serve accompanied by Skylan and Tui's floor defense allowed Micah to use the Quick Attack, which no team in the 14 & Under Division had been able to stop. While Enrique Ugalde was stuck in the back row and being short-served to limit his Pipe-attack, Keenan, and then Noah, scored on transition ball after transition ball until Ka Ulukoa switched sides, taking the first set, 25-17.

In the second set, the Mexicans' OH2 served first, so that Enrique could still have three full rotations in the front row, starting at left front. Baja was clever. They mirrored Ka Ulukoa's first set tactics. Everyone but Enrique served Tui short, to shorten his approach on the Go-attack in the front row and the Pipe-attack in the back row. Enrique hit his tough topspin-jump-serve. Sebastian Castro started to use his own Quick Attack against Ka Ulukoa. The tempo of their Middles was much slower because of how long Castro held the ball, but they were much more athletic so they could jump up and hit around or over Ka Ulukoa's Middles. Again, Baja put the Hawaiians in some early trouble using those tactics. It was effective for the rest of the team, so between the first and second set, Coach Pono told Tui to switch to a jump-float-serve. Once Austin subbed in the back row, Ka Ulukoa developed a nice serve-receive rhythm, using Evan, Tui, Skylan, and Austin in a four-person passing system. Micah continued to use the Quick Attack in transition and now had the passing to add it in serve reception. The Quick Attack worked like a charm. Keenan and Noah attacked the Front-1-set close to Micah, and then moved away to the *Gap-set away from Micah. Ka Ulukoa kept Baja guessing with their offense and kept scoring. They brought it back even at 10-10. Enrique took the momentum away after he sided-out on the right side and went back to serve. Baja scored four straight points on his topspin-jump-serve. Once Ka Ulukoa was able to get Baja into some longer rallies, Baja used tactic again. When they couldn't get the ball to Enrique or their Middles, they tipped the ball over the block so that Tui would have to come behind the block from area-four and scoop it up. It was left to Evan and Adrian to pick up the offensive slack. And they did. Evan attacked smartly on the Pipe-attack, hitting only the one-box and five-box corners. Adrian used his heavy arm to blast the ball off the blockers' hands for *tools, or off of the defenders' bodies and down, to score. Ka Ulukoa's string of points persuaded Baja's coach into his first timeout of set two.

Tui served the next few points. Enrique Ugalde was stuck in the back row and Ka Ulukoa made the necessary plays on his Pipe-attack, digging Big Circle. He eventually made it back into the front row and Baja made a thrust forward. Baja sided-out well with Enrique in the front row with Castro. Poor serving by their teammates is what prevented them from having the chance to capitalize in defense. Skylan got his feet stopped and dug up a cross-court hammer by Enrique. Micah set Go, and Evan controlled it over to the one-box, setting up Keenan to get a stuff block on Ugalde in transition. That play pocketed the momentum and allowed Ka Ulukoa to close out the match a few plays later. With a 25-18 win, the boys clinched a place in the tournament finals against Southern California Volleyball Club (SCVC). How appropriate.

The Hawaiians exited through the doors of the ASC into the parking lot with their signed bid to Junior Olympics and the spherical glass trophy representing the SCVA Junior Invitational tournament championship over SCVC's 14-Quicksilver team. They were on a roll and playing good volleyball. Everyone played his role and Coach Pono was happy with his team's showing at its first qualifier. Skylan dragged behind the group, wrapped his hands behind his neck and took a satisfying deep breath, proud of himself for the courage he showed by pulling himself through the grueling three days of volleyball in Anaheim. The tournament was finished and Hawai'i was calling. Everyone went back to the house for one last overnight before flying to Oahu in the morning.

Chapter 11 - Humbly Qualified

Evan arrived back just in time to start the first day of his second semester at Kamehameha Hawai'i. He also had to hurry home to prepare for his tryout with the USA Volleyball High Performance Pipeline the following weekend. Carla Kabalis, a USAV director on Hawai'i, spoke with Evan before he left to Oahu and convinced him that it would be beneficial for him to attend. The spring semester was shaping up to be special. Guy Enriques decided on stepping away from coaching at Kamehameha Hawai'i to take a place as a Big Island city councilman, so the spring season would be the last time that Evan could be coached by his dad and play with his brothers at Southside.

Skylan carried his confidence into the spring. He asked his dad if he could come to the gym at Maryknoll on his off days from Ka Ulukoa and play with his boys' junior varsity team. His dad agreed, but once Skylan had spent two days in the junior varsity gym with his father, the head coach of the Maryknoll program asked Dave if Skylan would play at the varsity practices. Skylan felt like he had prepared himself, and although he wasn't an official member of the team, that was his time to give a preview of where his skills could go. He attended the practices eagerly, and then began to attend their weight-lifting schedule, and before long he was tagging along to whatever team event his dad was attending. He saw what it looked like when his role was minimized, so he pursued everything within his power to make certain that it was maximized.

Tui, Micah, and Noah entered their first intermediate volleyball season together at Punahou. The boys realized quickly that the three of them, mixed in with their intermediate volleyball teammates, created a team stacked in young talent. Most of the players in the league weren't involved in club volleyball, so the competition was scarce. For that reason, Punahou's intermediate competition occurred primarily in practice. The coach introduced an incentive format. The statistical leader in each category of play was given a bag of candy. That lost its spark when Micah started complaining of being robbed every time that he wasn't in the group of boys given candy. Micah used the intermediate volleyball experience, as a whole, to act rascal. He saw any opportunity outside of his dad's training to show his backside. He came to practice with plastic bags of food in his pockets, and he pulled from his stash of snacks constantly. His coach would catch him and tell him to run laps. After 30 minutes, his coach would call him back in, and Micah would refuse, saying that he didn't want to stop, and he'd spend the remainder of their two-hour practices running laps.

USA Volleyball High Performance results were sent out in April. Evan checked the list and saw that his name was absent. He ran into Carla Kabalis a week later and gave her the news.

"Not on the list?" she asked. "Nowhere at all? On any level?"

Evan said disappointed, "I'm afraid not. It's okay, though. I really appreciate you getting me out to the opportunity."

She was shocked. "No sir. They aren't getting off that easy," she said viciously. "I don't know how you slipped through the cracks. I will give you a call later this week."

Evan wasn't sure what that meant. He just smiled and thanked her again.

The call didn't come later that week, so Evan erased his mind of disappointment and put the verdict in the past. Coach Pono and Coach Charlie were still conducting Ka Ulukoa practices for the boys who didn't have intermediate volleyball, but once that season ended, work ensued. School finished, and for the majority, 8th grade was officially over. Evan's bags were already packed for Oahu and this time Kaehu was coming with him. Kaehu met Evan and Guy at Big Island Airport with his mom. As they walked away from checking in, Guy got a call on his cell phone.

He passed the phone to his son. "Evan, they want to speak with you."

"Okay — Is it Uncle Cyrus?" Evan asked curiously as he took the phone. "Hello."

A lady spoke, "Hi Evan, this is Carla Kabalis. I have some good news for you. I spoke with the USA Volleyball committee from the Big Island tryout. It was a mistake that your name was missing. You've been invited to the A1 Select Camp. Check your or your parents' email when you get a chance."

Evan's face lit up. "Oh, wow. That's an honor. Thank you so much for calling."

It was a true honor. A1 was the highest level for the Select age group, under the Select National Team.

"Who was that, Evan?" Kaehu asked.

Evan said, "A lady named Carla Kabalis from the USA Volleyball tryout."

Guy stashed his phone back in his pocket. "Good news?"

Evan picked up his duffle bag. "Yes, it was," he replied, glowing.

Coach Pono and Micah were waiting when Evan and Kaehu

arrived. Kaehu's grandparents pulled in and exchanged big hugs with everyone, and then they took Kaehu to their home on Oahu. Micah and Evan picked up where they left off. Once Evan's bags touched the floor in Kaneohe, he called his mom, brushed his teeth, and the boys left. Micah took Evan to the local deli to pick up their favorite snack, Red Brick Oven Pizza and white rice.

The club always had an open tryout for the second half, after the high school season. Coach Pono offered that for his team as well, but no one ever showed up who illustrated the potential to keep pace with his 14 & Under group. Keenan, Adrian, and Austin spent the spring training with Ka Ulukoa consistently. Now that the full group was done with intermediate sports and the Big Island boys were back, the coaches could implement team tactics. Not as quickly as they had hoped.

Coach Pono and Coach Charlie were surprised to see how sloppy their boys had become. They couldn't complete a *One-Contact* drill without the ball hitting the floor. The boys weren't holding their moves and one-arm digs were spattered all over the gym. *Quick Hitter Timing* had continuous misconnects. Noah pointed his thumb up in the air, telling Micah to set him higher. Coach Charlie's patience had run out. He grabbed Noah by the arm and brought the group of boys over to him.

"Never show up your setter," Coach Charlie shouted, disgusted. His eyes were filled with rage. "Never!"

He couldn't believe the audacity. All of the intermediate volleyball boys were in bad form. Coach Pono was frustrated and he wasn't willing to move on from the necessities of the boys. Team tactics were put on the back burner. Technical partner drills kept their place in the practice plan. *One-Arm Digging*, tedious freeball drills, and *Quick Hitter Timing* warranted an extended stay.

Evan's record was as clean as a whistle back home on the Big Island. That didn't stop him from enjoying a good time on Micah's influence and getting into shenanigans. Micah and Evan took the bikes and tried ordering through a Taco Ball drive-thru window. They were denied. Evan suggested that they go to his cousin's house.

"It's ten minutes away," Evan said.
"Okay, shoots. Let's go," Micah said willingly.

Ten minutes passed and Evan said, "We are close. It's right around here."
The boys kept pedaling down the streets.

Ten minutes after that, Evan said, "Now, we are almost there. Around the corner."

Micah's facial expression became annoyed.

Another 10 minutes passed.

Evan said, "Almost there. A few more minutes."

Micah's annoyed expression turned tired and angry. An hour and a half after leaving Micah's home, the boys arrived at Evan's cousin's place. By that time, they had to turn around and leave for dinner. At the end of the day, all of the other emotions faded and both boys were glad to have a brother figure just one room away.

Coach Pono consulted Coach Charlie before the next training, and together they felt that the boys had returned to a satisfactory level in their technique. They started to add the *back row Three-on-Three*, two contacts, and then they progressed to three contacts. The *Primary Passing* was added in and that led to the addition of the starting six working through serve receive and transitioning freeballs.

The Pipe-attack was a helpful tool at the SCVA qualifier. Micah saw that and the Outside Hitters did, too, so they got creative. During *back row Three-on-Three*, anytime a right-back, area-one defender dug a ball behind the 10-foot line, the middle-back, area-six Outside Hitter would wrap around to area-one and call for the *D-attack, which was the equivalent of the Pipe-attack to the right side. The set resembled a Red-set, only set seven or eight feet away from the net for the back row hitter.

Coach Pono and Coach Charlie appreciated the creativity and problem solving, so they said nothing. Ka Ulukoa's fast-tempo Quick Attack was opening up the middle of the court, so the team added on X routes for the Outside Hitters as well. The X1-attack was an inside *Lob-set, 10 feet in from the left antenna. The X2-attack was in the middle of the court, four feet in front of the Setter. The X3-attack was four feet behind the Setter, usually 10 feet in from the right antenna. Ka Ulukoa was never the tallest team in their tournament, but the more and more tournaments that came, the further they were from being the tallest team. It was important that they developed ways to spread the opponent and keep their taller blockers out of rhythm.

Before the boys left each practice, Coach Pono reminded them, "We add these things in to help us be successful. Remember though, success will come from us being simple. We can only execute these things we want to do if we control the ball."

Five days from leaving to Junior Olympics, Coach Pono huddled the boys at training.

"Coach Charlie put together a team, so today we are going to scrimmage. Tournament warmup, and then we'll play."

The boys looked around haphazardly as they followed the order. They went through their jog and stretch, then *Partner Setting*, then *Partner Passing*, *Shoulders*, *One-Contact*, and as they prepared for *Quick Hitter Timing* and serving, their opponents walked into Palama Gym:

Sean Carney, a three-year starting Setter at the University of Hawai'i. Mau LaBerre, a two year starting Middle at UH. Jaylen Reyes, a local talent of Kamehameha Kapālama at Outside Hitter, committed to play Libero at California State University, Northridge. Jordan Inafuku, a Libero from Stanford University in Palo Alto, California. Brothers, Kawika and Erik Shoji, a Setter and a Libero at Stanford University, sons of the historic University of Hawai'i Women's coach, Dave Shoji.

Keenan and Noah reached frantically toward each other's shoulder to grab the other's attention. Skylan turned his head toward the entrance and gulped hard. Micah was the last to look.

He shined a big smile and said, "Shoots! Heck yeah! Let's do this."

For the majority of Ka Ulukoa, the feeling was much more intimidating than anything these boys felt their first time squaring off against Borinquen Coqui, or against Baja. Coach Charlie's group of Hawaiian Island superstars arranged themselves with Sean Carney and Kawika Shoji setting and hitting in a 6-2 offense. Erik Shoji and Jaylen Reyes were featured in the Outside Hitter positions. Mau LaBerre played full-time front row Middle, and Jordan Inafuku took the Libero spot.

Ka Ulukoa lined up with Micah setting the 5-1 offense, and Adrian as his Opposite. Tui and Evan played the Outside Hitter slots. Keenan and Noah were in their usual Middle roles. Skylan played the Libero position and Austin subbed into the back row for Adrian. The change in speed from Ka Ulukoa's game to their opponents' was obvious. The combination of being stronger, faster, longer, and having more experience, gave the opponent an edge before Ka Ulukoa could get the ball across the net. They knew where the ball was going to be before it was en route. Erik Shoji had to admit to Coach Charlie that his team's power and ball control were impressive for their 14-year-old age. However, that didn't change the fact that Erik Shoji's group was going to roll them. Inafuku made the game look much more simple than Skylan did as a Libero. Carney and Kawika Shoji set more consistently than Micah in good situations and out-of-system situations. Erik Shoji and

Jaylen were more athletic and more technically developed than Tui and Evan. Keenan and Noah were both no match for LaBerre's 6'7" block and nearly invisible when he attacked.

Between points and between sets, Tui looked over at his coaches and asked, "What could I have done there? Am I not finishing left pocket? Should I have hit that somewhere else?"

Coach Pono continually put his arms above his head and showed Tui the Big Circle. He rolled his finger in a loop, symbolizing movement to the next point. The Ka Ulukoa boys took a licking. They had no expectation verbally, but the fear in their eyes was apparent, the way that a young boy makes a fictional monster in the closet, real. Coach Charlie knew that a butt kicking was likely for his 14 & Under club boys, but they had not played as well as they were capable. He wanted them to learn, but they had to learn through their own experience.

The two teams played a total of four sets. With each new set the Ka Ulukoa boys learned and with each new set their game improved, along with the score. Skylan and Austin watched Jordan from across the net and learned to be more still and more patient. Micah watched Sean and Kawika deliver. He began to see the times when he could take chances and when he should be simple. Tui and Evan watched the result of Erik and Jaylen passing the ball well and making hitting a secondary activity. Keenan and Noah focused their energy on the way LaBerre used his eyes to read Micah's setting decisions, which made his physical job so much easier. Whether Adrian was on the court getting his own swings blocked and touched, or watching Kaehu have the same result in the next game, he saw the benefit of attacking the ball at a high point and aiming for a deep spot. The lower he swung on the net, the faster the stuff-blocks hit his court, and the more out of control he swung in bad situations, the more points he gave to the opponent. Each player had something to learn and Coach Pono and Coach Charlie had things to learn as well. They wanted to know how their team would respond in a tough position and they wanted to know if their team could continue to learn in a position of punishing defeat.

Coach Charlie asked his invitees to share what they felt the boys could focus on to improve the most.

Sean Carney spoke up first. "You guys are good," he said coolly, running his fingers through his wavy brown hair. "My advice is to make sure you always take the extra step."

Kawika Shoji backed him up. "Yeah, there were a lot of balls that one of you could have chased and made a play on, but all of you have to go in order to find out."

The Ka Ulukoa boys nodded their heads and gave their appreciation for the older guys coming in to scrimmage. Coach Pono sat the team down on the bench inside of Palama Gym.

He asked, "So what did you guys learn from today?"

Austin joked, "Not to stand under one of Mau LaBerre's hits."

The other boys laughed.

Tui brought the focus back to the question. "I think — for me — trust the teaching."

Coach Pono stopped the comments there. "That's a big one that Tui just said. Boys, we want to make sure that we stay in the *present* moment — not focusing on what you could have done and not asking about the corrections, like left pocket or hitting a different shot — just playing in that moment." He dropped down to a knee and placed his clipboard on the ground. "I learned three things from Karch Kiraly that helped me to become a better player: One: *Always bettering yourself.* I realized that I could never worry about anyone else unless I always bettered myself first. Two: *Helping others to get better.* If I didn't add value to anyone else while I was on the court then I wasn't helping the team be better. Everything that we do on the volleyball court should benefit the other players, too. Three: *Reframing.* Changing the picture that things are broadcasted in. We may be physically out skilled by every team that we play, but as long as each of us does our job the best that we can, and each of us works hard in practice and makes the players around us better, then we can do pretty well in the tournaments."

Auntie Maile was prepping the boys' travel information at the house. When Tui walked through the door with his dad, Maile began to ask, "Tui, did you..."

Her eyes shifted down to his hand. "Why are you holding your back?"

"Oh —" Tui stood up straight. "It's nothing, maybe a little tweak at practice or something. Training was fun today. Coach Charlie brought —"

His mom stopped him. "Boy, don't change the subject. What happened to your back?" She looked over at her husband to examine the language of his body for information.

Tui's voice grew nervous. "It's been bothering me the past week or so. But really, it's nothing," he faltered.

"Where is the pain?" Maile demanded.

"Mom, it's nothing." Tui did his best to shorten the discussion before it became a lecture.

Maile walked toward the phone. "We leave for JOs is in five days.

I'm making you an appointment to see the doctor tomorrow."

Tui thought it best to say no more.

Maile accompanied Tui to the doctor's office the next day. Tui approached fearing the worst, fearing that the doctor would deliver the news that he could not participate in competition. He decided that he was going to do his best to make the symptoms appear minor. That was going to be a difficult task with his mother near, playing the role of lead detective. Tui stood up and removed his shirt. The doctor looked at his spine and ran his finger up and down his vertebrae.

"Slowly bend forward," the doctor requested. "How does that feel?"

"Fine, no pain," Tui said as he felt his back tighten.

"Slowly bend backwards," said the doctor. "Any discomfort there?"

Tui started to bend and shot back up straight when he felt the familiar pinch in his lower back. Maile's eyes widened and she looked tautly to the doctor.

The doctor asked, "Feel a little pinch there?"

Tui couldn't avoid being honest about what the three of them had just watched. He nodded his head.

The doctor's expression was vacant for a moment. "Okay, lay down on the table, on your stomach."

The doctor applied pressure with his thumb to different spots on Tui's back.

He said, "I think I have an idea of what is going on, but let's get you an X-ray."

Tui and his mom sat in silence while the doctor fetched the X-ray results.

The door opened slowly. Tui and Maile sat up, alert.

The doctor said gingerly, "Alright. The X-ray doesn't show any serious problems with the bone alignment. It appears to be an issue with the sciatic nerve in his back."

"Okay, and what does that mean?" Maile asked.

The doctor pulled his pen from his coat pocket. "It means that he should be fine. He is going to have to maintain it and take it easy this summer." The doctor looked over his file. "It says here that you play football and volleyball?"

Tui rushed to speak before his mom. "Yes, my team has a big tournament next week. I can play, right?"

"Volleyball or football?" the doctor asked.

Tui thought for a moment if one answer would be better than

the other. Regardless, he planned to be honest. "Volleyball."

"You should be alright for volleyball since it isn't a contact sport," he said. "But you will have to pay attention. If you start to feel pain when you play, then stop. I'm going to write you a prescription for Ibuprofen."

"Okay," said Tui rapturously, trying to get out of the office as soon as possible, as if the doctor was going to change his mind.

Maile extended her hand. "Thank you, Doctor —?"

"Fey," said the doctor. "Ronald Fey."

Chapter 12 - Close Doesn't Count

The heat of Austin, Texas was a change from the cool breeze of Honolulu, Hawai'i. Auntie Maile scheduled for the team to go sightseeing in Austin while they waited for their house to be available. She and Coach Pono dropped off their rental vans and led the team out into the city. The 98-degree heat with 50 percent humidity was too hot for the boys. They would have preferred to have been inside, and Coach Pono's heavy breathing and soaked t-shirt said that he felt the same way.

Jestingly, Micah said to the group, "Looks like Coach Charlie is the only smart one. He never gets put in these situations."

The team laughed at the kernel of truth to Micah's joke. Coach Pono decided that it would be alright to ditch the sightseeing and head over to the convention center to pick up their tournament passes. The group walked as if they were walking through the Sahara Desert in July. The pace was slow. The feet dragged and the sweat poured.

"Is this heaven?" Micah continued his solo-comedy show as the group walked through the doors of the convention center.

Coach Pono handed each boy his pass and walked with Auntie Maile into the playing site. The boys followed.

It was the afternoon wave of teams, the time when the Club Division plays its competition. The 18, 12, and 13 & Under teams were deep into their pool play. Coach Pono weaved through the courts, maintaining the slow pace from outside. The boys paused behind their coach.

"This is Court 1," said Coach Pono.

The boys gazed at the court beside their teammates. The setup was just as magnificent as the year's prior. The metal grandstands rose high in the air, surrounding a 60-foot-long and 30-foot-wide court of red court tiles, outlined with a rectangle of black. Across the net, behind the end line and the black end zone, was a stage, tall and wide with a circular volleyball decorated with the stars and stripes of an American flag. Under the ball it read, *USA Volleyball*. Auntie Maile looked down at her cell phone.

"The house is ready," she said.

Coach Pono began to walk away. His team held one last gaze at the court before they followed him outside of the playing site.

The next two days of practice were exhausting, not because the training was anything the boys weren't used to, but because they avoided drinking the fountain water. In fear of sounding ungrateful, the boys didn't dare say anything to their coaches or their chaperone, but it was a consensus. None of the boys enjoyed the taste of the Austin tap water, so they decide not to drink it.

When the boys woke up the morning of the tournament to their packed bags and their initialed water jugs, the reaction was unusual.

"Why are you all acting so funny?" asked Auntie Maile, forcefully.

"What do you mean?" asked Skylan in his best innocent voice.

Auntie Maile lowered her eyebrows. "Don't play. You are all hugging me and holding on and putting a little *extra thanks* on your thank you."

Micah walked up and linked his arm with hers. "We just really appreciate all that you do." The goofy grin on his face was obvious.

She smirked quickly and returned to a straight face. "Mhm — I've got my eyes on you."

As the boys walked into the arena filled with teams in their own age group, the feeling was immediate. The stares felt like lasers piercing through their clothes. The whispers started quiet like a kitchen mouse at midnight, and the volume grew to sound as loud as someone yelling in a sanctuary. There was no escape. When Ka Ulukoa sat on their court, the other teams stared as they passed. When they jogged, when they took a bathroom break, the whispers were nearby. The atmosphere wasn't uncomfortable like a feeling of distress. The Hawaiians just didn't have frequent encounters with such obvious visual judgment. Ka Ulukoa advanced undefeated through the first two days. The boys didn't speak to each other about the staring and the whispering. The way that they exchanged looks with one another each time told the story of what they were thinking well enough.

The boys sat down to dinner and Keenan said, "I didn't see Vaqueros there today."

"They aren't in the tournament," Coach Pono replied with no explanation.

Noah smirked, "Maybe they were tired of us beating them."

"Woah!" Micah said as he joined Evan in a lean backwards. "We don't talk like that, Brah. This guy —"

Tui raised his eyebrows. Evan and Micah smiled and shook their heads in playful disappointment. The other boys continued to eat their pasta.

Coach Pono sent the boys to bed. Tui, Evan, and Micah shared one of the three bedrooms on the top floor of the house. They were making a big racket up there.

"I'm sleeping on one of the two beds," whined Micah, standing up straight in the middle of his room.

As he lay down on the bed furthest from the door, Evan said, "Yeah right, Ficus!"

Micah jumped on top of Evan's bed and they started to wrestle. Coach Pono yelled up, "Cut out that noise and go to sleep!"

Austin and Keenan were in the bathroom at the top of the stairs brushing their teeth. Micah kept on with his attempts at winning over one of the beds from Evan and Tui.

He was yelling by this point, "Come on! You guys got them the last four nights. It's my turn!"

Tui just laughed on his bed while all of Micah's attention was focused toward Evan. Micah jumped again on top of Evan's bed and his knee collided with Evan's thigh.

"Ouch!" screamed Evan.

Coach Pono bolted out of his room and whipped around the corner to the bottom of the stairway. In his sight were the boys brushing their teeth.

"Austin! Keenan! Get your butts to your room and go to sleep, now! I'm going to be ticked if I have to come out here again."

The house was silent. Austin and Keenan didn't even wash out their mouths or the tips of their toothbrushes. They dropped the brushes in the sink and walked briskly to their room, with mouths full of toothpaste. Tui, Evan, and Micah quietly giggled to themselves about the misdirected blame that was being handed out because of their noise.

On the third and warmest day of the trip, the team walked into the convention center feeling fresh. Ka Ulukoa saw more California teams in their first two days than they had ever seen in their three seasons together. They were fortunate to have moved by their opponents unblemished. In fact, other than SCVC 14-Quicksilver giving Ka Ulukoa a tough match, scoring 21 and 23 points, no team scored above 18 in the first two days.

"Why is that older guy staring at us?" asked Skylan.

"He looks like a coach. Puerto Rican, maybe?" Micah added.

"Everyone is Puerto Rican to you, Micah," Evan joked.

Micah smiled, "You guys all hear that? He called me Micah. Write that down."

Tui said, "That guy is definitely Puerto Rican. He is staring hard."

"Eyeing us out, right?" Skylan asked, goggling back at the man. "Let's go. We are on Court 18."

"Do you know who we play?" Noah asked.

Micah responded sarcastically, "Do we ever know?"

The Manhattan Beach Surf 14s were the first opponent of the day. Ka Ulukoa made quick work of them, 25-10 and 25-13. That was a surprise, considering that MB Surf was the second-highest-ranked team from Southern California, behind High Line, and their number-one Outside Hitter (OH1), Louis Richard, was as tall and strong as any 14-year-old kid they had seen. Coach Pono's boys had already proven that they were unlikely to let one player be the deciding factor for a team, especially because that team would have to pass to the net consistently first. On break, the boys caught the older, dark-skinned man staring at them from across the gym.

Skylan noticed and turned to his teammates. "Brah, that guy is eyeing us out again, look."

"Maybe he likes you," Micah toyed with Skylan. "After all, you are — Da Kine."

Adrian and Austin laughed. Evan and Tui tried not to stare back.

Keenan threw his arms around Adrian and Tui's shoulders. "Speaking of Da Kine, did you guys see who we play next?"

The group shrugged their shoulders, waiting to see if Keenan planned to spill.

"Brah, KU'IKAHI them, with the RoShamBo jerseys," Keenan said ecstatically.

Tui sounded excited, too. "What? Not another California team? We've played like six in a row."

"Rajah. Island battle," said Kaehu, flashing a Hawaiian Shaka with his thumb and pinky.

KU'IKAHI 14-RoShamBo was a good ball-control team, better than Ka Ulukoa had seen through the first half of the tournament, but they were small. Two sets to none, Ka Ulukoa swept the local foes.

"Brah, what is this guy's deal?" Skylan asked Evan as he noticed the large Puerto Rican man cutting his eyes at them. "Is he following us around or what?"

"No good dat kine," said Adrian.

Evan glanced over as he put on his backpack. "Yeah, that guy is different. Don't sweat it, Braddah."

"I still think he likes you," added Micah, holding a smirk as he walked away swiftly.

"Let's go. Get in the hall," Coach Pono ordered.

Tui was lying on a heating pad in between matches because of his aching back. Adrian was having a nice tournament in his first JOs as a starter, so nice that Tui really only had to snap balls around the court and hit off-speed shots. Adrian only had two swings that he used often, but he was hitting so hard that no one had found a solution. He was either going to hammer the ball down the line, somewhere in the direction of the five-box, or if the opponent had a bigger block, he was going to take the same exact swing down the line and blast it off the hands and out, for a tool-kill. Auntie Maile left Tui alone with the heating pad to go get the boys' snacks. On the way, she ran into Coach Pono.

"How's Tui's back doing?" he asked. "I see he's got the pad on there."

Auntie Maile said, "It's a little sore. I am just worried he won't be able to hit hard. He seems tentative out there."

The boys were close, so Coach Pono spoke softly. "It would be denial to say that being physical and hitting hard don't contribute to Tui's success as an athlete. That's not his gift, though. His ability to understand the situation at his young age is — his timing of when to give and when take is exceptional. That is his gift."

Auntie Maile smiled. "Yeah, he just better make sure he is out there to help his teammates."

The boys rose from rest and snack slowly. As they made their way to Court 18 for the last match of the third day, they noticed the same large and dark Puerto Rican man staring at them. With each time that the boys glanced over, his look became more intense. His eyes squinted a little bit tighter to lock in his gaze. His chin dropped toward his neck and the corners of his mouth turned down. The boys didn't comment. It was like they had become used to his unexplained gawking.

Torrimar 14s waited near the side of the court for the match before them to end. They stood as a team, and without saying a word to one another. They held the presence of a group that was waiting for something more. Their stances said that they were impatient and their faces displayed the look of urgency. As the final whistle blew, Torrimar hurried onto the court in a half-run to make sure that they started their warmup before the Hawaiians. Ka Ulukoa didn't have a warmup that was common to them. In fact, it was quite sloppy, especially in *Quick Hitter Timing*. Micah was locating the sets well, but the attacks didn't do the sets justice. Tui was hitting the top of the net-tape on all but one swing. Without any blockers, Kaehu, Keenan, and Noah must have hit seven balls out of bounds. Adrian was pounding balls consistently near the 10-foot line; the problem was that they were two feet outside of the court. Coach Charlie's patience was being tested. He paused the drill.

In a tone of erecting frustration he said, "One-box! Five-box!

This isn't Hollywood."

Torrimar jumped out on Ka Ulukoa and took the first set 20-25. Coach Pono held onto his timeouts, as per usual, in hopes that his team would mount a late-game comeback as they did so many times previously. The second set didn't start much better for Ka Ulukoa. On the fifth point of the second set, Torrimar set the ball outside to their best left side Hitter, Sergio. Evan peeled off of the net in area-four and got stopped to face toward the attacker and play defense. With two Ka Ulukoa blockers up, Sergio blasted Evan in the face on a sharp-angle swing inside of the 10-foot line and sent him to the floor. That drove the Torrimar fans into frenzy.

"Let's go! Next! Sideout! Sideout!" yelled Coach Pono.

The next play, a shaken-up Evan passed to Micah and got the set in return. He snapped it off the edge of the block and out for a kill. Coach Charlie made eye contact with Evan.

Coach Charlie unfolded his arms, exposed his empty palms to Evan, and said, "A point is a point."

Some timely serve-receive kills by Adrian and Micah's crafty decisions led to few transition Quick Attacks and kept Ka Ulukoa closer than the rowdy atmosphere (full of Spanish shouting) would have made it seem. Skylan's eyes browsed the crowd as he left the court for Noah to rotate to the back row and serve. His browse stopped abruptly when he saw a face that had become unpleasantly familiar. It was the dark-skinned Puerto Rican man, standing up from his front row seat and walking away. Subconsciously, Skylan felt more comfortable, even if only a little bit. Once Noah finished serving and Torrimar sided-out, Skylan took his place back on the court. Down 19-20, Ka Ulukoa sided-out to put the set back deuce, 20 all. Adrian was playing exceptionally well, so Micah stayed with the same tactics until the end of the second set, which Ka Ulukoa squeezed out 25-23.

The match was not a must win for Ka Ulukoa. They, along with Torrimar, were already in position to advance into the Gold Bracket Semifinals on the fourth day. However, Ka Ulukoa's streak was on the line, as it always was. No team had ever beaten Ka Ulukoa at Junior Olympics. And no boys' team had ever beaten them in a regional competition. Adrian found something special in his game, and Micah took notice. There hadn't been any boy or any team the entire tournament that could find a solution for his offense. The match against Torrimar produced no change in that, or in their undefeated standing. Loads of late-arriving spectators, hoping to be live witnesses to the team from Hawaiʻi's first loss, left disappointed. Ka Ulukoa departed the arena with a 15-11 third set win over the Puerto Ricans.

After volleyball ended each day, Coach Pono and Coach Charlie rarely allowed volleyball to be a topic of conversation in the group. He wanted the matches forgotten and their minds to be clear. The boys weren't even sure whom they would play in the semifinals the next day. All that mattered was pointing at the owl outside of their window, eating as much pasta as they could fit in their stomachs, and preventing another episode of Austin and Keenan going to bed with toothpaste in their mouths.

The arena was filled by the time Ka Ulukoa walked inside at 9am. The 15 & Unders were deep into their third day of competition, 16 & Under on their second, and 17 & Under just starting their tournament. The boys walked to Court 6 for their match. They waited behind a big crowd of referees and tournament officials in a ruckus.

"Why is Borinquen on the other side, Coach Pono?" asked Austin.

Coach Pono didn't look back at his player. "They are the opponent," he said, keeping his gaze ahead at the crowd of officials.

Austin's eyes widened as he said, "What? I thought they were the 1st seed in the tournament. We are 2nd so we play the 3rd seed."

Tui poked Austin's back. "Chill Brah, we gonna have to play them anyway, might as well be now."

Coach Pono turned around, but his eyes were still looking above Austin's head.

"Borinquen lost in their last match yesterday, so they are 3rd seed, now. That doesn't matter, though. Warm up."

When the boys returned from their jog the court was finally clear of extra officials. Just the two in charge of the semifinal match remained. Coach Pono called the boys over to the bench.

He said, "Listen, we are going to start with some points before the first serve. Don't worry about it. Just play."

The boys figured they wouldn't get an explanation from Coach Pono. They shifted their bewildered looks to Coach Charlie. He flashed a closed-lip smile and returned to his signature poker face. The boys lined up in their areas of the court and the boy at the scorer's table flipped the scoreboard to say 12-0 in Ka Ulukoa's favor. Borinquen carried their argument from the bench onto the court and on throughout the first set. Ka Ulukoa finished the first set before Borinquen could reach double digits, 25-8.

Borinquen was so familiar to Ka Ulukoa by then. This was the fourth time that the teams faced off at JOs and it had grown into the largest rivalry in their age group. In the first three days, Borinquen took straight set wins over the 8th-ranked team from Rochester, New York, the 7th-overall-ranked team in the tournament from San Diego, California, and the 6th-overall-ranked High Line Volleyball Club. So, it was clear that Borinquen hadn't lost their skill with each new season that came. What was fading, or rather never present, was true leadership. The players continued to bicker through the second set and the coaches accompanied them in the arguments. Ka Ulukoa didn't have to play their best volleyball to finish the match against their rivals in the second set, 25-17.

That win guaranteed a Gold or Silver Medal for Ka Ulukoa. The team walked out to the convention center hallway, unsure of who took Borinquen's place for the first time as their opponent in the finals. Auntie Maile walked beside Coach Pono and Coach Charlie.

"So what happened with the points situation?" she asked. "I'm curious."

Coach Pono let out a short chuckle. "Borinquen was 22 minutes late to their refereeing assignment at 8am. USA Volleyball says your team loses a point for every minute that you are late to the start of a match. It was supposed to be 22-0, but their coach negotiated it down to 12-0."

"Pretty interesting, huh?" asked Coach Charlie.

Coach Pono turned to Auntie Maile and asked, "Hey, will you grab the snacks for the boys? We play the finals at 1pm." Then he turned to Coach Charlie. "Any thoughts?"

Coach Charlie paused. "Yes. I think it's time that we read to them."

The team picked its favorite spot, away from the doors to the arena, the furthest corner they could find. They sprawled their bags out randomly and sat on the floor. Some boys sat up and anxiously waited to eat the snacks that Auntie Maile prepared for them, and some laid their heads down. The coaches approached their group of boys.

Coach Pono said, "It's 10:45 now. We play the finals at 1pm. Whoever wants to eat can eat. Anybody that that wants to sleep can do that, too. First, everyone sit up." He pulled out a small book with a checkered, gold outline and a maroon center. In white letters it read, *The Precious Present.*

An hour before the match, Auntie Maile woke the boys who were asleep. The coaches were inside of the arena, gathering the information they wanted for the finals. They came back outside to the hallway and all of the boys were together, standing up with their backpacks on and water jugs hanging from their hands.

"We play on Court 1," said Coach Pono.

Inside of the arena, the boys put their bags down and checked the score of the match prior, to estimate how soon they would start their warmup. Ka Ulukoa took their jog around the arena and returned to their spot on the concrete for their stretch. The hairs on Skylan's arms shot up when he looked up from his hamstring stretch to see a man glaring at him. It was the same man who had been creeping around them the entire tournament. Behind his penetrating gaze was a group of dark, Puerto Rican players who looked like they belonged in the 18 & Under Division. In that moment, Skylan realized that the man who was watching his team was the coach of that 18 & Under team. Except, they weren't 18 & Under. They were Ka Ulukoa's opponents in the 14 & Under Gold Medal match.

San Juan Volleyball Club was from San Juan, Puerto Rico and they warmed up on the concrete, right beside Ka Ulukoa. The illustration began producing clarity for Skylan, and by the uncomfortable looks on his teammates' faces, clarity was forming for them as well. The purpose for the older man staring all of that time wasn't a coincidence or a mental illness (which was the boys' original hypothesis). It was a scare tactic; he was trying to intimidate the young Hawaiians, the defending champions. The previous match ended and the boys walked onto the court as the officials lowered the net for the 14 & Under Open Division Finals.

"Did you see that man eyeing us out again?" Micah asked.

"Ho Brah, did I ever?" Keenan replied sarcastically.

Skylan said softly, "Yeah." His face still held the look of discomfort.

San Juan took the court for their four minutes. All but one of the players had crispy, dark brown skin, like they spent too much of their springtime in the sun. The boys turned back toward Coach Pono to hear what he had to say.

He dropped to a knee and said, "Coach Charlie and I have watched this team and they are good. They wouldn't be in this position otherwise. But, what sets us apart from them is our ball control. We have used our time, putting in the effort while it was boring so that when the game time comes we can be automatic. No flashy stuff out there."

There was a moment of silence, and then Coach Charlie said,

"Okay!" and the boys stood up to take their four minutes on the court.

Court 1 was loud when the starting lineups took the court. The Puerto Rican fans held true to their expectation. San Juan's fans were ready to make a lot of noise, and every other Puerto Rican team's fan base joined in to represent their country. The American spectators piled into the grandstands as well; although, they were unsure which club they would give their cheers. Every 14-year-old boy just wanted a spot in the crowd so he could watch the kid from Hawai'i with the big ponytail. That was Tui, but even Tui didn't match up well in stature with this team.

The three players who started the match in the front row for San Juan approached the net with sweat dripping from their shoulders down their exposed and uncommonly well-defined biceps. Skylan felt the pressure of their serves and the strength of their attacks from the beginning. They were undeniably strong. Tui was less worried about any of the players from San Juan. He had issues to worry about on his own side of the net. With how tightly his back was locking up, he wasn't confident that he was going to make it through the match. Tui couldn't use his topspin-jump-serve. Putting any real power behind his swings was uncomfortable, and jumping any higher than six inches would have been asking too much. At the end line, he served a standing-float, in the front row he struggled, and in the back row he wasn't much better. San Juan celebrated with their lurid fans and jogged circles around its half of the court with each point that they scored. Ka Ulukoa went down 7-13 at the start of the first set and Coach Pono called his first timeout of the tournament. He avoided timeouts because he saw them used as a crutch, as an excuse. He felt that timeouts didn't slow momentum or cause an opponent to miss their serve, like so many coaches claimed. He felt that a timeout should be applied only for rest, or if there was a message to deliver that was better left unsaid to the entire arena from courtside. He did have a message and it wasn't complex.

"Get water," he said. "Let's get one pass. Micah, talk about the play you want to run and keep it simple."
Coach Pono saw that his star Outside was in trouble. The weapon that Tui could always return to was the strength of his swing. Now, that was absent.

Coach Pono said to the team, "Whatever you are doing out there — blocking, digging, setting, etc.," he glanced at Tui, "— just do your job."

Coach Pono's last statement struck a chord with Tui. On San Juan's next perfect pass, Keenan did his job and followed San Juan's Middle to the Quick Attack, away from the Setter, and commit-blocked.

The San Juan Outside Hitter approached inside to the middle of the court for a medium-height *X-play, right on top of the net in area-three. Ka Ulukoa's blocking system was to get in front of the hitting shoulder and press straight over the net with no reaching left or right. It was too late to front the Hitter, so Tui took all of the six inches of vertical he had and jumped straight up where he was in area-four. The net was left wide open for the OH1 to hit. He cracked it. As it headed toward the floor in front of the 10-foot line, and the Puerto Ricans prepared for a few celebratory laps, Skylan was stopped under it in defense and dug it straight up in the air. Micah set Tui in transition and he snapped it between the block for a kill. Tui treated the rest of that set like a *One-Contact* drill. He was attentive to all of his skills and while his hitting stayed below mediocre, the rest of his game elevated. Micah reverted to the offensive things that brought his team there: the arm of Adrian Faitalia to sideout and the Quick Attack to score in transition. Ka Ulukoa capped the first set with an eighteen-to-nine run and changed sides.

Coach Pono's team escaped the first set with an impressive comeback. He wondered, though, if his team could survive another slow start against a team with San Juan's size and energy. Ka Ulukoa took the court first in the second set. San Juan's coach sat in the first chair on his bench and stared through the net at the boys from Hawai'i as he wrote down his lineup.

Micah walked over to Skylan and said, "I still think he likes you. I'm telling you, man."

Skylan was not amused. San Juan called an early timeout after Micah softly dumped the ball over on two (second contact) to take a 6-4 lead. The boys sat down on the bench and drank water.

Coach Charlie made a comment to Micah. "Good timing, but okay, that's enough dinks (soft tips) for this match. Set your hitters." The boys walked back onto the court. The very next play, Skylan made an awesome one-arm dig on a cross-court cut-shot and Micah dumped it over on two. Before San Juan scooped it up and transitioned it out to score, Coach Charlie was nearly all the way on the court to grab Micah. Coach Pono extended his arm to hold his friend back.

"Frickin' rascal," Coach Pono said under his breath, with a vicious gleam in his eye.

San Juan evened the score and teams traded points until double digits. At 12-12, Tui made a defensive move in area-six from behind Evan's block, so that he could see the attacker. As he saw the hitter's arm come forward, Evan pressed over onto San Juan's side of the net and stuff-blocked the ball straight down.

The American fans in the crowd yelled, "Ohh!" and applauded Evan's cunning blocking move.

The crowd erupted after the next point when Keenan solo-stuff-blocked the San Juan Middle even harder. That was the dagger. The momentum carried to a final score of 25-17, and after the last point, Ka Ulukoa didn't run, jump, or scream. They met in the center of the court and waited for Coach Pono to put his hand in the huddle. In a volume no louder than they would use at the dinner table, with elated smiles across their faces, together they said, "Koa!"

Evan took a seat on the bench with Kaehu on his right and Tui on his left. The boys sat back in their chairs and took in a deep breath. Evan looked over at the San Juan boys who were still spread out on their side of the net, pouting. Then he looked straight ahead to the parents of his team walking onto the court to congratulate their sons.

Evan said, "Man, we are going to suck on the eight-foot net next year."

Tui and Kaehu laughed.

"Ho Brah, tru dat," said Tui.

Coach Pono called the boys over to him one-by-one. He decided that he wasn't going to wait to conference. He wanted them to be immediate and he wanted the content to be heavy.

He told each boy as they walked over and sat with him, "Very few teams get the privilege to win. Even fewer get to win three, so getting ready for next season starts now. This is when the reach starts. We can start to truly separate from other teams. I don't want us to be satisfied." And then he asked them, "How do you feel?"

Skylan came first, and he said, "It feels good to be a champion. It feels good to be a part of the team and have a role. I was intimidated by the San Juan coach eyeing us out all these days, but all of the work paid off."

Adrian came over, then Austin, then Noah, Micah, Keenan, Evan, and Kaehu. Tui was the last to conference.

He said, "The system is really important, and everybody doing their job. Honestly, I trusted our diggers already, but after Skylan made that play in the first game, that was big. Before, I would feel bad if I didn't make a touch for the diggers, but after today — I trust — you know, that they can do it themselves. Whatever I am doing on the court, I want to help the team in any way I can. Just contribute."

Coach Pono didn't reply to Tui. He looked in his eyes and gave him one nod. Coach Pono stood up and Tui walked over to his mom and gave her a big hug and a thank you.

Ka Ulukoa was presented the trophy and their 14 & Under Open Division Gold Medals. For the first time, there was an All-Tournament Team and number eight, Adrian Faitalia, number 18, Evan Enriques, number 13, Micah Ma'a, and number five, Keenan Meyer, were chosen. Number four, Larry Tuileta Junior, was named the tournament's Most Valuable Player. Coach Pono took the group to the waterpark that afternoon and Coach Charlie brought steaks over to the house for him to cook for everyone — everyone except for young Enriques. The same day, Evan returned to the airport in Austin to fly through Los Angeles and make his way to the Big Island. The opportunities were running out, so he maximized the two days he had to spend with his family before departing to Wisconsin and accepting his invitation to the USA Volleyball Boys' Select A1 Program.

Chapter 13 - Academy

Tui returned to the doctor and enrolled in a short period of physical therapy, for his back. Two weeks later, he left to the *Tom Martinez Football Camp*, hosted in Hawai'i. Tom Martinez was Tom Brady's personal Quarterback coach, a professor of Quarterbacks. Tui immediately fell into his teachings of new mechanics on how to throw the ball properly. By the end of the camp, Tui showed so much progress that he was invited to attend The *Football University Camp* in West Virginia for the top 100 players of each high school class. The camp was scheduled for late June, ten months later.

Pono took Micah to pick up a membership from The Outrigger Canoe Club in Honolulu. The Outrigger was a historical club on the sands of Waikïkï Beach, which was built to promote the water sports of old Hawai'i. It grew to foster the most successful volleyball club that Hawai'i harbored. Many of the young girls and boys on those teams were raised playing beach volleyball on The Outrigger's three private beach courts. Micah put in a call to Skylan.

"Sky, it's Micah. Cruise down to Outrigger tomorrow and try to get one membership. Can your mom or dad bring you down?"

"Howzit, Braddah Micah? Er — Uh — I can ask. What time you going to try and go?" asked Skylan.

Micah said, "Not too early, maybe like 11, yeah? Need to get my beauty rest."

"I guess you'll be sleeping for a long time, then," Skylan chuckled. "But yeah, I'll try to get a ride there around 11."

"Okay, shoots!" Micah hung up the phone.

Skylan made it down the next morning and brought Cullen Mosher with him, a light-skinned friend from his neighborhood, who was an only child. Cullen played volleyball, as well. One year older than Skylan, he was headed into his 10th grade season at Kamehameha Kapālama. Football soaked up the majority of Tui's summer availability, so Skylan played his beach volleyball with Cullen. The boys went to the beach too often for their parents to drive them. Once they learned how to use the bus system, they could cruise down to the beach every day.

Tui moved onto the academy at Punahou, so Micah decided that football wouldn't satisfy his sweet tooth in fall sports without him. Instead, a few 8th-grade classmates convinced him to try out for the intermediate water polo team. Micah didn't have any experience with ball-sports in the pool, so he played goalie. There, he basically hung on the goal waiting for action on defense, and took every opportunity to try to heave full-court shots at the opponent's goal. Punahou's academy didn't allow any 9th-graders to play on the varsity football team. In fact, it was a rule for the entire Interscholastic League of Honolulu. In the ILH, regardless of whether Tui was ready for that level or not, playing football in the 9th grade meant playing on the junior varsity.

Dave and Arlene volunteered to be the girls' junior varsity volleyball coaches at Maryknoll, where their son enrolled for 9th grade. Skylan had spent enough time in the gym at Maryknoll the previous few seasons for the girls to remember who he was. He walked into school as a proud boy. He assumed that winning three national titles in club volleyball was going to make him popular. He thought that he'd have lenience and if he decided to do anything mischievous, people would turn the other cheek. It wasn't long before Skylan realized that the combination of that attitude, Cullen Mosher being at another school, and no one there having a single care for what happened prior to high school, would lead to a challenging time in making friends.

The start of high school wasn't a smooth transition. Evan was coming away from his first season having spent no time playing with his brothers or beside his dad. Tui played another fall season of football and lost every one of his games. Skylan was feeling the pressure to change his mental structure at school, and Micah was stuck in middle school without the boys that he saw as his peers. The boys were buoyant about the start of the 15 & Under season. It couldn't have come soon enough.

The 2010 meeting for Ka Ulukoa was more of a reunion than a tryout for Coach Pono's team. Having no volleyball at the tryout wasn't for lack of want. Literally, there wasn't a single new boy who came to try out. It seemed that even showing up in an attempt to join the reigning champs was too intimidating for anyone local. Rather than training, Coach Pono decided to order pizza for the boys and talk with them about the structure of the season. Practices were going to be smaller, consistently, even smaller than the previous season because extracurricular schedules became even thicker with the start of high school. He offered all of the returning boys a spot on the team. Evan and Kaehu were back on the Big Island, so Coach Pono presented his offers in front of the group.

Going from left to right, he said, "Noah, Adrian, Austin, Micah, Tui, Skylan, Keenan, you all have a spot on the team again. If you want to try out elsewhere or make another decision then you can talk with me after, or call me."

They all shook their heads that they weren't going anywhere

else.

Coach Pono continued, "For the fall, we'll have practices two days a week for now, and we'll add in Sunday practices, later. Most days will have three or four guys, but the guys who can get in the gym should be taking the opportunity."

Auntie Maile walked in with the pizzas.

"Okay, we pau. Eat up," said Coach Pono.

The boys rushed over to Auntie Maile near the door. They spent the next hour eating and talking story until their parents returned for pick up. On the way out, Lee Lamb brought all of the teams together and reminded them of Ka Ulukoa's mission. He also added in the reminder for the Grade Point Average minimum to compete. It was a good thing, too. After a championship season and starting an unfamiliar chapter of schooling, grades were the last thing on most of the boys' minds.

Coach Pono and Coach Charlie got straight to work in the practice environment. The rusty volleyball converted itself much more quickly. Everything inside the practice plan stayed the same, except for one addition. Coach Pono added significant time on blocking. From his own playing experience, he remembered that blocking became more of a factor in every level that he progressed. His thoughts for his own team were that the only way they could keep their defensive prowess at the top of the charts was to have a disciplined block to funnel the ball, as the opponents got taller and stronger. *Tennis* got put on the shelf, and every day after stretching they did *Blocking Trips*, slow paced and one at a time. They did shuffle moves, then crossover moves. Every player had to do the footwork in area-four as a left side, area-three as a Middle, and area-two as a right side. Sometimes the coaches would stand on a box. The blocker had to see the toss, line up on the hitting shoulder, and press straight over the net. Regardless of how the block resulted, if anyone reached even an inch inside or outside of his body, Coach Pono would stop him and say, "Don't be selfish. Just take away your area."

Micah was the only boy on his team who hadn't moved on to high school. He had a mom and three sisters all putting in time to their lifestyles and growth. Staying busy was important in his brotherless household. He decided that he'd stick with intermediate basketball for the winter season. Micah wasn't an 8th-grade superstar in basketball, but being able to hang, in a game of two-on-two against full-time basketball players, made him feel good. Coach Pono played different sports growing up, and it provided him more opportunity. That made it easy to support his son playing multiple sports. He was Micah's volleyball coach, so naturally his direct involvement put volleyball in the highest position of regard. But he allowed it to be Micah's decision what he drifted toward playing. Pono wasn't going to stop making breakfast for his son if he woke up one day and decided that volleyball wasn't for him.

He did, though, remind him often as he left the house, "You better not get hurt screwing around."

All of the fall high school sport banquets ended by early November and more Ka Ulukoa players could come out and train. The coaches added 8am Sunday practices. They saw that the boys understood what to do, so Coach Pono yelled much less. Yet, the atmosphere was so intense. Not intense by the typical application of voice, but strictly by the intense nature created by the visual attention to detail. The way that Coach Pono and Coach Charlie stood over them and watched was more powerful than anything verbal could have been. It made them feel as if extra movement after a contact or missing a partner's forehead on a freeball pass or missing a dive after an attack was sinful. The system was their law.

Scheduled for the second week in December, Evan was invited to the five-day *USA Volleyball Holiday Camp* in San Diego. Meanwhile, Coach Pono set up some scrimmages against the older Ka Ulukoa teams to gauge the competition level of his boys. It was the third week in December by the time Evan arrived to Oahu. However, this time he came alone. Kaehu decided that he was going to stay on the Big Island and play. He didn't say it, but Coach Pono and Coach Charlie figured that it was because Adrian had taken over the spot that he used to play. Losing Kaehu was going to put a kink in their armor as a team. There wasn't much to be said, though; it was a long distance for Kaehu to travel and Adrian earned his time on the court.

Through the first half of the six practices that the team had with Evan, they kept the emphasis on introducing the blocking and transition system. The second half was spent on restoring and confirming their ball-control skills, as individuals and as a team. The boys completed their laps, their stretching, and then their Blocking Trips, with the coaches making sure that they landed square to the net and opened up to react quickly to a dug ball on every repetition. They moved through *Partner Setting*, *Partner Passing*, *One-Arm Digging*, *Freeball Passing*, *Shoulders*, *One-Contact*, and *Three-Man Pepper*. After they finished up *Quick Hitter Timing*, *Partner Serving*, and back row competition drills, the coaches guided the boys back into the new focus.

They trained their *Primary Passing* drill with blocking schemes against the Hitters. One play at a time, they practiced blockers switching positions and transitioning out the touched or dug balls. Everyone had to block. Each boy had to dig. Each one had to set. The boys' ability to maintain discipline and maneuver through their practice without yelling and with few direct orders influenced the coaches to keep that culture consistent for tournaments and add symbolism. The last thing that Coach Pono and Coach Charlie gave to their players before departing to the qualifier was: *The Focus Triangle.*

"This is The Focus Triangle," said Coach Pono as he raised his hands in front of his face to place his thumbs together and his index fingers together, creating the shape of a triangle. "We'll use this to remind each other of our training and to keep our mental toughness."

Ka Ulukoa repeated their lodging from the 2010 SCVA Junior Invitational. The Anaheim house was furnished just as they remembered it. The American Sports Center assumed its usual mystery during the two days of practices.

"How can it be 80-degrees outside and freezing in here?" asked Micah, grimly.

"Brah, this has to be where Santa Claus lives," Austin said jokingly.

The boys laughed, rubbing their hands together as they left the gym. Auntie Maile laid out the jerseys at the house.

"Make sure everyone has the right number," she said.

"You only ordered black jerseys, right Auntie Maile?" asked Skylan.

She looked up at him with a menacing glare in her eye. "Boy! Just make sure your number is correct."

The team pulled up in their vans the next morning and ran into the same parking lady. She had on a white hat, a red vest, and khaki pants, like a vehicle valet.

"There you guys are," she said with a smile. "I saved you all's spot, right over there."

Micah rolled down his window and handed her two bags of macadamia nuts. Skylan hopped out of the van and pulled out the hand warmers that he'd stashed in his bag. He handed them out to his teammates. Skylan made sure that Micah was the first to get his.

Practices at the ASC brought up reminders about the eight-foot net and how the team hadn't played any tournaments together on the higher net. Those worries were put to rest quickly. All of the teams that Ka Ulukoa squared off against hit the ball as minutely over the tape as they could, trying to create a more impressive bounce. It didn't work out for them as well as it did in 14 & Under Division, on the 7'4" net. A ton of opponent attacks either went out because they tried to hit so sharp, hit the top of the net-tape and slowed down, or were flat out hit into the middle of the net. It was going to take those players time to change their depth perception and the angle at which their hand consistently contacted the ball. Coach Pono and Coach Charlie's system was designed to hit spots on the court — and not spots over the net, but spots deep in the court that required the same angle of hand contact, regardless of the height of the net: the one-box and the five-box.

Tui and Evan were the best 15-year-old Outside Hitter duo that any coach could want. Evan was smooth, with court vision, and Tui was strong, with control. Adrian had another year of polishing under his belt. He had become a more complete player. The combination of those three Outside Attackers, along with Tui, Evan, and Skylan passing nearly flawlessly in a three-person serve receive, made it so that Micah had effective and efficient options everywhere on the court.

Coach Pono realized that his team was rolling into a good rhythm. They were giving teams fits. Enough that the Head Coach of Florida's Orlando Gold 15s was booted from the tournament for continuously screaming during their match that Ka Ulukoa was cheating and that Tui was on steroids. Word spread fast through the ASC. By the end of their morning pool on day two, even before their evening crossover match to advance to the quarterfinals on day three, Ka Ulukoa's matches on Court D1 were the most packed matches in the gym. Every young team in the gym suddenly wanted to talk story with them. When the boys sat humbly on the bench after their matches, players frequently walked up and asked if they just lost, because they were sitting so quietly. They made it into the quarterfinals on day three, qualified, and stayed their course all the way into the SCVA Junior Invitational 15 & Under Tournament Championship.

Chapter 14 - Transparent

First place belonged to Ka Ulukoa, and it was done without dropping a set. The overnight was fun for the boys. They filled it with jokes and countless games of Mini-ball. Departure the next morning had a mood more desolate than their typical sendoffs. The year 2011 was the first in which all of the boys broke away from Ka Ulukoa training because of the high school season. They wouldn't see one another as a full team again until the end of spring. Each boy got a taste of what Evan felt every time that he had to leave the team for home.

Carla Kabalis called Evan at his home on the Big Island to confirm that he was trying out for the USA Volleyball High Performance Pipeline, again. He confirmed that he was. Skylan made the decision to do the same on Oahu. He attended the tryout in Honolulu the next week. High school tryouts came around one week after Valentine's Day. All of the boys were nervous how the evaluations would fair.

Evan was chosen to join the varsity team at Kamehameha Hawai'i. His mom and dad were very excited for him. So was his Head Coach, Tom Poy, who assisted for Guy Enriques since the program's beginning in 2002, before Guy stepped away to City Council. Tui made the varsity squad at Punahou, a program that was returning half of the starting players from a successful 2010 season. Skylan was also picked for varsity at Maryknoll. He knew the poor history of the varsity program and had high hopes of changing the team record and the reputation in the ILH. Micah chose to add another middle school sport to his already intricate list. He talked with his family, and his dad decided that, as a 7th grader, intermediate volleyball made Micah's game sloppy and he didn't want his son playing those months on a 7'4" net. Instead of volleyball, Micah went out for Punahou's intermediate track and field team. His events were pole vault and triple jump, interesting choices for a short and scrawny boy with no mentionable vertical jump.

Basketball was the premier sport at Maryknoll. Skylan's only sport at his high school was volleyball, and in his mind he began receiving more attention than the basketball players. He noticed that more people greeted him with hellos and he added more contacts to his cell phone every day. He didn't see it as a natural effect of being in a different territory with new faces. No, he figured that his name was spreading because of his court presence in athletics. Skylan was the lone 9th grader to make the varsity team, and he wasn't treading softly. He allowed comments to slip from his mouth that weren't earning him the respect of the upperclassmen.

He bragged, "The girls are asking me to hang out and skip class, so I must be doing something right." *He knows who I am, so I guess I am that cool*, he thought.

He offered unrequested advice to the senior players in practice on how they could improve their technique or something that could have been done differently on a play. None of his teammates wanted to hear it from a little 5'3" Libero, especially since he was a 14-year-old high school first-year. His intuition said that helping to guide his teammates was the right thing to do.

Tui was entered into the starting lineup during Punahou's preseason tournaments. Punahou hosted an annual tournament called *Clash of the Titans*. A few top-rated Mainland teams were invited down to Oahu for a two-day tournament plugged inside of a four-day-long vacation from school. Southern California volleyball powerhouses, Mira Costa and Corona Del Mar, were invited to the tournament in 2011. Tui was more excited than any other player on his team because it was going to be his first time playing against high school guys outside of his age group. Things went well the first day, and Punahou beat Corona Del Mar. The second day didn't go well. Punahou played its second match of the tournament against Mira Costa, led by their 12th-grade Outside Hitter, DJ White, and got trampled. Tui struggled in the match; worse, it was the first time he felt like he got shut down.

Micah caught a bad case of bronchitis and was sidelined for the rest of the intermediate track season. Schoolwork was sent to his house. He stayed home and played video games in his spare time. Micah was already missing volleyball, so if being confined to the house would make the time pass faster until club, then so be it.

Skylan remained unsatisfied with his team's progress in the league standings. Maryknoll won a match against `Iolani High School. That was uncommon from the years past, but Maryknoll wasn't getting over the hump against the 2011 league favorites, Kamehameha Kapālama and Punahou. That was frustrating for Skylan.

At home he complained. "Mom, the other — players — just don't get how to win. It's like — we get the opportunities, but don't do it."

"They don't convert?" asked Arlene.

"Yeah, like we don't convert," Skylan said frustrated, as he rubbed his tough head of hair with his palm.

She looked up from the floor and said softly, "Well, everyone isn't perfect, Sky, and neither are you."

Skylan said back, "I know no one is perfect and I'm not either, but..."

His mom cut him off. "Remember how you felt when your dad used to criticize you in the gym for making mistakes? Think about that before you... Hmm?"

Skylan pulled his head up and stopped the rubbing. The look in his eyes illustrated an epiphany.

He said, "Okay, Mom," then stood up and left the room.
Arlene feared that her son hadn't understood the message that she was trying to convey.

Punahou completed an undefeated season in the ILH and moved into the Hawai'i State Tournament hosted on the Big Island. In the semifinals, Tui matched up with Evan and Kamehameha Hawai'i. Kamehameha Hawai'i won their league consistently, but that didn't validate their volleyball skills. Even in that season, the 9th-grade Evan Enriques was their captain and best player by a big margin. The top teams in Oahu were expected to take the win over any team from the Big Island in the State Tournament. Evan and Tui shared some laughs and a game of Rock-Paper-Scissors at the net during their televised match. Tui's team moved on in the end. Punahou and Kamehameha Kapālama faced off in the state finals. Punahou looked to add another win to their three-matches-to-none regular season record over their ILH foes. The best volleyball player in Hawai'i, Micah Christenson, led Kamehameha Kapālama. They weren't interested in another loss. Skylan sat in the stands and watched his best friend's (Cullen Mosher) high school team beat Punahou 3-0 in a best-of-five-sets match.

USA Volleyball emailed out the results of the 2011 tryouts on the week of Hawai'i high schools' final exams. Evan was pleased to read that he was invited to the USA Boys' Select National Team for the summer. Skylan logged onto the computer and read through the email with his fingers crossed. He came upon the line,

The USA Volleyball High Performance Committee would like to congratulate you on your selection to the 2011 USA Select Aloha Region Team.

"Mom, I made it," Skylan shouted from the family room.

Arlene walked out of her bedroom to the computer desk. "Made what?" she asked.

"USA, I made High Performance, the Aloha Region Team," Skylan said as he reread the sentence of acceptance aloud.

"Oh — my — gosh," Arlene said with a big smile. "That's an accomplishment, baby. Nice work!"

Skylan turned to his mom and tried to hold back the big grin he felt coming on. He wanted to act like it was expected, but inside he was ecstatic. The Select age group was the youngest group of the USA Volleyball Pipeline with a National Team. However, in that age group the National Team didn't play international tournaments, so Skylan was going to have the chance to compete against Evan and the Boys' Select National Team that summer, in the High Performance Championships hosted on the Mainland.

Tui went over to Micah's house that Friday after his last 9th-grade exam. They sat down on the couch and turned on the NBA basketball game.

Tui tapped Micah on the arm. "Brah, you feeling better now? That sickness knocked you out, huh?"

"It was Da Kine, for sure," said Micah. "But yeah, I am better now."

"Good thing," said Tui. "Man, this school year passed so fast for me."

Micah clapped his hands and agreed. "Right? Mine too. Even though I was home for like two months. It still went by so quick." Micah said with a smirk, "Sucks for you though, 'cause you know I'm gonna go big at academy next year."

Tui replied humorously, "Brah, you must still have that sickness. Let me check your temperature." He boyishly reached for Micah's head.

The end of school was a subtle reminder for the Ka Ulukoa boys that their bond was just a few days from being restored. The crossover into high school gave each boy a tool that he may have never received inside of Ka Ulukoa's system. Tui played for a varsity team where he wasn't viewed as the best player on his team. On the other side of the net he matched up against some older players who exposed the holes in his game and he was affected while learning to bounce back from that exposure. On the contrary, as a 9th grader, Evan alone was his team's serving, passing, offense, and defense. If he didn't play well, then his team wasn't going to win, no exceptions. Skylan was obligated to re-humble his persona. He had become so accustomed to each teammate around him adhering to the same system and handling his responsibility without interference from peers. At Maryknoll, each player was a different age, came from a different background, and lived different experiences through the game of volleyball. Accepting others for who they were, including maximizations and limitations on the court, was a lesson that was required of him if he were to ever build success there.

For Micah, patience was the imperative practice. He was stuck in middle school. The boy who always played up an age group, the one who always wanted to prove himself at a higher level, was forced to wait to be involved.

The boys had become used to no new auditions coming to the club tryouts for the second half. They were surprised to see a tall and lanky Haole-looking boy standing at the door of Klum Gym with his mom. Coach Pono and Micah walked into the gym with Evan, who had arrived two days earlier. They finished greeting Lee Lamb near the door and met their group on the furthest court from the door. The pale-skinned boy hesitantly separated from his mom and walked over to the 15 & Under court. Around 6'4" he stood, and his dark brown hair was cut low, almost buzzed. His eyebrows peaked just over the top of Coach Pono's head.

As he stopped, Tui said, "Dan?"

Tui's teammates looked over, confused.

"You know him?" asked Skylan.

"Yeah," said Tui. "Dan played intermediate with us at Punahou last year — Micah and me."

Micah put his closed fist up to his mouth. "Oh crap. Howzit Dan?" he asked.

The boy smiled and said, "Hey, guys. Hi everyone, my name is Daniel Andrews. I am here to try out for the team."

Coach Pono stepped forward. "Nice to have you, Daniel. Everyone introduce yourselves and let's get going."

Daniel had the body control of a baby deer, and he was not strong. What he did have was height, and Ka Ulukoa was missing that. Coach Pono talked with Micah after the tryout and Micah said he was a good kid, so Coach Pono called Daniel and invited him to join the team. Daniel politely accepted. It took a short time for the boys to restore their cleanliness. However, it was clear that intermediate volleyball wasn't the only level that gave the boys problems staying technically sound. High school volleyball returned a group of untidy players to Coach Pono and Coach Charlie, and having a new Middle who was going to take a while to develop was a reminder that the training had to be tight. Coach Pono gave a notice to the boys.

"Remember our few rules." His thumb extended from his fist. "We always show respect to our family and our teammates. From the time we walk into practice to the time we leave, we are focused on getting better. If any ball touches the floor around us we always give a dive." Austin teased Adrian with a soft elbow. "Fourth, we treat every play and every point with the same care." Coach Pono surveyed the group with his eyes, making sure he got a nod from Daniel, as he looked his direction. "Remember this, and what it represents." He raised his hands into The Focus Triangle. "Always focused."

Micah and Evan set their alarms for early morning Ping-Pong. Every day, they caught the bus down to Outrigger and Micah used his guest pass to get Evan inside to play sand volleyball for hours. In the evenings, the pair got hooked on the NBA playoffs and getting them away from the television for dinner became as hard as pulling teeth. They would place bets on which team would win, then they'd head out to the hoop in the driveway and the winner of the bet would get first shot in their pickup basketball games.

Micah told Evan, "Ho Brah, did I tell you I got bronchitis for — like — months? And I couldn't leave the house. It was gnarly."

"Hmm —" Evan bounced the basketball and took a shot. "Sounds like something that would happen to you, Ficus."

Micah jumped toward to edge of the driveway. "Oh! Give me the ball. You are going down!"

Micah and Evan left the next day for Outrigger. They always made up new rules to keep the games interesting.

"You only get a point if you tool off the block on offense," said Micah.

Evan agreed, "Okay, but you can only get a point on defense if you get a block. Otherwise there is no point in blocking."

"Good thinking," Micah said as he went back to serve underhand.

Three plays later, Micah stood on the ground and smashed a spike up into Evan's hands.

"Ouch!" he yelled out as he dropped down on his knees and clutched his left hand between his thighs.

Micah stopped celebrating his successful tool swing and dropped to a knee. "Brah, what happened?"

Evan managed to mumble out, "You got my finger." He stood up, wincing in pain with his hand still between his thighs.

"Frick!" said Micah. "My dad is gonna ruin us. He just told us not to get hurt."

"It will be alright," said Evan. "Don't say anything. I will be alright."

The team had Ka Ulukoa practice that night. *One-Arm Digging* had just become crisp and the boys were consistently remembering to open up after their moves, and now Evan's pinky finger was so swollen that he couldn't even hand set a ball in practice. Fortunately, the pain and swelling wasn't the cause of a more serious injury and Evan had two weeks to ice it back to normal. The team was in a nice flow. The only time that Coach Pono lost his cool was if the team was running their six-person defense drill and an off player allowed a ball to roll onto the court.

Two weeks from Junior Olympics, Auntie Maile was putting the finishing touches on the trip for the boys. The schedule for JO's in Minneapolis made the management unusual. Tui would have to meet his team in Minnesota because he was leaving Hawai'i six days early for his five-day camp in Virginia, with The Football University. Coach Pono and Coach Charlie were leaving the boys early as well, to travel to the end of the year tournament for their girls' team. Dave Engleman invited out the A level men from the open gyms to scrimmage the Ka Ulukoa boys. Coach Pono thought they could add a lot of flavor to the gym and get the boys' minds ready for competition. Tui left for Virginia at the end of the week. Coach Pono and Coach Charlie left the next day after practice.

Coach Pono said, "We have three practices left this week. Coach Charlie and I will meet you all in Minneapolis. Tui will as well."

"Who is going to coach us?" asked Skylan, importantly.

"He is sitting over there." Coach Pono pointed to a man observing, sitting in a chair near the corner of the court. "See you in Minnesota."

Chapter 15 - HI Life

Coach Pono had asked his college teammate and long-time friend, Mike Among, to come take over the practices. Mike held the head coaching job at `Iolani High School and was freshly out of his spring season with the boys' volleyball team there. He graciously accepted Coach Pono's request to stand in while he and Coach Charlie were away. He spent just three practices with the Ka Ulukoa 15-Mizuno team, but he was intrigued by the one practice that he observed just two days prior. Coach Charlie worked with Mike at `Iolani for a season. Mike was familiar with Charlie's way of breaking down each skill into the smallest detail and his ability to teach his players to self-correct. He knew Micah and Tui from visits to the Ma'a's home in Kaneohe. The gym setting was different, though. He didn't know them as athletes. Immediately, he could tell the team was something special. He told Micah to start their warmup and the practice was like clockwork. They knew each drill in order and how long it extended. They knew the run-time, and the effort and focus were apparent in every repetition. It was nothing like the substitute teaching experience that he imagined he would have. Mike was completely impressed. In truth, he would have liked to copy everything and take it back to his team at `Iolani.

The boys stepped out of the baggage claim in Minnesota to Auntie Maile in the driver's seat of a 12-passenger van. She attempted to tell the boys about the house she had rented for them, with no success. Like Auntie Maile, the residents walking through the clean streets of Minneapolis had no choice but to listen to a van full of boys, all belting songs from Keenan's heavily-Michael-Jackson-featured mix-CD.

The van pulled onto a dusty gravel road that contrasted the clean look of the area just outside of the airport. The gravel led to a wooden house that seemed, from the exterior, as wide as half of a football field. The dark brown wood kept its strong color until it faded to the much lighter shade of brown that was the garage, big enough to fit four cars. The garage had windows filling the exterior, more windows than they'd ever seen. Auntie Maile invited her boys into the house to see a surprise.

The interior was made of wood, as well, dark brown in color. It was three stories with the main floor on the bottom. Before any one of them could make it onto the second story, Auntie Maile's surprise was exposed. The players were excited to pass the kitchen and turn the corner to a long, glass window. Behind it was a heated, indoor swimming pool with two slides. The boys grabbed their bags and divided up through the house. Noah, Keenan, and Skylan stayed on the bottom floor in the main room, hoping to convince Coach Pono on his arrival to allow them into the swimming pool. Micah pulled Daniel along with him to the second floor and dropped their bags in a bedroom with one queen-sized bed. Evan walked up to the second floor and turned back around once he saw only two bedrooms left. Coach Pono and Auntie Maile would surely have those. Adrian was following Austin up to the third floor attic when Austin let out a scream.

"Holy crap!" he yelled down, "You guys gotta come see this."

All of the boys rushed upstairs. Auntie Maile took her time trailing behind them.

"Check that out," said Austin.

On the mantle piece hung a tattered green dress from a wire hanger. It was collecting dust and looked as if it had belonged to a seven-year-old girl in a Halloween movie.

"That's trippy," said Skylan.

With his bag still in hand, Austin turned toward the attic door. "Yeah, I am not staying up here," he said.

"Just don't bother it," said Auntie Maile with a disgusted look on her face. "Let's go. Dinner in an hour."

Coach Pono pulled up to the house on a shuttle halfway into dinner. He gave Auntie Maile a greeting kiss on the cheek.

"Everyone get settled in?" he asked.

"Hey, Coach Pono! How did the girls do?" asked Skylan.

"They played well." He asked Auntie Maile, "Tui's not here yet, right?"

She replied, "No, we pick him up tomorrow night after practice."

"Okay," said Coach Pono. "Hey, I saw a Dairy Queen on my way over. You guys want to go for dessert?"

The boys looked at Coach Pono like he had a fever and spots on his face, but they weren't going to turn down an offer for some ice cream.

Micah stood up from his chair and said, "Shoots! Auntie Maile, try pass me those keys to the van, yeah?"
Everyone laughed.

Once the group returned from their dessert, a game of Mini-ball ensued.

"Where is Adrian?" asked Auntie Maile, while she was preparing the boys' bags.

"Good question," said Skylan.

Austin said, "I think he is upstairs."

"What do you mean — upstairs?" Auntie Maile asked, confused.

"That top room upstairs," Austin clarified. "I think he is sleeping up there."

"The attic — with the green dress?" asked Noah.

Auntie Maile walked up the stairs, past Coach Pono's room, and up to the attic.

"What are you doing up here, Adrian?" she asked worriedly.

"Umm — about to go to sleep," said Adrian normally.

"Up here, with that weird dress on the mantle? That doesn't bother you?"

"No, it's no big deal to me."

"I will leave it up to you," Auntie Maile said as she scowled at the dress once more before leaving.

"Was he up there?" Noah asked Auntie Maile before she got both feet back into the main room.

"Yes," Auntie Maile sighed, "he is going to stay up there tonight."

"Alone?" Skylan whispered. "Seriously?"

Austin shrugged his shoulders and said, "Let's get back to the game."

Auntie Maile interrupted, "Uh, no — how about let's go rest. Go get ready for bed, all of you."

The next day, Auntie Maile dropped off Coach Pono and the team to the house before going to pick up her son from the airport.

Skylan jumped out of the car and asked, "So what do you think Coach Charlie does at his hotel all day after we practice?"

Obnoxiously, Micah said, "Definitely practices his Jedi mind tricks."

"Probably does night shows with a band," Keenan said sarcastically.

"I bet he reads a lot," Skylan replied to Keenan, seriously.

"Yeah, could be," said Keenan. "Didn't know we were asking for real."

Tui gave his mom a big hug when he walked through the doors of the baggage claim.

"Hi, son. How was the camp?" she asked.

"Hey, Mom," he said as she squeezed him more tightly. "Ah!" Tui winced and held his shoulder.

Auntie Maile stepped back. "What is it, Tui?"

"My shoulder is a little sore. Nothing serious, I think."

"You think?" asked Auntie Maile impatiently.

"I'm all good, Mom," he said surely.

She wrapped her arm around him and walked outside. "Let's go, boy. Your teammates missed you at practice today."

Coach Charlie met the team in front of the convention center the next morning. Coach Pono walked the team to Court 1. By then, they knew the drill. They looked at it and knew Coach Pono's purpose. That is where he wanted them to end up. That is where they wanted to end up.

After practice, Keenan asked, "Coach Pono, can we go to Dairy Queen again? On the way back to the house."

"He's brave," Tui whispered to Evan. "What's he mean, again?"

Coach Pono thought for a moment in the driver's seat. "Okay, yes we can go. Last time though, so enjoy it."

Evan replied back to Tui in a whisper, "Yeah, Coach Pono took us to DQ when he came on the first day, too. And it was his idea."

Tui raised his eyebrows and whispered, "He must have a fever."

Evan snickered, "Braddah, that's what we said."

"Tui, did you know you can flip the Dairy Queen Blizzard upside down and it won't fall out?" asked Micah, as Tui took his ice cream from the cashier.

"Thanks for the info," said Tui sarcastically.

"No seriously, check it out." Micah reached for Tui's DQ Blizzard and turned it upside down. "See? I told you."

Tui looked un-amused. Micah shook his hand, just slightly. The ice cream slid out in slow motion and hit the concrete outside. Tui's eyes opened wide and he let out a frustrated sigh.

"Are you freaking kidding me, Micah?!" yelled Tui.

Micah bent over to the ground trying to scoop the ice cream back into the cup. "Oh man, I'm so —"

Tui cut him off, "No. Don't even talk to me, man." Tui walked away to the van.

The team rode in silence all the way to the house. Most of the boys stayed to themselves in the main room or in the bedroom, until Auntie Maile called them down for pasta. Skylan said the grace and the boys dug in. Coach Pono was the last to get his plate, but the first to finish eating and leave the table. The table was quiet, until Coach Pono returned a few minutes later.

"Gather 'round when everyone is finished eating," he said.

The boys finished quickly, and hurriedly put their plates in the sink. The team formed a scattered seating arrangement in the main room to listen to Coach Pono. In his hand was *The Precious Present* book.

He said, "I am going to read this, and afterwards, I want you each to tell me what the message means to you."

The boys walked into their first day of the tournament with their black Mizuno sweat outfits on and their backpacks freshly packed. Once their feet touched the tiles on Court 9, Ka Ulukoa 15-Mizuno was all business. The team rolled, crushing the same teams on day one and two that pushed them in long-lasting, tight sets during the seasons past. Coach Pono even managed to sub in Daniel for the last four points in all three matches on day one.

Numerous kids passed by, trying to talk story with Tui, Evan, and Micah, asking, "Who is that tall, gangly, white kid? He doesn't even play. You guys just got him so you have enough players to play."

Evan and Tui just ignored the comments and politely half-smiled with no reply.

Micah chose to speak his mind. "He's our teammate, man, and he goes on the court. Don't talk junk, Brah."

Micah defended his teammates in the gym without hesitation. His shenanigans at the house were less admirable. Before leaving the morning of the second day, he waited for everyone to walk out to the vans first, and then he ran up to the attic and took the green dress. All of the boys were spooked when Adrian called them up and showed them the dress' disappearance.

"What's up with that?" asked Skylan, staring at the empty mantle piece.

"See, this house is haunted," said Austin, standing farthest from the mantle.

Micah held back his urge to laugh at his teammates' fear, which only he knew, was unwarranted.

As the house prepared for bed, Keenan let out a scream, "Ahh!"

Auntie Maile rushed from the second floor to the main room downstairs, where the boys slept.

"What? What is it?" she asked.

The boys downstairs were already huddled around Keenan when Micah and Daniel trickled in from the second floor.

"That creepy green dress is sitting in my bag. Look." Keenan was shaking.

"Did one of you do this?" asked Auntie Maile.

The boys looked around at each other in search for a confession. And nothing.

Auntie Maile sighed, "It's not funny. Stop messing around and go to bed."

All of the boys walked back to their spots for bed.

"Pretty weird, huh?" Daniel said to Micah as he sat on the edge of the bed they were sharing.

Micah smiled and said, "Have a good night, Dan."

Ka Ulukoa continued to roll through day three. The boys illustrated their creativity inside of their simple and efficient brand of volleyball. Tui, Evan, and Skylan received serves in a wonderful sync to help their team sideout quickly. The offense was fluid with consistent serving, accompanied by aggressive, yet smooth defense. The boys froze after each movement on the court, and finished it before moving onto a new job. They trusted one another. When the opponents were in an unfavorable offensive position to hit hard, the Ka Ulukoa blockers would pull away from the net and all six players became diggers. Every effort was synchronized and Coach Pono rarely used The Focus Triangle. He just repeated himself, softly.

Before serve receive and attack he said, "Next. Next. Sideout. Everybody sideout."

If the opponents made the mistake of hitting softly at the tournament's best defensive team then Coach Pono yelled in the middle of the play, "Easy!" and his team scooped up the soft attacks and converted them into points. The team sunk into autopilot.

Leaving the gym, Coach Pono joked with Coach Charlie, "The boys are playing so well. The biggest job for you and me is taking the cleaning towel from one court to the next."

The only team that came close was Balboa Bay Volleyball Club 15s, from Orange County, California on the second day, losing 25-23, 25-23. The Hawaiians redressed that close call with a beating of Balboa Bay, 25-19 and 25-16 in the day-four semifinals. The 2nd seeded Manhattan Beach Surf 15s were upset in the other semifinal. Ka Ulukoa received the news from the hallway outside of the convention center. Borinquen Coqui was back into the Junior Olympics Open Division Finals.

For the third time in four years, Ka Ulukoa matched up with their biggest rival in the biggest match of the season. The rivalry's past proved to be rather one-sided. However, both Borinquen's difficult road to the 15 & Under Open Finals and their past rubs with Ka Ulukoa demonstrated them a worthy opponent. Besides, the Puerto Ricans were rumored to be different. Even three years after their first meeting, Danny Rivera and Ricardo Pidilla were still the best left side duo that Tui and Evan opposed. They'd just never been enough. Borinquen Coqui's new weapon was a 6'5" Setter, named Brian Negron. He was a strong server, and an imposing blocker at the net. He set a consistent ball that was set from a higher point, which made it easier for the hitters to contact. Most importantly, he was groomed as the leader Borinquen was missing. His presence was demanding and his teammates responded well to him.

The Ka Ulukoa boys hadn't seen him play. Coach Charlie's brief explanation of Brian Negron during the four-minute warmup was enough to fervor Micah's competitive instincts into a mission to prove himself a more necessary influence to his team than Negron was to his. As the teams lined up for the referee to check the rotations, Micah walked onto the court and extended his massive right hand to his teammates. Unaware that his motivation would begin a tradition for his teammates, he gave each of the other five starters and his awaiting Libero an intense handshake with an equally powerful hug. Ka Ulukoa started in their standard rotation one. Micah gave the first set of the match to Tui on the right side. He hit deep, a few inches out of bounds. The next play, Tui took the set again. Borinquen's Middle closed the block to Danny Rivera, the OH1, and they stuffed Tui straight down. Micah stayed persistent on the third play and set Tui again. He finally took the kill, down the line to the five-box. That was the icebreaker. Ka Ulukoa played a terrific match. Skylan lined up the back row defense, Keenan and Noah got up early to hit in serve receive and transition, and Evan and Tui got comfortable against Negron's big block and attacked his arms with a wrist-flick and a left pocket finish for continuous tools off the block and down.

The X-factor was Adrian Faitalia. For his three rotations through the front row, in a deuce second set, every dig that the Hawaiians took from Borinquen attacks got set to Adrian and he blasted the ball over the block to the corner, where the one-box would lie. Three kills in row, Adrian brought his team from an even score to a one-point advantage, until the final ball of the match, when Austin Amian subbed in to serve. Austin ran to his defensive position and dove to dig up Brian Negron's Dump-attack. Micah stepped away from the net from area-two and targeted his set to Tui, who wrapped around from area-six to area-one, to approach the back row D-attack. The set was a complement of the dig before it. Tui struck the ball and it rattled through the block and down. Ka Ulukoa won the battle 30-28 and smiled to one another in front of a roaring crowd on Center Court.

The 2011, 15 Open Division, Junior Olympic Champions finished the tournament 11-0 in matches and 22-0 in sets. To the boys, beating Borinquen was another satisfying win, nothing more. To the fans, it was impressive. To Coach Charlie and Coach Pono, it was the kind of special that only a person involved in the process could understand. An evening session of laser tag and Coach Charlie's celebratory home-cooked steak dinner didn't do the experience justice. The entire year, no team won a match; no team took a single set from them. The training, the system, was ingrained into the team.

Chapter 16 - Early Departure

Evan and Skylan's summer participation with USA Volleyball caused them to miss out on an exciting piece of news at the Ka Ulukoa Luau. Lee Lamb announced that the club was closing the deal on their own facility, and it would be ready by the boys' club tryouts in late September. The boys brainstormed how they could make their summer pass more slowly. The solution that each one came up with was cruising to the beach as frequently as possible. With more age came more risky behavior. The boys never hesitated to duck-dive into the ocean waves covering the rocks, or body board into a close call with the front end of a passing surfer's board. But that was part of the Hawaiian culture. Growth and learning happened faster when there was a little bit of risk involved.

Arlene got a call to her house phone the last week in July. Her son was on the line.

"Hello?"

"Mom?" Skylan asked.

"Of course it's your mom." Arlene sounded annoyed. "Where are you calling from?"

Skylan could hear the displeasure in her voice. "Uh — Grandma's house," he said. "I think my arm is broken —"

"What!" Arlene shouted as she shot up from her chair. "How in the... Stay there! I am coming!"

Arlene arrived at her mom's house, to her son leaning back on the couch holding his arm in a homemade splint, with a bag of ice.

"How did this happen?" she asked, feeling agitated.

Skylan flexed his neck to pick his head up from the shoulder of the couch.

"My cousins and I were playing basketball at the park by our house, and I pump-faked. Then I got undercut and fell on my arm."

She sat down next to him and shuddered, "Did you call 911? How did you get here?"

"No. You and Dad said if anything happens don't call an ambulance, because there is a fee."

"That was a joke!" she said, about ready to smack him. "This is serious. How did you get here?"

"We walked, after I laid on the ground in shock for a while." Skylan chuckled.

Arlene tightened her face. "Stop laughing. We are going to the hospital now."

The doctor said that Skylan dislocated his elbow and fractured his radial head. He would be out for a while. Skylan's eyes watered as he walked out of the doctor's office with his mom.

Arlene rubbed his back. "Why are you crying, Sky?"

He said, "Now I can't play volleyball. This is all messed up."

As they sat in the car, his watery eyes turned to a flow of tears.

Micah decided to enter high school at Punahou with no intention of playing a fall sport. It was a first for him, but it was a good plan in order to get his grades off to a good start at the academy. He wasn't going to be without training, though.

Micah's Uncle Keli'i came over to the house three times a week through August and September to get Micah in, as he called it, "Big boy shape."

Keli'i had Micah in the backyard doing push-ups, pull-ups, sit-ups, jump rope routines, and running in the streets. Afterwards, Micah always walked upstairs to shower and looked down at his skinny body, exposing his bones.

He said to himself, "I should have just played a sport if I was going to do all this work."

Keli'i's workouts were far less time consuming.

In August, Tui started his summer training with Punahou Football. He returned from another Tom Martinez Camp and was excited to show what he'd added to his skill set. His brother and six sisters showered him with praise after Tui was chosen to the varsity football roster. By then, he and all of his siblings were integrated into volleyball, so it was a treat for his family to watch him do something outdoors. Tui was happy about the promotion, too. The return from Tom Martinez's camp accompanied him with his last three seasons of football in mind. Tui planted his cleats into the ground and didn't shy away from being a leader. Although he was just a sophomore and a first-year varsity player, he left training camp with the role of Punahou's starting varsity Quarterback. His football squad was off to a nice start, winning their first three games. In Tui's life experience as a football athlete, he hadn't been on the winning end of games. Early season success with Punahou Football gave purpose to his work in the summer.

Evan called Tui at his home on Sunday.

"Braddah Tui! How's it going?" Evan asked joyfully.

Tui smiled, "Ha! Hey, Evan. We are just coming in from church. We had a football game last night."

"Auntie Maile said you made varsity... and you are starting. Good work, boy!"

"Thanks, Evan. Yeah, it's going okay so far." Tui said modestly.

"Hey, so I called to see if you got the email."

"What email?" asked Tui.

"I guess not," said Evan. "USA wants you to come to the Holiday Camp this year. It's in December."

Tui raised his eyebrows, surprised. "Oh, sweet. But I don't know. I have football and stuff. I think playoffs might be in November or December or something."

"Rajah," said Evan. "I'm going to call Coach Pono and give him a heads up. Let me know if you get the email and talk to your parents. If you go, then we can cruise Mainland together."

Ka Ulukoa held its boys' tryout on the following Sunday. Lee Lamb had already funded the rental space for the club facility in a redeveloping area of Kaka'ako, for an incredibly low rate. The understanding was that the facility rental would be temporary. Before closing down its school, Word of Life Academy was the previous owner and Lee decided that it required a few more weeks of development before it was a finished product to host his club. Instead, the boys' tryouts were held at Palama Gym.

Tui walked into the gym in street clothes, with a small bruise on his leg from his game the night before. Coach Pono turned around from the registration table and wrapped his arm around Tui.

He said, "Good to see you, Tui. Good work over there at Punahou. Your dad is proud."

Skylan walked into the gym wearing his cast.

Keenan dropped his jaw and said, "Brah?"

Micah smiled and walked over to him. "I heard you broke your elbow, flying on the basketball court."

"That's why we are gonna call him Sky Man," said Tui, sensing Skylan was bummed about his situation.

Skylan still hadn't spoken. He was disappointed that he couldn't play with his team, but it was nice to hear that his teammates didn't hate him for his injury. He looked at Coach Pono nervously. He hadn't seen him since the luau.

"Appreciate you showing up, Skylan," said Coach Pono.

Micah said, "Where is Dan?" He spun in a circle looking around the gym.

Daniel walked into Palama a few second later.

"Over there," Coach Pono said, pointing to the court where he wanted his 16 & Under group to meet.

Micah whispered to Tui as they walked over, "You seen Adrian?"

Tui shook his head, no. "Been busy with football. My dad hasn't said anything, though."

Micah shrugged his shoulders.

No new players showed up to the 16 & Under tryout. That night, Coach Pono confirmed his son's return, and then put in calls to Tui, Keenan, Skylan, Noah, Daniel, Austin, and Adrian. Pono talked with his wife before bed.

Lisa asked, "Are you all done with calls? Did everyone confirm for the season?"

"All except for one," Coach Pono said.

In the middle of September, the Ka Ulukoa facility was stripped down to bare bones. Lee took a group of six other helpers in, five days per week for a month, to build, install, paint, and clean. Coach Pono and Coach Charlie met the team at their new practice facility for the season. The front door opened to a beige two-story office, each floor separated by a thick red stripe, with white outlined glass windows. The top floor housed a small conference room and space for storage. The bottom was equipped with a bathroom for each gender and a lobby with black furniture for lingering parents. Through the entrance of the gym were four bright blue courts, side-by-side, outlined with grey tiles and divided by black nets. The walls were freshly painted white and padded blue on the lower half for protection. It was a small fraction in comparison to the size of Anaheim's American Sports Center or any United States convention center, but it was theirs and it made them proud.

With no question, the boys assumed the court on the furthest wall from the entrance. The boys all gave one another a handshake and a hug before the coaches spoke.

Coach Pono said, "A few things. First, welcome to the new facility. Lee Lamb worked hard to get this for us, so make sure that we take care of it. Always leave it better than when we came. Second, it's important that everyone comes to the first practice and you are all here. As you can see," Coach Pono looked at Tui and Skylan in street clothes, "players have injuries and high school sports, so everyone won't be able to practice all the time. But take the opportunity to come when you can." Coach Pono glanced at Coach Charlie, whose arms were behind his back, and then turned back to the boys. "So that it is clear, Adrian won't be with us this season."

The boys said nothing and kept their still eyes on Coach Pono as he explained.

"Our training was getting too serious for him and his family. If you see him outside of the gym, make sure to thank him for helping us. Anyway, now Noah will train for us on the right side."

Coach Charlie looked at Daniel and gave a single nod from his split-leg stance.

"Let's get to work," said Coach Pono.

Whenever Micah came out of the shower from a backyard workout with his Uncle Keli'i, Pono asked him to come downstairs and sit on the couch. Every time, Pono spoke to his son intensely.

"Micah, you are going to have to take more responsibility and help to get the team going. Tui is in football and Evan isn't here. Skylan can only do so much from standing on the side. At this time, you've got to take the leadership and make the boys take it seriously. Other teams are playing just to have fun. It's your job to help the team understand that each person has a job to do. They've got to commit to that mentality."

Micah sat and listened to his dad. He nodded anytime his dad's voice grew louder.

Tui led Punahou Football to the league title and prepared for the State Tournament. Meanwhile, Micah said goodbye to workouts with his Uncle Keli'i and tried out for basketball at Punahou. Micah didn't have formal training in basketball, but his adoration in watching the professionals and his knack for copying the moves he saw on TV pushed him to give playing in high school a try. Unexpectedly, Micah was chosen to the varsity roster of Punahou Basketball as a 9th grader. Pono felt good about his son's accomplishment. However, that didn't stop him from making sure Micah stayed true to their conversations. Basketball ran through the first half of the club season. With Noah being new to the right side and Daniel having only six weeks of experience with the team from the previous season, Pono told Micah that he would have to attend both.

Skylan attended every practice in his cast to shag balls and remind his teammates to stay in the ready. Other than him, most of their evening practices had only Micah, Daniel, Austin, and either Noah or Keenan. Small numbers on a court with Coach Pono and Coach Charlie's unyielding eyes made the intensity of the atmosphere even more apparent. The boys had their mental toughness tested. This was especially true for Micah, who was leaving from school to basketball practice and conditioning, to another 90 minutes of joke-free volleyball, then home for homework in a house shared with his head coach.

Tui finally resumed club practice the last week in November. After the league title, he had led Punahou Football for three more weeks, all the way to the state finals, before losing to Kahuku High School in the season finale. October and November were spent on the Ka Ulukoa boys cleaning their ball control as individuals. Tui's attendance turned the page to the team's weakness: blocking. From the start of high school volleyball, on through the college level, most high quality teams in the country taught read blocking. The blockers were asked to wait and pick up tendencies of the opponent's Setter and react accordingly. That was a good option for teams with experience and perhaps the best option for teams with height. Coach Pono and Coach Charlie felt their team was better off without it. Getting over the net when the opponents set close to the net was the biggest priority for their undersized team. If the opponent set the ball far away from the net, then the Hawaiians didn't block and just prepared to dig. The coaches had the boys scheme and predetermine their blocking decisions to the probabilities of whom the opponent was most likely setting. The times when the opponent didn't set the ball close to the net was a benefit for Ka Ulukoa. It took away random net-touch violations and eliminated more potential tools off their block and out of bounds. When they did block, Coach Pono and Coach Charlie wanted them disciplined, with no selfish turning or reaching.

For two weeks, the team spent 30 minutes of their practice blocking. They blocked without a ball. They blocked without transition. Each boy stepped in and prepared, made his blocking move over the net, landed, and opened up. Then he went to the back of the line. Coach Charlie watched intimately and corrected movements.

Coach Pono repeated himself every few minutes, "Straight over, low and tight. Simple. Simple."

Tui left Sunday night to meet Evan in San Diego for the USA High Performance Boys' Youth Holiday Camp. For his room assignment, Tui was paired with a blonde-haired Libero named Erik Sikes. He hadn't seen his friend in months and figured trading places with Evan's roommate wouldn't cause a fuss. The camp was competitive and was Tui's first opportunity at six-versus-six for the fall or winter. At the end of the first day, the camp had roulette with the room keys to decide which room would do the laundry for day one.

"Room 319!" said the camp's assistance coach.

"Ahh, come on!" said Erik Sikes, miserably, realizing that 319 was his room.

Evan looked at Tui and raised his arms in celebration. Tui kept his head down, to keep a low profile.

The camp coach said, "319, that's Sikes and Tuileta," looking at his sign-in sheet.

Erik Sikes looked at Tui and said, "Wait, no. He's not..."

Tui signaled for Erik to stop talking. The camp coach walked over and asked what was going on. Tui stepped forward and told the camp coach that he switched rooms and was staying with Evan.

The camp coach thought for a moment and said, "Hmm — Alright, well you and Enriques have laundry duty for the rest of camp."

Evan shook his head at Tui and took on the same low profile body language that his teammate had, just moments ago.

Evan and Tui stayed up for hours collecting all of the laundry after dinner and preparing to rotate the loads through the single machine. They sat on the floor and waited for the washer to finish so they could load the dryer. Finally, at 1:30am the first load finished washing, so Evan and Tui loaded the dryer and left. Half an hour later, they smelled something unusual from their room.

"Do you smell that?" asked Evan.

Tui nodded, and they walked out of their door to a crowd of people leaving the third floor in a cloud of smoke. The entire hotel was evacuated until the smoke cleared at 3:30am. Tui and Evan cautiously came back to a basket in the laundry room full of wet clothes.

Tui shook his head and said, "Forget this. I want to go to sleep. Come on."

He grabbed the shirts and Evan followed him up the elevator. They dropped off the shirts and shorts in front of each pair of players' door. Evan managed a laugh out of his sleepy face as Tui left a note for the last two doors that read:

Your shirts are soaked... and we don't care.

Evan and Tui returned to Oahu from their five-day camp on Saturday. Lisa picked the boys up from the airport with Micah and dropped them off to Pono at the club gym. The boys walked into the gym to Coach Pono and Coach Charlie on the far court doing *One-Contact* with the girls.

"What the crap is that?" said Micah.

Evan asked, "Have they been doing that all this time?"

"That's our stuff!" Micah said, getting more upset.

Tui said calmly, "Yeah, that's pretty annoying they are copying."

The boys walked back out into the lobby and sat until the girls' practice was finished. Micah jumped up as soon as his dad walked into the lobby.

"Why in the heck are those girls doing our stuff?" he asked.

Pono looked at him sideways. "You better cool it, Micah."

Micah deflated his chest a bit.

"What stuff?" asked Pono.

"All of the stuff we do in practice. The girls were doing it."

Tui and Evan walked to Micah's sides. "Hey, Coach Pono," Evan said quietly.

Pono turned away from his son. "Hi, Evan. How was the camp?"

Micah held his position, standing impatiently. He softened his body language again once Charlie Jenkins walked into the lobby from the gym.

"Hi, Coach Charlie," the boys said together.

Coach Charlie said softly, "The techniques have been successful The club wants us to make it a standard for the club."

Micah was unhappy, but he knew, that was the end of the conversation.

Report cards came in the mail and every boy and girl in the Ka Ulukoa program was required to bring in their first semester grades to their coaches. The 16s brought report cards along to Sunday practice. All eight of the players earned above a 3.0 grade point average. The 2.75 minimum was exceeded and the entire team was eligible to play in the California qualifier.

The team had just three practices to put in finishing touches on the system for the SCVA Invitational. Daniel was preparing to start his first match ever for Ka Ulukoa. That stripped the idea of Micah using the Quick Attack as often he had in the past. That reality, in concert with clarity that Noah wouldn't be an offensive threat as an Opposite, encouraged Coach Pono and Coach Charlie to make additions to the offense. Similar to the addition of the Pipe-attack from the previous season, the coaches input another back row route. They would miss the front row prowess of Adrian on the right side. Without that ability to spread the offense, teams would become savvy to Ka Ulukoa's game. The coaches prepared a set for Tui and Evan called the *C. The C-attack was a set for a back row Hitter, in the area between the Pipe-attack and the D-attack. The route was far enough to act as some form of a right side offense to open up the Quick Attacks and the left side attacks, yet not so far that Evan and Tui couldn't transition back to defense in area-six. Good news came at the arrival of the second to last practice of the winter season. Skylan showed up to practice without his cast. He was cleared to play for the qualifier. Jerseys were taken care of by Auntie Maile, who also collected breakfast ingredients and booked the travel arrangements. The team left for Anaheim.

Coach Pono finally bent on his *no swimming pool* rule in Minneapolis, so the first order of business in the Anaheim house was changing into their board shorts and running out to the pool. Micah stuck his foot in and yanked it out quickly.

"This pool is freezing!" he exclaimed.

Austin Amian was the last to walk out to the backyard.

"What are you guys waiting for?" he asked. "Jump in."

Skylan walked up to the edge of the swimming pool and kneeled down to stick his hand in.

"What do you think, Sky Man?" asked Tui.

Skylan looked at Micah and Micah looked at Skylan.

Together they said, "Nooo!" shaking their heads.

The typical early arrival gave the boys two practices in the ASC to get their feet wet with the additions in the system. Playing only one scrimmage together before leaving Oahu may not have prepared Ka Ulukoa for the competition they were yet to face. Although the boys were adjusting to a new lineup, they did find comfort in every player being a returner, familiar with the expectations.

Skylan found himself sluggish in his return to training and hesitant to dive for balls, in fear that his elbow might fracture again. Adding insult to injury, he spent the two practices and the first day of the tournament sick. A cold sweat ran down his face throughout the day and he constantly couldn't catch his balance. After each practice and the night before day one of the tournament, he returned to the Anaheim house, showered, ate, and slept in his uniform and game socks.

The morning of day one, Keenan asked, "Brah, how do you keep getting sick at the qualifiers?"

"I think it's the yogurt," said Skylan. "I am lactose intolerant." Auntie Maile turned her head quickly. "What? If you are lactose intolerant, then why would you eat yogurt?" Her eyes were wide, waiting for an answer.

Skylan said, "It usually doesn't cause a problem."

Tui laughed. "Clearly it does," he said.

Even feeling ill, Skylan was still the first awake and the first to Auntie Maile's breakfast. Skylan hadn't missed any practices, so regardless of his injury, if he was the best player for the position then he was going to start. He always kept in mind the way he felt when he was the backup, versus the way he felt when he earned the starting position. Those recollections spoke to him when he was injured or ill. Other boys could play additional sports or spend the year on different parts of the island and still perform well in the system. For Skylan, he felt he had to be at everything and take in every ounce of knowledge possible and always play. If not, then his level would fall, and so would the position that he earned.

Ka Ulukoa played the most technical volleyball in the gym, all age groups included. That didn't prevent the first day of the tournament from having more violations and misconnections than tournaments past. Daniel was very raw in every part of his game, and Noah was working out a lot of old habits adapting to his new front row position. The team was fortunate that Coach Pono and Coach Charlie warned Micah in advance, and he cunningly adjusted his habits. Micah had a new game plan. It was to occasionally set Keenan on the Quick Attack; otherwise, get the ball to Tui and Evan. Those two knew when to be patient and when to go for it. Ka Ulukoa wasn't going to be in trouble defensively. Evan and Tui still held down the middle-back in area-six. Micah played area-one along with Austin, who subbed in for Noah. Keenan played defense for half of a rotation when he served, but Skylan could serve for Daniel and defended left-back, area-five for the other five and a half rotations. The back row defenders hadn't changed. Therefore, without Adrian on the right and Noah in the middle, the most important job was to make smart decisions on offense.

Micah rode that plan through most of day one and all of day two. It worked wonderfully. Few teams had an answer for Evan and Tui's consistency to the one-box and five-box. For the few that did, they mixed in short tips and roll shots over the block. Once teams started to automatically send two blockers out to the left side, Coach Charlie signaled to Micah and he started using the back row C-attack. The opponents were being exposed. The team was happy. They were in a smooth rhythm, especially Tui. Physically, his playing style had always been aggressive. Now he brought some of his football-influenced attitude to the volleyball court. He'd let out the occasional roar as he killed the ball. He gave a short scream in excitement for his teammate if he made a block or a nice transition set. Tui was in a new zone and his teammates allowed him to be there. His instincts were guiding him, while his teammates remained who they were.

Being unblemished by the end of the second day was refreshing for the boys. They felt pleasure that Daniel could be on the court for it.

Micah said, "I propose a toast."

"What are you talking about, Ficus?" Evan asked eagerly.

"We should celebrate," Micah said, more seriously.

"Celebrate what?" asked Skylan.

"A good second day, of course." Micah pulled down his top layer of pants, exposing his board shorts. "Let's get in the pool."

The boys paused for a moment, looking around the room at each other.

Micah put his hands on his hips. "Dan?"

Daniel surveyed the room once more and said, "Let's do it."

All the boys cheered and ran to their bags to get dressed for the cold swim.

Auntie Maile loaded her car of boys on the morning of the quarterfinals.

"Everyone got his backpack and water?" she asked.

"Keenan, put in the CD," said Micah.

The van pulled up to the red-vested parking lady.

"My favorite crew," she said, waving at the boys in the back seats.

Micah extended his arm and handed her a bag of nuts. "We will bring you something different next time," said Micah.

She smiled. "These are just fine, honey. You all have a good day in there."

Court C2 was host to Ka Ulukoa's 8am match against Shorebreak 16s from San Diego, California. The team was tall and had a few high school 11th graders (young enough to play down), with good arm swings. The control in those arms was spotty, however, and they hit out of bounds, a lot. Ka Ulukoa passed them up with accurate serving, followed by a disciplined block.

Two hours later, Ka Ulukoa met Baja 16s in the semifinals. They were making their annual appearance in the SCVA Invitational. Even without the ability to accept a bid of qualification to Junior Olympics, Baja seemed motivated against the team from Hawai'i. Enrique Ugalde and Sebastian Castro were clever players. They hadn't forgotten how effective Adrian had been against them in the 14 & Under qualifier. Right from the start, their coach put two blockers on Evan and Tui when they were front row, and Sebastian worked with Enrique to reveal the weakness in Ka Ulukoa's right side blocking. Noah could take up space, but not nearly the kind that Adrian had been taking away. Micah's block was virtually nonexistent against Ugalde's attacks down the line.

Baja and Ka Ulukoa split the first two sets. Coach Charlie talked with his boys and told them that Tui or Evan, whichever was front row, was going to wait for the serve and switch with Micah to block in area-two, anytime that number 10, Enrique, was front row. Coach Charlie's tactic worked and the team made just enough touches on the block and digs to transition their way to a 15-9 win. Micah sat outside in the hallway of the ASC with his team, grateful to be playing on into the finals, yet upset that he allowed himself to be exposed, the same way that he tried to expose other teams' blockers. He didn't nap. He didn't eat. He sat for an hour, waiting for the finals.

Manhattan Beach Surf still had Louis Richard, the African-American boy from Los Angeles, leading the team with his powerful spikes. They still had the head coach's crafty son, Hayden Boehle, at Outside Hitter and the tallest Middle in the 16 & Under Division, along with a good vertical jump, 6'7" Cole Paullin. Who they had added was Jacob Tuioti-Mariner, a four-star football recruit who played Defensive End for Saint John Bosco, the best high school football team in the nation, a 6'5" Samoan boy who transferred away from Orange Coast Volleyball Club when his stud-Setter left the team.

Skylan walked off the court on C1 as MB Surf walked on for their four minutes and said, "That kid is like the taller, left-handed version of Adrian."

He was maybe the only Opposite in the entire Southern California 16 & Under Division who could hit an effective back row D-attack, consistently.

Ka Ulukoa snuck out ahead in set one on overzealous MB Surf hitting errors. Nothing changed in Micah's plan by the time that the Californians settled down and started to find the court. He set Tui and Evan all except two balls in the first set to win. MB Surf made an adjustment in set two and matched up Jacob Tuioti and Cole Paullin on the block with Tui while he hit in the front row.

Evan sided-out his rotations in the front row, quickly. MB Surf did the same with Cole Paullin each time they got a good pass to the net. Any swing that Paullin got good pace behind went around Daniel or straight over the top of Keenan and into the floor. MB Surf slowed down Tui's offense and when they did, they used Tuioti's thundering left-handed swing to finish the plays. Manhattan Beach edged Ka Ulukoa in the second set and forced a third for the tournament title, sending the spectators into a frenzy of whispers.

Ka Ulukoa kept Evan and Tui blocking on the left side because Jacob Tuioti was MB Surf's most effective Hitter on the right. After a tie at 5-5, Manhattan Beach made a mistake that would cost them the match. Their Setter went away from Tuioti on the right and set four straight balls to Richard on the left. Micah lifted his tiny body off the ground and crept his massive hands over the net for three straight stuff-blocks and a clean block touch that Ka Ulukoa transitioned out for a kill. Rapidly, 5-5 turned to 9-5 and the Hawaiians arrived at match point soon after. Micah tucked in his jersey and adjusted his shorts from his belly button down to his hips. He turned back to his teammates in the back row, flipped his floppy brown hair, and clapped his hands three times with a scowl on his face that said, *Let's finish this.* Skylan's dig of Enrique Ugalde's Pipe-attack led to Micah setting Evan Enriques on the C-attack for the transition kill. The Ka Ulukoa victory was so.

Fourteen & Under is when the Mainland teams started to be involved with volleyball, but 16 & Under is historically when they started to take the national throne. The Mainland boys were gaining the years of experience that they needed to win, plus they had a much larger pool to pick from to field teams of tall, physical, and talented rosters. That was especially true for teams from Southern California that had the large pool to draw from, the athletes growing up playing on the beach, and athletes following the generation of AVP Beach players who were predominately California residents. Leaving Anaheim the next morning, Coach Pono thought about some of the teams his group dodged during the qualifier. He and Coach Charlie hadn't even seen the talent that the east coast was bringing, yet. They knew that more work was going to be necessary if Ka Ulukoa was to defend their title at JOs.

Chapter 17 - Flip Of A Coin

Moving toward the spring, Pono was curious about the boys' development. Micah's decision-making for Ka Ulukoa was more important than ever before and he was only halfway into his Punahou Basketball campaign. He was going to be spending a while away from volleyball. Pono also considered how the club team's role players would rise or decline in their high school programs. Things were much more certain before high school, when his boys trained with Ka Ulukoa from the fall, straight through to JOs.

Evan was elated to come home to the news that his dad was vacating his city councilman job and returning to head coach varsity volleyball at Kamehameha Hawai'i. Tom Poy stepped down from the head coaching position so that Guy Enriques could coach Evan, as well as Emmett, entering as a 9th grader. Guy missed the strong volleyball relationship with his sons and they missed it with their dad.

The high school volleyball season was one week away. Evan and Tui received email offers to the roster for the USA Volleyball Boys' Youth National Team. Both were quite humbled by the offer to represent their country in the two weeks of summer training, and the one-week international tournament. Unfortunately, JOs fell within the block of the Youth Team competition. Both boys declined the offer and made the decision to play with Ka Ulukoa and attempt a fifth straight Gold Medal.

Punahou's varsity basketball team moved into the February state championship. Micah didn't grace the floor often as a 9th grader. He learned from the court in practice and from the bench in games. Unrelated to the minutes he played in the games, was the novel experience he took away from being involved with his team inside of the University of Hawai'i at Manoa's Stan Sheriff Center on their way to a state championship. The next day was Sunday. Micah took a day of rest from sports and spent hours talking story with his family in the backyard. It was a rare day in the Ma'a household that no child had a sporting event. Everyone returned to school on Monday. Sports resumed that afternoon: volleyball tryouts.

Skylan spent his four weeks after club, hitting the weight room with his dad and attending open gyms. At USA High Performance over the summer, Skylan set his sights on playing well and medaling. Instead, he played with a team full of good players who didn't care. His Aloha Region teammates snuck out of the hotel and got lost in the city, while looking for marijuana to buy. They took seventh place out of nine teams in the tournament and no one batted an eye. From that, he developed a softer feeling toward the guys on his high school varsity team. They weren't the caliber of USA High Performance Pipeline players, but at least they gave effort.

All eight of Pono and Charlie's club boys made their 2012 high school varsity teams. Evan's brother, Emmett, also made his dad's talent-thin varsity team at Kamehameha Hawai'i. Guy's first order of business was showing that there wasn't going to be favoritism toward his two sons. Each day, Evan and Emmett received the toughest treatment from Coach Guy. The treatment was an extent beyond equal. Guy made certain that every player in his program knew that Evan and Emmett would be the last to watch a ball drop, be late for a training, or take any discernible action of separation from the team values. Evan welcomed the responsibility. Any expectations were kosher with him. It was enough for him to have his dad back on the bench, instead of the stands.

At Punahou, Micah opened his varsity volleyball campaign positioned as a Setter, splitting time with an 11th grader. Tui moved forward into a role as the team's premier Outside Hitter. Head Coach, Rick Tune, took his team down to San Diego for California's annual *Best of the West Tournament*. Punahou's *Clash of the Titans* featured two of California's top ranked teams every season. In return, the tournament creators of San Diego extended an invitation to Hawai'i's 2011 State Finals runner-up to join them in the preseason. Punahou watched Mira Costa take on Southern California's new number-one-ranked team in the last match of day one, Loyola High School. Five of Loyola's six starters, and the Libero, were 12th graders signed to National Collegiate Athletic Association (NCAA) Division I universities. Regular season games in high school were played best of five sets. Because it was a tournament, the teams played best of three sets and Loyola cleaned Mira Costa's clocks in two quick ones, putting on a blocking clinic.

Larry Tuileta Senior rarely got to travel to watch Tui play. The Best of the West Tournament was one of those rare occasions. His dad being in attendance was exciting for Larry Junior. Punahou learned that Loyola would be their opening match on the second day.

Tui said to Micah, "Let's have some fun in this match. I'm gonna hit hard. No being scared. Let's go after it."

"Shoots," Micah said, flashing his friend a big smile.

Loyola won the match, and the tournament. Tui learned something in the match, though. Through the trees of big Loyola blockers and a 23-25 and 23-25 loss, Tui saw beyond the shade and found the light in attacking aggressively the entire match — not to mention the light cast by Loyola's OH1, Nick Porterfield's, crushed-swing blasting through the seam into Tui's chest and flying back over the net and down, resulting in a point. It led to his dad raising his fist in the air in pride for his son. Tui no longer felt that intimidation about the older California boys. He didn't feel that ounce of worry in what might go wrong if he took chances against a team like Micah Christenson's from last season's state finals. He found comfort. That comfort, he imagined, could lead to a winning result in the long-term.

   The blend did not come without mental challenges. Together, it was common practice for the Ka Ulukoa boys to conform to Coach Pono and Coach Charlie's system. There wasn't a power struggle between coaches or players. High school volleyball presented some of those struggles. Coach Pono insisted the boys stick to their Ka Ulukoa training during club season. He kept his finger out of the pots of his boys' high school programs and prepared to welcome their progressions and restore order in whatever habits were created that would damage the Ka Ulukoa system. The struggle belonged to the boys.

   Skylan often came home upset about the comments of his high school coach. Words like, "The level of club isn't good in Hawai'i. All of the learning gets done in high school," would ring in Skylan's ears. Skylan took offense to that. In his opinion, something more ridiculous couldn't be said.

   Tui and Micah were told consistently to use two arms while digging. That was a common critique for coaches all over the world if a play didn't result ideally. "Use two arms. Don't be lazy," they'd say. Tui and Micah would follow their coaches' demands and watch themselves, and their teammates, swing their arms on balls outside of their bodies and shank into the bleachers. They'd look at each other in frustration and return to the practice of one-arm digs and watch the very same attacks be dug perfectly on a dime, all while their teammates were still spattering two-arm swing-digs into the fifth row.

   Guy Enriques gave his son the same corrections and often asked him for his opinion of what the team could use or do to improve. Evan chose to stay tight-lipped and leave the coaching and ideas to his dad. That was frustrating for Guy; he desired more vocal leadership out of his physical leader and he wanted to learn from his son. Evan never needed to give his input in club and it wasn't a feeling of ease to adjust that in high school. He preferred that everyone handle his own self and his own job.

   Finally, in a rare car ride home with only Evan, Guy took the opportunity to ask his son, "It's clear that you feel Ka Ulukoa is the way. It isn't something you've said. I'm not saying it's anything bad. I have good feelings toward Coach Pono and everyone involved up there, or else I wouldn't send you there. But I want to know." Guy paused and turned to Evan. "Why do you feel Ka Ulukoa is the way?"

Evan sat quietly and murmured out, "I don't know Dad. I don't really want to talk about it."

The league playoffs in Hawai'i finished. Tui was awarded the league's Most Outstanding Player Award before the ILH division championship. Evan was awarded the Big Island Interscholastic Federation's (BIIF) Most Outstanding Player Award before beating Waiakea in the Big Island Championship. Kamehameha Hawai'i and Punahou advanced to the State Tournament on opposite sides of the bracket. Evan's team grinded through a first-round (quarterfinals) win in four sets, over its cousin school, Kamehameha Kapālama. Evan finished with 35 kills and three blocks for his team. In four sets, 35 balls put to the floor was quite impressive, considering that even just four kills per set was a high average and Outside Hitters rarely compiled more than 15 or 20 total attempts in a three-set match. That performance was nearly duplicated in the second round against Moanalua, when Evan left the five-set match with 31 kills on a whopping 98 attack attempts. Kamehameha Hawai'i acquired an 18-0 record on the season and proceeded to its first state finals appearance since 2006. Waiting for them was the Punahou Buffanblu.

After the second round (semifinals), Evan spent his post-dinner time icing his shoulder while Emmett watched TV. The finals were played the very next night. Blaisdell Arena was host to the State Tournament and had been filled all week with Hawai'i volleyball fans. Kamehameha Hawai'i had a great run toward the finals, but analysts said it was supposed to end, and end quickly. Punahou was the number-one seed in the land and boasted a more impressive résumé. Evan and Tui met at the captains' meeting for the coin flip. Evan smiled at his Ka Ulukoa mate.

Tui said cheekily, "Hey. Give us a good game." Then he gave a wink before pulling Evan in for a handshake and a hug.

Evan sensed the cheeky nature in Tui's comment and prepared himself to compete. Tui walked straight toward the bathroom and a single tear dropped from his eye as he started to wash his face. Tui had never been particularly sentimental. Something about the atmosphere and the brief encounter with his club teammate, a boy he saw as a brother, pulled at his emotion.

Micah burst through the bathroom door and said, "Here you are. Let's go. Warmups are about to start."

Tui walked toward the court with the thought that someone was going to have to lose. He wanted his Buffanblu team to win. At the same time, he couldn't deny the respect he had for the load that Evan was asked to carry for his team.

The match was closer than advertised. In fact, it was a barnburner. The teams reached a fifth set to decide the match. Just 22 hours since the start of his 98-attempt match the previous night, Evan's attempt count in the finals was piling up. Rick Tune was through with watching Micah get his wrists tooled on the block by Evan all night. Punahou sided-out and was ahead 12-10 in the set to 15, when Rick Tune subbed Micah out of the front row for the 11th grade Setter. It only took one kill on the left side from Evan Enriques, bringing the set to 12-11, to jolt Micah from the bench in a tantrum, screaming for Rick Tune to put him back in the match.

Pono stood up in the crowd from the third row behind the bench and yelled to Micah, "Sit your ass down! Now!"

Micah glanced back at Pono with a pinched look on his face and dropped back down into his chair on the bench.

By the end of the match, Evan amassed 42 kills on 114 attempts. Fortunately for Punahou, the most impressive performance didn't guarantee a victory. Tui, Micah, Noah, and Daniel took the 2012 Hawai'i State Title, 15-13 at Blaisdell Arena. However, Evan didn't leave empty handed. After an incredible 10th-grade season, Evan approached the awards table wearing his drenched jersey, exposing his beloved number 18. His name was announced and he graciously accepted the award for 2012 Hawai'i State Player of the Year.

CHAPTER 18 - BOYZ

On the car ride home from Blaisdell Arena, Micah said few words. He wore a big closed-lip smile, complemented by his squinty eyes to show his sisters how satisfied he was with winning the Hawai'i State Title. Misty, Mehana, and Maluhia didn't hesitate to respond to Micah's proud body language with their displeasure that Evan Enriques hadn't come out on the winning end of the match.

"Ugh — Evan played so well. He deserved to win States," said Mehana.

"Yeah, at least he got Player of the Year, though," Misty said, poking fun at her little brother.

Maluhia added, "Did you see Ficus getting tooled by Evan?"

"Okay! Okay! We got it," Micah said sharply.

Pono and Lisa chuckled.

"Alright, leave your brother alone, girls," Lisa said, reaching back to rub her son's leg. "You did well tonight, Micah."

Micah restored his obnoxiously confident smile and pointed it in the direct of his sisters.

School concluded and club reconvened just one week later at the Ka Ulukoa facility in Kaka'ako. Tui walked in, just as Skylan was in the middle of talking story with the few boys who were already there.

"... Brah, our coach stayed having us run towels anytime we lost to Punahou guys. Felt like my legs were gonna tear." The others laughed at his stand up comedy as he continued. "My dad was like, 'No weakness! Keep going!' Freakin' military style, Brah. No good dat kine."

Just then, Coach Pono walked in with his clipboard, Micah and Evan following. Each team member was prepared with his report card in hand. Again, each card presented a semester GPA exceeding a 3.0, B average. Coach Charlie was the last to come through the entrance. The team smiled cheerfully as he walked slowly toward the court and put his backpack down.

Presumably talking to the Punahou players, he said, "Congrats on winning States; was a good game."

That was the last comment of the season about high school volleyball. It was ironic, but the boys never talked about high school after it was over. Perhaps it was out of uncertainty to the tenderness of the subject. Perhaps it was purely out of respect. Regardless of the reasoning, they simply didn't bring it up in conversation.

Micah and Tui had a glance of the teams in Southern California.

They both knew that the players in their age group were on some of those varsity rosters and were itching for their time to shine. Coach Pono and Coach Charlie knew, as well, that the Mainland teams were gaining the attributes necessary to challenge Ka Ulukoa for their seat on the 16 & Under Division throne. Daniel saw his only playing time in practice at Punahou and it was unhelpful that Noah spent the three months of high school hitting Quick Attacks and playing limited floor defense. The role players were going to need consistency to reach a fifth Junior Olympic Championship. As for Evan and Tui, they were going to have to be great inside of their roles, even greater than they were in the fall and winter.

The team got straight to work in cleaning off the inevitable high school rust. Every boy returned to his training as a complete player. Back into the *One-Contact* drills, back into the *One-Arm Digging*, back into the *Blocking Trips* and *Quick Hitter Timing*, attacking only the one-box and five-box. Most importantly, it was back to the peaceful quiet, facilitated by a focused group of individuals working and saying only what was necessary to improve himself or the few around him. Nothing changed about Coach Pono and Coach Charlie's training sessions. This was the beauty. They weren't required to add on to the system because no one had stopped it, few had only slowed it. The goal was instead to improve upon the traits they already used and recycle them into the same system, with more consistency.

On Tuesday morning, Micah and Evan finished breakfast after an early session of Ping-Pong.

Micah said, "Evan, try pass me that apple over there."

Evan grabbed the apple and threw the apple across the kitchen to Micah, playfully finishing to his left pocket and bending into the ready. Micah busted up laughing and grabbed his bag and flip-flops on his way out of the door. Jaylen Reyes had been on summer break from his freshman season as a Redshirt-Freshman at Cal-State Northridge. He planned to transfer during the upcoming fall to Brigham Young University in snowy Provo, Utah and was eager to spend his summer in the Hawaiian sun. Every morning, Jaylen came to the Ma'a house in Kaneohe and picked up Micah and Evan to cruise down to Outrigger Canoe Club. Three nights per week the pair had indoor practice with Ka Ulukoa. Two weeks out from departing to Dallas, Texas, Pono caught Jaylen at the door.

"Hey Jaylen. Before you run out, do you think you can get a group together to come scrimmage next week before we leave to JOs?

"No problem," said Jaylen. "I'll get some guys together."

The 16 & Under boys' practice court began to fill during the team's last week in Oahu. As the players walked in, they saw their scrimmage opponents waiting with Jaylen. Coach Charlie was near the corner, talking story with Jordan Inafuku and Taylor Crabb, a messy haired, pale-skinned boy raised on Oahu, who followed his older brother Trevor to play indoor volleyball at California State University, Long Beach (Long Beach State). Taylor had played for Coach Charlie at Outrigger Volleyball Club a few seasons back, and he was using his effortless leaping ability and beachy playing-style to make quite the name for himself at Long Beach State. Jaylen invited a foreign Outside Hitter from Germany, named JP Marks. Marks was starting as an Outside Hitter at the University of Hawai'i. He had a volleyball friend from his hometown visiting him in Hawai'i, so he brought him along to the scrimmage to fill in as a Middle Blocker. The last to arrive was Micah Christenson, coming home after being chosen as the National Freshman of the Year by Volleyball Magazine, and setting those USC Trojans to an appearance in the NCAA Championship.

In comparison to two seasons prior, the sight of Jaylen's group of young college studs intimidated the boys much less. Coach Pono and Coach Charlie's boys weren't without admiration and respect. The 16s were excited to compete against a group with strong pedigree. More exciting was the simple fact that competition time had come, no matter who it was against.

Coach Pono spoke before the first serve. "We will play three or four games. Find your rhythm during the match," he said.

The 16s played Jaylen's group tough. The coaches were glad to see the boys' confidence was unblemished by a slow start, and they didn't fall into a black hole of critique questions. After Skylan's serve, JP Marks whacked a ball that bounced off Skylan's one-arm dig attempt and rocketed to the ceiling. Skylan, Evan, and Micah covered their mouths and said, "Ooh" at Skylan's almost-dig. Austin Amian flipped the scoreboard to 21-25 in the visitors' favor.

As the team went back to its bench, Tui said with a laugh, "Almost had him, Sky Man."

"Man, I know, right?" Skylan replied. "He left me this, though," he said, exposing the four-inch welt on his forearm.

After the scrimmage, the coaches thanked everyone for coming to help out. Coach Pono and Coach Charlie were both leaving the next day for their girls' team tournament. The boys were circled up with their flip-flops on their feet.

Coach Pono put his hands together. "We played those guys

tough. Not bad volleyball today," he said. "So what did you guys learn from them?"

Keenan said jokingly, "How to get a fat welt on our arms."

His teammates laughed and Coach Pono cracked a smile. Coach Charlie was un-amused.

"Crabb had a good line shot off the hands," said Evan.

Skylan added, "Er — Christenson had good footwork on his setting. He made every pass look perfect, even when it wasn't."

Coach Pono gave his team a once over; to make sure that was all they had to say.

"Coach Charlie and I are leaving tomorrow morning. Two trainings left here, Mike Among is going to come for those. We will meet you all in Dallas for trainings."

The team put fists together and headed for home.

Auntie Maile met the team at the airport. She handed every boy his ticket and was given in return, five cups of rice and a can of spam, each.

"You got the CDs, Keenan?" asked Skylan.

"Duh, Sky, you know I'm on it," Keenan said, flashing two discs from his backpack.

Evan said, "Any Island Jamz this time? Michael Jackson was great and all, but..."

"Patience is a virtue," Keenan said slyly.

Evan replied, "Yeah, so is compliance," playfully thrusting his fist into his palm.

Auntie Maile interrupted the laughter and said, "Let's try get through security, boys."

In Dallas, Evan and Tui sprinted to take dibs on the room of their choice. They made their choice without research, and five minutes later, were trying to convince others to trade their spots.

Keenan smirked at Evan and Tui from his bed, saying, "Slow and steady wins the race."

Tui gave a quick laugh and restored the tightness to his face. Evan rolled his eyes. Coach Pono arrived to the house just one hour after the team. The boys didn't bother asking how the girls' tournament went, still bitter about their imitated techniques.

The house was well structured with a classic Texas red brick exterior. A set of carpeted stairs from the hardwood on the bottom led up to the completely carpeted second floor. Through the U-shaped hallways upstairs, there were five white-walled bedrooms. Located on the bottom floor was an open kitchen with a dinning room table, and behind that were three back rooms. One room surrounded a billiard table and two video game consoles from the 1990s. Another room enclosed a miniature version of a movie theater, including six reclining chairs. The third was an additional white-walled room that Auntie Maile slept in, located nearest to the kitchen. The boys took the billiard sticks and a few billiard balls to the top of the stairs. Micah put a plastic red cup at the bottom of the staircase for each player to take turns holding. A creative game of billiard-stick golf ensued. The game even progressed into having a commentator who would lie down by the shooter at the top of the stairs, who was sprawled like a sniper on a roof with his stick behind the billiard ball.

Coach Pono was in his room upstairs making a phone call to Mike Among. Mike answered.

Coach Pono said, "Hey there. Feels like I haven't seen you in a while. How were the trainings?"

"Good," said Mike, "the boys were focused. They said they had fun with the scrimmages against Reyes' group. I just talked with them a little about serving areas."

"Yeah. Yeah. That's all good," said Coach Pono.

"So I'll see you back on the island?"

"If I survive these rascals," Coach Pono said half-jokingly. "They are out here playing golf on the stairs with billiard balls."

Mike busted up laughing on the other end of the phone.

Coach Pono quieted his own laughs and said; "See you on the island, Mike. Mahalo."

The next day, after practice and a visit to Court 1, Coach Charlie joined the team in a trip to *The Grassy Knoll*. Coach Pono left to get a tour guide. He came back with a tall African American man wearing blue jeans and a wrinkled grey t-shirt. His facial hair was short and curly, but looked like it hadn't been combed in a decade. He wore white K-Swiss tennis shoes and walked with a small limp, which clearly wasn't from a handicap. The boys tried their best to hold back laughter at the first sound of the man's voice.

"Is this our tour guide?" asked Micah, holding onto his half-straight face.

The guide said in his thick southern accent, "Let me tell ya' here, boy! I've worked this spot for years — probably since y'all were born — I know everything there is to know about what went down here."

Tui raised his eyebrows, unsure of whether to be surprised or confused. Coach Charlie hid his smile, pretending to adjust his mustache. The guide walked the team around the hill. He did have a good knowledge of The Grassy Knoll. Either that, or he was a fantastic storyteller. His enthusiasm and role-playing made the tour much more interesting. He crouched down at the top of the hill and pulled Micah and Austin down next to him. The group inched in closer as the guide looked at Micah to his left and Austin to his right.

"This is right where the shooter lined up and centered his gun in on the president. This is right were he laid before he assassinated John F. Kennedy."

The boys kept their faces straight as the guide went quiet for a moment. The coaches and Auntie Maile turned and smiled at each other.

"Bam!" the guide shouted, making the boys nearly wet their pants. "Just like that. He got JFK. Moment of silence, please."

The guide took the team back to the entrance and popped his collar as if he were in a Will Smith rap video.

"Thank you. Thank you. I know I got skills," he said flippantly.

As the team walked toward the vans, Coach Charlie said, "That guy was actually really good."

"Unexpected," said Auntie Maile.

Coach Pono replied, "You've got to pick the one that looks like he has lived the story."

After dropping Coach Charlie at his hotel and arriving back at the house, Keenan and Noah noticed a wasp nest on the tree outside of the front door. The boys grabbed a handful of rocks to throw at the hanging nest.

"It's not working. Get the hose!" Micah said boldly.

"Heck no. He's crazy," said Noah, pulling Keenan in the house with him.

Evan and Tui followed but didn't walk all the way inside. They stood at the edge of the door, watching Skylan and Austin help Micah unwrap the hose from the side of the house. Austin twisted the nozzle while Skylan was working any blockage knots out of the hose. Micah pointed it right at the nest and doused it. At least 20 wasps escaped the nest in a hurry. The boys screamed as the wasps flew in a frenzy over the tops of their heads. Auntie Maile power-walked toward the door from the inside and shoved Evan and Tui into the front room.

"Get your butts in this house and quit screwing with those things!" she yelled angrily.

Micah hurried inside behind Skylan and Austin.

"Thank you. Thank you, Auntie Maile. Thank you for saving us," they said, pretending to kiss her feet.

"Stop messing around," she said, unpleasantly. "Dinner will be ready soon."

The start of the tournament two days later was uneventful for Ka Ulukoa. The excessive amounts of hitting errors by the three east coast opponents expunged the optimistically tough perception of their height and strength. The Hawaiians moved through pool-play on day one with few calories burned. The stares of envy from frustrated potential opponents were their only parting gift.

As the second day of competition came, Coach Pono was still thankful that his boys hadn't run into any of the equivocated teams from California, worthy and eager for their chance at Ka Ulukoa's record. *Missouri Thunder* was another team, in the second day's pool play, whose physical stature was developed and whose warmup appeared advanced. The match, however, didn't provide the same story. Again, the Hawaiians left the arena with an untarnished day of pool play, happy about returning to their red brick shelter with food and Mini-ball.

Keenan came downstairs to The Breakfast of Champions, befuddled. His teammates looked at him sideways; a few laughed.

"Boy, what is wrong with you?" asked Auntie Maile.

Keenan seemed nervous. "Umm — My bag is shut — I can't open it."

"Bring it down," said Auntie Maile. "Actually, you eat. I will go up and look at it."

"Okay, it's the black one."

The boys ate quietly, occasionally looking up at Keenan's uncomfortable facial expression.

Auntie Maile walked back in and said, "The bag was glued shut. It's not going to open." She looked around the room, scanning the boys' faces, and then back at Keenan. "What's in the bag? Something you need today?"

"Yeah. My jersey. And my shorts," he said without hesitation. "Er — yeah — just my jersey and my shorts."

All of the boys kept their heads down to avoid getting grilled by Auntie Maile. She decided not to ask the question that she surely had on her mind.

Instead, she said, "We are going to have to cut it open then."

Keenan woefully nodded his head, knowing that no other

options came to mind.

Coach Pono came down from his room and said, "Load up the vans."

To advance to the quarterfinals, Ka Ulukoa had to get past just two teams in the third day's three-team Power Pool. California was on the agenda, with a match against Shorebreak 16s, the team of unusually classed students from San Diego. The third team in the pool was Chicago's Sports Performance. Shorebreak was building their way back from a terrible start to the tournament, coming in as the 6th overall seed and dropping to the 28th after day one. They grinded their way back into the top 12 by making it into one of the four Power Pools. The top two teams from each Power Pool made it into the Gold Bracket Quarterfinals on the fourth day. The pressure was on.

Shorebreak played much better than they did in the opening stages of the SCVA Invitational matchup, but ultimately, their untimely hitting errors after 18 all, in both set one and set two, cost them a loss to the reigning champs. As the highest seeded team in their Power Pool, Ka Ulukoa took their break while Sports Performance battled Shorebreak for its Gold Bracket tournament life. Coach Pono and Coach Charlie stayed in the convention center to watch the match while Auntie Maile followed the boys out to nap and snack. Thirty minutes into the boys resting in their standard spot, a group of players came through the backdoor making a racket. Skylan read 17 *Open Athlete* on one of the player's tournament entrance passes. The players were throwing ice at each other and it spewed across the floor. By then, all of the Ka Ulukoa boys had their eyes open. When the group of 17s' concessions cups were empty, they threw the cups and their food wrappers at each other. As that team walked into the gym, likely unaware of the mess they'd made, Coach Pono walked out into the hallway to wake his team.

He yelled out, "Pick all that stuff up now! What the frick is wrong with you guys?"

Micah started to say, "But Dad, it was those —"

Auntie Maile was ready to back Micah up. Coach Pono cut him off.

Dropping his volume only slightly he said, "It doesn't matter whose it is. What kind of people are we? It really doesn't matter who did it. It's not the janitor's job to clean up after nonsense. If we have the ability to do something and we know it's the right thing to do, then we do it."

The air was sucked out of the hallway and no one dared to

breathe too loudly.

"Get up — clean this up — and let's go. It's almost time to play."

Sports Performance was massive, more so than any other team in the tournament. They started a 6'5" Setter, a 6'8" Opposite, and a 6'9" Middle, who his teammates called Jeff J each time he thumped a ball in Hitting Lines over the spectator seats. Even their six-foot Libero was tall. There couldn't have been a front row player on their team smaller than 6'4". The real surprise was that the passers and Setter had good touch on the ball. Ka Ulukoa's serves didn't pull them out-of-system as easily as they'd hoped, which translated to Ka Ulukoa having to watch Coach Pono rotate his finger, *Next! Next!* And round his arms overhead, *Big Circle! Big Circle!* through a ton of Sports Performance bounces. Tui was playing Junior Olympics with a healthy body for the first time since he could remember, so he used his tank of an arm to sneak past the big block to the one- and five-box. He would have had to tip the ball too high over the Sports Performance block for it to actually hit the ground on their side. Evan's tactic was staying patient. He popped the ball into the big block and covered himself, repeatedly. Evan was waiting for them to either touch the net illegally, or wait until the set felt right and use the line chop he learned from watching Taylor Crabb, to tool the reaching arms of the Setter and Opposite. Ka Ulukoa's usual ability to serve the ball in and pass the ball well made the difference in their win over Sports Performance.

It wasn't until after their own match that the boys learned of Shorebreak beating Sports Performance in three sets. Coach Pono never gave his boys information that wasn't directly useful to succeeding in the match immediately in front of them. Skylan was shocked that a team as good as the one his team had just played could be out of the Gold Bracket for the fourth day; though, he was glad, not to be in the same situation.

The team left a sushi lunch, to the vans and traveled toward the house. The boys mostly talked about how big the Sports Performance guys were and how wild it was that Shorebreak made it into the quarterfinals over them. The vibe was good.

That was until Coach Pono said, "I want it quiet. No more talk about volleyball."

The boys followed instructions and said nothing more. At the house, Coach Pono parked and told his boys to sit still. He walked around to Auntie Maile's passenger door as the boys were opening it and told them the same. He spoke loud enough for everyone to hear him.

"I know about the suitcase this morning. If you did it, stay in the van. Everyone else can go inside."

Keenan, Daniel, and Noah walked out of the van and into the house. Coach Pono kept his eyes on each boy as he exited the vans. Austin and Skylan followed inside. Micah paused for a moment, knowing that his dad suspected him of gluing the bag. Just behind Skylan, Micah also got up and walked out, making sure to flash his dad a big mischievous smile on his way in. Coach Pono was not amused. Only two boys were left sitting. The irritation was building on Auntie Maile's face, looking back only once at her son as she walked inside. Coach Pono's face held a look of surprise and disappointment.

"Seriously? You two are the ones?" he asked, hoping it was another hoax.

They knew it was not the time for jokes.

Chapter 19 - Old Fashioned

Evan spoke quietly with his head down. "Yes. Tui didn't do anything, though. It was my stupid prank."

Tui sat in silence, thinking, *The less said, the better.*

Coach Pono looked, at a loss for words. He managed to say, "Just why y - ... never mind. Just go inside."

Evan and Tui realized that Coach Pono's disappointment was much worse of a feeling than any screaming or workout he had ever put them through. On his walk inside, Evan looked back to apologize, but like Tui, thought better of it when he saw Coach Pono hunched over the passenger window of the van.

The fourth day was new. The gym reeked of excitement with fans and foes whispering about Ka Ulukoa's 16 & Under team. The quarterfinals were at 9am against another Chicago team out of Power Pools, called *Ultimate Volleyball Club*. The boys came through the entrance with focus about them. Micah came through with the look of an upset stomach. What quickly took over his thoughts was the news he heard in passing, that MB Surf was knocked out of the Gold on day three, and immediately he thought about how he wouldn't get the chance to prove that his six-block match from the qualifier wasn't a fluke. After a noticeable groan of his midsection, he was sharply reminded of his unsettled stomach.

Ultimate 16s resembled a slightly shorter version of Sports Performance, yet an identical style of play. Coach Charlie made an adjustment for Skylan and asked him to come off of the area-five sideline to dig their left-handed Opposite, who was hitting his line shot over Evan and Tui's blocks. Evan and Tui were fortunate to save their legs as Micah flipped in more transition Quick-sets for Keenan and Daniel than he had the entire span of the tournament. Ka Ulukoa took the match in straight sets and progressed onto the semifinals. Micah made his way to the bathroom and sat on the toilet.

Shorebreak continued its remarkable run from their self-imposed hole and won their quarterfinal match in three sets to take over the 4th overall seed, lining them up to face the 1st overall, Balboa Bay Volleyball Club's 16s. Ka Ulukoa kept the 2nd seed that they'd held the entire tournament, and threw their hands in the air with a small laugh as Coach Pono told them they drew a Puerto Rican team, San Juan 16s.

Micah was still laid out on the floor as the rest of his team stood up from snack and nap for its 11am semifinal.

"I'm up. I'm up," he said lying there, not even pretending to stand up.

Skylan and Evan grabbed him and put him on his feet.

Evan said, "Let's go, Ficus. You aren't Michael Jordan (flu game). Sky has had worse."

"But I'll dunk on you like Jordan," Micah said with a sly smile on his face.

Evan let his arm go and Micah stumbled a bit.

The Hawai'i versus Puerto Rico semifinal on Court 2 was much more filled by spectators than the Orange County, California versus San Diego, California semifinal on Court 1. San Juan was still pretty big. San Juan was still pretty strong. No longer were they the biggest that Ka Ulukoa had seen, though, and no longer the strongest. The Hawaiians were confident about their chances against the Puerto Ricans, even taking into account their new Opposite and raw Middle. If Micah's sickness stayed at bay and they didn't have to sub Skylan in at Setter and have Keenan and Noah play six rotations, all the way around, then the Hawaiians could win.

For a boy sick with food poisoning from sushi, Micah was playing quite aggressively. He was dumping the ball and going over on two more than his dad had ever seen him do. The way he pumped the Quick Attack in the quarterfinals and the way he was dumping on two for kills in the semifinals, would have led one to believe that he was counting the seconds he could subtract from the run-time of the match by keeping the ball out of the air.

Coach Charlie asked him at San Juan's first timeout of the second set, "You trying to get to the bathroom faster or something, Micah?"

Skylan shrugged his shoulders and said, "Hey, if it works. A point is a point."

After the timeout, San Juan sided-out and served the next ball to Skylan. Micah jumped to set Skylan's perfect pass. San Juan's OH1 jumped with Micah to block his Dump-attack and Micah flipped a set over his head to Evan on the back row C-attack. Evan saw the open net with no blockers and crushed the ball to the one-box for a kill.

After touching hands with his teammates and resetting at the net for his team to serve, Micah looked through the net at the frustrated San Juan Outside Hitter and playfully said, "I see you."

The Hawaiians opened up a nice lead, and Micah gave a few sets to Daniel and Noah, to whom the Puerto Ricans were paying no attention. Keenan served the ball for match point. San Juan set the Quick Attack and he crushed it deep, right inline with Ka Ulukoa's area-six, middle-back. Evan extended his left arm for a one-arm dig that sat nicely on top of Micah's head. He set a Go, out to Tui, and he ripped toward the five-box for the win. Tui calmly walked over to Evan and gave him a powerful five-high, while Coach Pono huddled the boys to slap hands with San Juan.

As Auntie Maile pulled the snacks from the cooler into the hallway, Micah had forgotten all about his aching stomach and decided he wasn't going to nap during the break. Instead, he and Keenan saw some unoccupied rolling chairs and went for a ride down the hallway. Micah and Keenan raced down the hall in their rolling chairs, pedaling their feet quickly as if they were Flintstones characters. Keenan got out in front, so Micah accelerated his feet as they closed in on the end of the hallway. Keenan turned the corner and came to a halt. Micah followed in pursuit and fell over as he turned the corner and hit Keenan's chair.

Micah looked up from his face-plant and started to say, "Hey, why'd you —" then, like Keenan, he began to stare.

Balboa Bay's 16s were huddled around a video projector displayed on a large wall. They all turned their heads to Micah and Keenan, who were laid out on the floor.

Micah looked at the screen and said uncomfortably, "Hey, that's us," referring to the video of his Ka Ulukoa team from just one day earlier.

He then sprinted off with Keenan back to his own team and told them the embarrassing story.

Producing some of the best to ever grace the NCAA, USA Men's National Team, and international professional leagues, Balboa Bay Volleyball Club was a well-oiled machine inside of the volleyball world, and a man named Rich Polk was the person who supplied the oil for their top 16 & Under team, every season. Rich Polk's 16s won the previous season's 16 & Under Open Division Gold Medal and medaled each year in the five seasons before that. He was to Balboa Bay, what Pat Riley was to the 1990's Los Angeles Lakers. He was a lot of the reason that a Balboa Bay team, that had never beaten Ka Ulukoa, could come into the tournament as the 1st overall seed, demoting the team that had never lost a match to 2nd. Who could argue? His group was back into the finals and they, like Ka Ulukoa, hadn't lost a match the entire tournament.

Polk's team was led by Outside Hitter, Brenden Sander, the younger brother of Brigham Young University superstar, and USA Men's National Team member, Taylor Sander. Next to him in the serve receive was their Libero, Ben Oxnard, often labeled, along with Sander, as half of the best passing duo of their class, inside the state of California. Both boys spent more than their two seasons with Balboa playing together, even years before the first time they faced Ka Ulukoa at 14 & Under while they were with High Line Volleyball Club.

Polk was in his first season coaching the 6'3" stud-Setter who transferred in that season from Orange Coast Volleyball Club, Eric Matheis. To complement their already stacked Middle position, headed by fourth-year Balboa player, 6'3" Lucas Lamont, Rich Polk's team acquired its newest addition in the spring, Noah Blanton, the 6'6" African American nephew of Beach Volleyball Olympic Gold Medalist, Dain Blanton.

Coach Pono's team lined up in their standard rotation one, with Micah as the first topspin-jump-server. Micah tucked his shirt and formed a ring around his waist with his hands, adjusting his shorts. The referee blew the whistle and Micah threw up the toss for his topspin-jump-serve. Approaching the end of the first set, three Ka Ulukoa real points (points scored while serving) later, Balboa watched their 16-14 disadvantage grow to 19-14. Balboa finally sided-out from Noah Hayashida's standing-float-serve and Austin Amian subbed in for him. Although Skylan passed the serve perfectly with his hands, Balboa dug Ka Ulukoa's attacks and transitioned successfully to inch closer, getting to 16 points. Skylan passed the next serve, equally as perfect, with his hands and Balboa made another dig to give themselves a chance to creep within one — but Sander hit out, deep, 20-16. Evan Enriques served his jump-float, while Micah and Keenan shuffled out to concentrate on Sander. Tui shuffled over from area-four in front of Lamont and solo-blocked his Front-1 Quick Attack.

The next ball went to Sander. Micah and Keenan were waiting for him, and he hit into the middle of the net, trying to avoid the block. Balboa was sinking fast but responded with another Front-1-set to Lamont, which tooled off of Tui's solo-block and out of the Court 1 end zone, 22-17.

Another perfect pass from Skylan's hands led to an inside Lob-set from Micah to Tui, which he tipped deep over the line defender into the home corner of the one-box. Balboa's serving and defensive substitute, Tommy Casey, ran it down but shanked it into the crowd, 23-17.

Balboa had its opportunity for a late push at 23-18 when Evan stayed patient, getting set three straight times in the rally on the Pipe-attack and just snapping it around; but again, Sander hit out deep.

Coach Pono crouched with his hands on his knees, yelling, "Next!

Next!"

Balboa squandered that opportunity, as well as the next, when Micah topspin-jump-served game point in Oxnard's direction. Matheis delivered an average Go-set that Sander was forced to *roll-shot. Noah Hayashida dug it — Tui got a Go-set from Micah — it rattled the block. Skylan covered — Micah flipped the Red-set back to Noah — that was dug... but too tight to the net. Tui two-step approached hard and bounced the overpass right off of Blanton's forehead and into the stands, erupting the crowd.

Coach Pono seated his boys after the side change. They drank from their water jugs as he spoke.

"Same game this next set. Dig it when they set the Quick from away from the net, and then they gotta go to number 15 (Sander). Press over, low and tight, no reaching. Same game."

The boys walked onto the court and gave a handshake and a hug to each teammate. Micah walked to the net in rotation six and put his hands on his hips, waiting to sideout so he could be Ka Ulukoa's first server. Micah opened the set by setting to Daniel. He didn't kill his two swings in the rally, but at least he put Balboa is some sort of trouble. Tui got the third set of the rally and hit it with no spin, sending the knuckling ball far out of the arena. Luckily, Balboa touched the net and Micah giggled as he trotted back to serve, 1-0.

Both teams traded points for a while. The only real points came at 2-1 when Tui topspin-jump-served, starting a long rally of good volleyball that ended in Balboa stepping under the net, and at 5-4 when Evan passed perfectly and Tui blasted Micah's Pipe-set into the net. The boys glanced over at the crowd and noticed some fans in Balboa shirts mocking Coach Pono, putting *Big Circles* above their heads during the match.

The points continued back and forth. Balboa didn't have a back row D-attack so the Hawaiians stayed with their scheme. Tui or Evan would shift over alone from the left to commit-block on the Balboa Middle's Quick Attack, while the Ka Ulukoa right-front and middle-front shuffled out to block Balboa's left side Go-attack. Balboa prevented Ka Ulukoa from scoring real points by learning that they could use their own Pipe-attack to Sander to hit on an open net. Ka Ulukoa wasn't making digs on Sander's Pipe-attack. After Ka Ulukoa's sideout, to reach 8-7, Coach Charlie was flashing serving targets at Micah, signaling him to serve away from Oxnard.

The Hawaiians scored some real points once they started to make a few digs. Micah used his sneaky set-over on two in the back row and his aggressive Dump-attack on two in the front row to try to score. The few times that he didn't score, Balboa was forced to scramble on defense and gave deep roll-shots or freeballs back.

Each time, Coach Pono yelled, "Easy!" and his team dug and set to Evan or Tui to finish the play.

Ka Ulukoa went ahead 10-7 in the second set. Rich Polk didn't look nervous.

Sander rotated into to front row and finished a long rally with a kill down the line, 10-8. There was confusion on the next play, and Noah didn't jump to block. Sander bounced the set from Matheis in the middle of court on the 10-foot line. The momentum shifted quickly. Balboa Bay was back within one, 10-9.

The crowd was coming alive. Everyone in the 16 & Under Division definitely wanted to see Ka Ulukoa lose. Most of the spectators outside of the 16 & Under Division had respect for whatever they knew about the team from Hawai'i, but they still preferred that the Mainland team took the Gold. As the match extended, the crowd gravitated their cheers toward good volleyball plays, regardless of which team made them. Before long, the capacity crowd on Court 1 was backing a close and exciting volleyball match.

Balboa knotted the match at 11 and the crowd kept their eyes wide. Balboa proceeded too fancy, eventually running Sander on an inside-out approach from the right, as Evan stood still in his blocking position and solo-stuff-blocked Sander's low-seam swing, surging the Hawaiians ahead 14-11.

But then, Sander sided-out on the right for Balboa and back-to-back blocks on Evan by Noah Blanton led to a 14-14 tie. The fans sat on the edges of their seats while more heard the noise and sauntered in from distant courts. Coach Charlie, standing at the end of the bench with his arms folded, was likely the only person in the arena off the court who wasn't fidgeting.

Tui rolled the ball short over Balboa's three-person block and to the floor for a kill, 15-14. Sander blasted the Pipe-set from Matheis for a kill, 15-15. Evan tipped the Go-set just over Balboa's Opposite and Lamont for the kill, 16-15.

The best two 16 & Under sideout teams in the country were putting on the most impressive passing display. One could only imagine what sort of meltdown a single service ace in the match could've caused. A cross-court kill by Tui in transition put the Hawaiians ahead 18-16. Balboa's OH2, Cameron White, tagged the line on a Go-attack for a kill, before being subbed out serving. Off of Tui's perfect pass, Micah tapped an easy ball over on two and Oxnard dug it up for the quick Balboa Bay Gap-attack in transition — kill, 18 all.

Oxnard dug Tui cross-court on the next play and Matheis set the Gap-attack for Lamont again. Daniel was frozen on the block — kill, 18-19 Balboa Bay. The Californians took their first lead of the match and Coach Pono had seen enough, timeout.

"Drink water," said Coach Pono as he dropped to one knee in front of his seated team. "Keep passing. After we sideout, remember: just get in front of number 15 and go low and over. Everyone be ready to set."

Cameron White's serving sub floated his next serve deep, out of bounds, over Austin Amian's head. Micah hit a topspin-jump-serve that trickled over the top of the net-tape. Lamont dove in to pass it and Matheis Go-set out to Sander. His swing down the line missed the area-one corner, deep by inches, 20-19 Ka Ulukoa.

"No reaching! Low and tight!" yelled Coach Pono, waving his arms from the sideline.

Balboa sided-out on a double-contacted freeball that Tui set over during a long rally. Then, Tui sided-out after a long rally and went back to serve. Tui's topspin-jump-serve was passed a little too tight to the net and Matheis fluffed it out of bounds trying to save it. A 22-20 Ka Ulukoa lead triggered a timeout from Rich Polk.

Out of the timeout, Coach Pono rested his hands on his knees. Tui snapped his topspin-jump-serve into the court and Matheis set Blanton on a Front-1, which scraped through Daniel's block and headed to the floor. Evan lunged out from area-four with his right arm and popped the ball up. Tui gave his best effort from middle-back, area-six to deliver a good set to Evan, but Evan's only option was a freeball to Balboa. Oxnard handled it and Matheis jumped up and two-hand Dump-attacked it on two for a kill, 22-21.

A long rally ensued on the next play. Evan was playing his patient style, chipping the ball into the block and getting covered repeatedly. Finally, Micah ran forward and set Tui over his head on the Pipe-attack. The set went far behind the 10-foot line, so Tui jumped back out of rhythm to control it over the net. Matheis made the dig in area-one, but Blanton netted, point Ka Ulukoa. Balboa sided-out the next play with a Go-attack in their own rotation one, 23-22.

Coach Pono raised his arms. "Big Circle! Big Circle!" he said.

Sander cracked his tough topspin-jump-serve. Evan passed it

well. Micah set the Pipe-attack for Tui. His swing nicked the tape and slowed the ball down for Oxnard to dig. Matheis set Sander on the Pipe-attack — open net — left arm stab from Tui — the ball was up — Noah dove in to save it — freeball for Balboa — Front-1-set for Blanton — tip, and a kill. Coach Pono called for time.

"Pass this serve, get the sideout, and dig one after our serve. Blockers: everybody one-on-one; they've got all three attackers front row, so everybody just get your guy."

The boys sat and drank water for the rest of their 60-second timeout.

It was 23-23 and the crowd rose to their feet to see the end of a spectacular match, or to see it extend into a decisive third set. Sander threw his toss in the air... into the net. Tui stepped over and gave Evan a one-arm hug after the ball headed in the direction of their passing seam fell into the net.

Coach Pono whipped his finger in a circle. "Next! Next!" he yelled.

Noah served his standing-float straight ahead. Oxnard passed it on a dime. Matheis set for Blanton on the Gap-attack — Keenan commit-blocked — his swing grazed the tape and Noah popped it up low with one arm. Micah followed and used one arm to pop it up higher. Noah stood up and sent the freeball over the net. Evan was bunched in, waiting for Blanton to get set. Blanton dug it and Matheis set overhead to his front row Opposite. Open net! He hit it hard. Tui made a step-dig into his line of approach and popped it up... it fell into the antenna, though, 24-24.

Parents had kids on their shoulders trying to see over the enormous crowd. Tommy Casey subbed in and served for Balboa. Tui passed and Micah set to Evan on the left. One-on-one, he swung for the five-box. Tommy Casey dove in to dig it, but shanked it 40 feet backwards into the stage.

Coach Charlie held up his exposed area-one serving signal for Evan, clear as day. Coach Pono dropped his hands to his knees and watched Balboa's formation. Evan served cross-court toward area-one at Oxnard. He passed it well. Matheis set the Pipe-attack for Sander. Tough swing into area-five — Skylan dug it inside the court — Micah chased it and bump-set out to Tui, who rolled the line toward the one-box — Matheis dug and Oxnard stepped in to set Balboa's Opposite. His approach was out of rhythm so Tui pulled off of the net. Skylan dug the open net swing with his hands — Micah set to Tui — he ripped the Go-attack cross-court outside of Balboa's two-person block. Oxnard made a fantastic dig that led to a joust at the net between Tui and Balboa's Opposite. Tui covered himself and Micah approached and hit it hard on two. Sander dug it from middle-back and Matheis Go-set out to Cameron White — off-speed swing over Micah and Keenan, right into area-six — Evan dug it with his hands — Micah jumped and dumped it over on two. He dropped to a knee and pumped his fist as the ball hit Balboa's court. Coach Pono and Coach Charlie quietly raised their hands in the air. Tui wrapped both arms around Evan and gave him a big hug. Micah drifted in behind them and wrapped his arms around the two of them.

After the team cheered Balboa and passed the net to slap hands, Skylan stood and drank from his water bottle. Just then, two coaches passed requesting a handshake from him before they moved onto Pono and Charlie. A young fan approached Tui and asked for a picture with him. The Ka Ulukoa boys sat down on the bench and leaned back. For the second season in a row: 11-0 in matches, 22-0 in sets, perfection.

Coach Pono and Auntie Maile took the boys to the local video arcade that afternoon. Tui really let loose and conceded to Micah's dare of jumping into the miniature basketball cage, kicking the basketballs all around the arcade. Afterwards, Coach Charlie took a cab from his hotel to the grocery store and brought steaks over to the house. Tui, Evan, and Micah decided to play a game of billiards after dinner. Micah proceeded to get lost in the heat of competition and threw a billiard stick through the wall, yet again. Coach Pono heard the thump and stormed downstairs. Micah grabbed the stick out of the wall and jumped onto Evan and Tui, who were already sitting on the couch trying to act inconspicuous. Micah's couch-surf caused a small lamp to fall off of the table and burst. Coach Pono didn't have to ask. He screamed at Micah until he started crying.

Coach Pono stormed out of the front door and got in the van, murmuring, "Freakin' rascal is going to give me a heart-attack."

No one knew where he went. The team enjoyed their last night together. For, in the morning, it was back to Hawai'i. Coach Pono was downstairs in the morning when the team woke up. All had been forgiven. The boys bailed to the airport — back to Da ʻĀina — but not without their team photo.

Chapter 20 - Acquired Education

Evan stayed in Dallas with his dad for one more day while his brother, Emmett's, team finished competing. From there, Guy took his and Julie's four sons along with him to Oregon, to help coach his girls' volleyball camps. After three days on Oahu, Skylan flew off to Iowa for a six-day volleyball camp at Grandview University with the USA High Performance Pipeline's A2 Training Group. He made it back to Oahu just in time for the Ka Ulukoa Luau. Tui, Keenan, Noah, Austin, and Skylan met for three straight days to practice their dance routine for the families and friends. They held the stage for six minutes of provocative and humorous choreography, dancing to a mix-CD created by Keenan, undressing from their black sweat pants and white tank tops down to only hula skirts with shirtless chests. The performance was definitely a fan favorite. At one point, a young girl even approached the platform and threw dollar bills onto the stage.

Now that Tui'd had a first successful football campaign with Punahou, football consumed his thoughts as soon as the plane from Dallas touched down in Oahu. Tui left to San Francisco the last week in July, headed to Tom Martinez Football Camp for his third straight summer. Even after his return from camp, Tui talked about football so much that Micah decided he, too, would try out, seeing it as a potential fall sport. Two-a-days with football in August were going to cut Micah's beach time at Outrigger short, but anything to avoid another summer of Uncle Keli'i's backyard workouts. Micah made the varsity squad as a Free Safety on defense. On Micah's very first play of the preseason, a 5'10" and 230-pound Tight End came across the middle of the field and laid Micah out, flat on his back. Tui laughed from the sideline and waited for Micah to limp off the field.

"Welcome, Lightweight," he said facetiously, rubbing Micah's back before jogging on for offense.

Punahou had another nice start to the 2012 fall season. Tui had already gotten two or three offers from small football colleges on the Mainland. He began to notice the University of Hawai'i at Manoa's assistant coaches at his high school home games. Soon after, Norm Chow, the head football coach at UH began to show up and Tui believed they were interested in him. Almost every time he glanced up, the coaches' eyes were already on him and he knew it wasn't a mistake, because his long, bushy ponytail made him easy to spot. Midway through Tui's 11th-grade season, Norm Chow invited Tui up to the UH campus for an unofficial visit with him and his six assistant coaches.

Norm Chow knew of Tui's connection to volleyball and Chow told Tui that the head coach for men's volleyball, Charlie Wade, approached him about the potential of Tui playing both sports at UH.

"What's your feel on it?" Chow asked Tui. "Give me your perspective."

Tui was still in disbelief that he was having this conversation with the head coach of Hawai'i's football program.

"It would be an honor – amazing – if it were possible," Tui replied, almost blushing.

Just then, Charlie Wade walked into Chow's office with his two assistant coaches. In two weeks, Tui went from trying to confirm that the men in flowered, collared shirts at his football games were the University of Hawai'i coaches, to being in an office with 10 coaches asking his opinion on playing two sports at the university.

With two games to go in the regular season, Norm Chow called Tui at home and offered him a scholarship to UH, with his blessing on playing for the men's volleyball program in the spring seasons. Tui was astonished. His mom and dad's words from the beginning of his sports endeavors were coming to fruition. Of course, he took some days to contemplate the offer with his family. It was early in the recruiting process for standard volleyball protocols and he hadn't been in touch with any other big universities, but Tui was strong-minded about being a dual-sport student-athlete. After one week, considering the unlikelihood of another program offering him the opportunity to play both of his affections together, Tui returned Norm Chow's phone call and verbally committed to the University of Hawai'i at Manoa.

The following Friday, Punahou Football bused home with the ILH league title after going undefeated in league. Auntie Maile sat with Tui at the breakfast table on Saturday morning.

"Do you feel better having it off your chest?" she asked her son.

Tui looked up luminously. "Definitely. I haven't done all that I want to do, but this feels like a step."

"Just so you know, your dad and I are proud of you."

"I know, Mom. Thanks for having my back," he said, playfully putting his hand up for a high-five.

"Whatever," she said, laughing at his gesture. "Don't think you are getting out of doing the dishes."

Tui palmed his forehead. "It was worth a try."

"Don't forget you got club tryouts tomorrow," she said as she walked to her room.

The same morning, Skylan got a call from Pono on his home phone.

"Hey, Coach Pono," said Skylan in a chipper voice.

Pono said, "How's it going, Sky? Hey, some guys said they already talked to you at Outrigger last week..." Skylan nervously swallowed spit as Pono continued, "Anyway, the guys left and I don't know if we'll have a team. But if you can stay — then we will make something work."

Skylan stayed quiet, with his head was down on his end of the phone, hoping it wasn't true. He remembered running into Keenan, Noah, and Austin at Outrigger the previous week. They were acting a bit strange when Skylan arrived, but they'd talked and joked about leaving the team. Keenan was leaving because he was too small to play Middle in college, Austin because he was losing time behind "*Superstar Sky Man*" and wasn't even serving anymore before subbing in games, and Noah because Evan and Tui got all the sets.

Skylan said under his breath, "I guess they weren't joking."

Coach Pono didn't hear him clearly but replied, "Wanted to give you a heads up. We can talk more at the tryout meeting tomorrow. You still coming?"

Skylan found his normal tone of voice, "Oh, for sure, I will see you there, Coach Pono. Shoots."

"Who was that, Skylan?" asked Arlene.

Skylan said, "That was Coach Pono," hoping that was all he had to expose to satisfy his mom's question.

Arlene stood there scrutinizing him, impatiently. Skylan gave her the short version of the story. As he'd expected the result to be, regardless of his story's length, Arlene dashed straight into panic mode.

"What! Oh — my — gosh. Those boys seriously... Er — Now we have to find you a new... Where is the phone?"

Skylan sat with his hand on his chin, watching his mom scramble around the room.

"Where is my book?" she continued. "We have to call your dad and get in touch with some other teams. Ugh, and it's already late in the tryout period."

Skylan realized the situation was chaotic and the news was going to cause mayhem. After all, Ka Ulukoa tryouts were less than 24 hours away.

Coach Pono and Micah walked into the Ka Ulukoa tryout to find just Coach Charlie, Tui, and Skylan sitting in the front office. Coach Pono didn't hesitate to tell his small group the reality of their situation.

He said, "I appreciate you guys showing up. The other guys decided to move on to other things, so this is our team."

Micah interrupted, "Why don't we just go out and get four guys that want to play and get better?"

Tui raised his eyebrows in Micah's direction, saying nothing. Coach Charlie and Skylan looked over to Coach Pono to examine his reaction. Coach Pono looked at the others.

"We can try," he said, "if you guys still want to play."

"Yeah. Let's do it," Micah said surely.

Micah and Tui began to brainstorm boys from their school.

Skylan said, "There was a Middle at `Iolani that seemed pretty good last season. I will ask my dad about him. I don't think he plays club anywhere."

Coach Charlie said, "Mike might have someone over at `Iolani. Tui, Micah, you guys think about prospects at Punahou." He turned back to Skylan, "Okay Sky, talk with your dad and I will talk with Mike Among. Call Coach Pono if you get anything new."

Everyone agreed that they would give their best effort to make it work.

As the group made their way out of the gym, Coach Pono said, "Hey, guys. No hard feelings if you choose somewhere else. We want you to do what's best for you."

All of the boys walked over to Coach Charlie, who was standing near Coach Pono, and put their fists in to touch.

That night, Mike Among called Coach Pono at his home.

"Hey, Pono. Dave Engleman called me today, asking about Preston from my high school team. What's going on?"

Coach Pono told him indignantly, "We had some of our guys leave, most of them, actually. We've only got Tui, Skylan, and Micah right now, maybe Evan too, if we can get a team."

"No way," said Mike, ominously. "The guys say why they left?"

"You know — a little unhappy with the roles, and some are looking to the future."

"I think it's a mistake for those guys to leave, Pono," Mike said in a dejected tone.

Pono said, "I do, too, but they have to fly free. We could only accomplish the things we did before, with total buy in, from every player. They all had that while they were with us."

Mike paused and soaked that in.

"Hmm — yeah — but hey — definitely. I will send a message to

Preston and his parents and get him over there to train with you guys."

Meanwhile, Micah was in his room upstairs, avoiding sleep, talking to Tui on the phone about who they could approach the next day at school before football practice. Just then, Micah's door cracked open.

"Okay, off the phone," said Pono. "Get some sleep. We will work on it tomorrow."

Training Tuesday evening was an anxious arrival for the three boys and the coaches. Tui and Micah were in preparation for football playoffs, so participating at Ka Ulukoa was out of the question. But they understood the importance of their faces being around if they were going to bring a rag-tag group of guys together and make a 17 & Under team. Coach Pono met them in the office half an hour before the start of practice.

Dubiously, he told them, "Guys, we don't know any of these guys who are showing up, but if we decided to take them and if they decide to come, then things are going to be different."

The guys nodded, hoping they understood Coach Pono's vague message.

A few new faces walked into the Ka Ulukoa facility over the next 20 minutes. The first to arrive was Preston Kamada, an 11th grader at ʻIolani High School who played his 10th-grade season as a Middle on the varsity team. He stood only about 6'0". His skin was light, like Micah's, and his body was long and skinny. His brown hair was cut low, unlike Micah's, and a widow's peak poked out of the front, pointing straight down to the gap between his eyebrows. He walked in with his chin and chest up, along with the most innocent smile that was reminiscent of an old Asian grandmother.

The next to arrive was a cheerful young guy of about 5'9" who resembled Jaylen Reyes. His brown hair was bushy and curled on top of his head like a plate of roasted marshmallows. His arms weren't big by any stretch, but he had a good physical build and should Austin Amian not have left, it looked like this guy could have easily taken Austin in an arm wrestling battle. His name was Kahiau Machado and Coach Charlie invited him to the first practice, after remembering him from a local community league volleyball clinic. He was only in his 10th-grade year of school, but he fit within the right age for the team.

Kainoa Quindica walked in third. He was a touch shorter than Preston Kamada with no bend in his knees as he walked. Kainoa had slightly darker skin than Preston and perfectly round ears. The line of his jaw was flat and he kept his lips closed as he introduced himself.

He was invited from Punahou. He had started the 9th grade only two months earlier.

The last to arrive was Trent Thompson, a Haole-looking 11th grader with light, almost pale, skin. He took off a goofy tie-dye hat, exposing his brown, short, and curly hair. He walked like a 50-year-old Hawaiian man and his entrance expression made him look a bit confused. He played his previous high school season, along with Kainoa, on the junior varsity team at Punahou. Tui and Micah mentioned him on Sunday night, so Coach Pono invited him out after talking with Rick Tune at Punahou.

Coach Pono took his eyes off of Coach Charlie's poker face and picked up his clipboard.

"Thank you all for coming. We won't play a ton of volleyball today. I think it is more important that we tell you all what we are about, but we will do some things with the ball, to see where your skills are." Coach Pono stuck his hand out to count the guys trying out. "Preston, Kainoa, Trent, Kahiau, you've all introduced yourselves already. Most of you know, but this is Tui, Skylan, and Micah. Tui and Micah are still in football so they won't practice until that ends, but they will join us as much as they can to help at evening trainings."

Tui and Micah smiled at the guys trying out. Skylan kept his face stoic.

Coach Pono continued, "Let's first go over the rules." He dropped to a knee and extended his fingers one-by-one.

After 20 minutes passed, Coach Pono asked Skylan to start the warmup. They played *Tennis*, which Skylan's side won, mostly because he was the only one not ripping balls into the net or 10 feet out of bounds with his platform. Tui and Micah stood on opposite sides on the net, each one on a corner where the end line and sideline met, and said as little as possible.

After jogging and stretching, Coach Charlie introduced *Partner Setting* and *Partner Passing*. As expected, balls flew all over. Coach Pono and Coach Charlie kept the critiques strictly technical. Tui and Micah continued to watch without saying much. Coach Pono had the guys pass freeballs for 45 minutes, first platform, and then hands. The guys had just gotten through Coach Charlie's explanation of *Shoulders* and threw a few balls and hit a few sad excuses for strokes before the end of practice time.

Coach Pono huddled the group of guys and said, "Again, thank you all for coming out. I would say that this may be new to some of you, but I guarantee that this is new for all of you. We do things differently here than I have seen anywhere else. But we get results. I will call you all tomorrow tonight. If we offer you a spot on the team, then please be ready and have an answer for me. We are sorry to rush you, but we don't have much time to get this together. If we offer you and you decide to join, then our director, Lee Lamb, will have some paperwork for you and academic standards to uphold."

The tryout guys waved as they exited the gym. Skylan made his way outside to his dad's truck, which Skylan was now driving alone since getting his license a week earlier. Auntie Maile came inside to say hello and pick up Tui. She got caught in conversation with her son and Micah in the front office while Coach Pono and Coach Charlie talked inside of the gym.

"So what did you think?" Pono asked Charlie.

Charlie fixed his mustache and pulled his hat down tighter over his head.

"I think it looks like we are starting over," he said.

"Do you think we take them all? Any stick out to you?" Pono asked curiously.

Coach Charlie chuckled, "Pono, I don't think we have a choice."

Coach Pono laughed, remembering that even if Evan returned and they got all four tryout guys to commit, Tui, Skylan, Micah, Preston, Kahiau, Trent, and Kainoa only gave them eight. That was barley enough for a full team with a Libero.

"I'll make calls tomorrow night and check in with you," said Pono. "Have a good night, Coach."

Charlie Jenkins said softly, "No worries," then he turned and walked out.

Coach Pono called each boy on Wednesday. The pace of the practice, just the night before, was slow. It was sloppy. There wasn't anything volleyball related that was particularly exciting about it. That didn't stop all four boys from committing immediately. Anyone and everyone who played volleyball in Oahu must have heard of Ka Ulukoa and the exclusivity of their success in that age group. They must have wanted to know what it was that created those years of dominance in the club world. For four young guys with no mentionable volleyball reputation, Coach Pono's offer was one that they couldn't refuse.

Yet, even with the happenstance of finding four age-appropriate volleyball bodies that weren't locked in elsewhere, and getting them committed, none of the returners were ecstatic with their developing circumstance.

Micah calling Evan, and hearing the words, "Yes, I am in if you guys are in," wasn't enough to relax the explosion of uncertain emotions that Micah, Skylan, Tui, Evan, Coach Charlie, and Coach Pono felt.

Coach Pono also called Tui and Skylan, to deliver the news from the new guys. He asked them, along with Micah, to meet early again the next night, before training.

On Thursday night, they met in the front office of the Ka Ulukoa facility. Tui and Micah still had on their shorts and cleats from walk-throughs at football practice.

Skylan asked perceptively, "Can you *ever* keep anything clean?" referring to the dirt and grass stains bled into Micah's practice uniform.

"I get these from crushing guys on the field!" Micah said proudly.

"More like guys crushing you," Tui joshed.

"Okay," said Coach Pono. "It's important we talk about your roles again. You guys have held a big load, but you are all going to have to really step up now. These new guys can only hear Coach Charlie's and my voice so much. The buy-in will come from you guys, and Evan. These guys have never heard of step-digging or *One-Contact* warmup. You guys have been here. You have to set the tone." Coach Pono looked to his guys for assurance.

Tui nodded his head. Skylan gave a smooth thumbs-up. Micah had already heard this talk at home, but he reassured his dad anyway.

"You guys didn't talk much on Tuesday. We don't want you doing too much and not focusing on your own skills, but these guys are going to need guidance from you guys. That's the only way."

Coach Charlie walked through the entrance of the building. He glanced over at Coach Pono and the guys' meeting and kept straight, toward the gym for practice.

The new guys showed up to the training in the same order as before, Trent wearing the same goofy hat on his head. One more followed into the gym after Trent. He was small, smaller than Skylan. He stood around 5'5". Micah thought he looked similar to Bruce Lee, the world-famous martial artist. The nervous look on his face made it seem like he had been outside waiting to come inside for an hour. A small lady followed in behind him, same eyes, same teeth; she had to be his mom. She walked up to the entrance of the courts and waved over to the group in an unorganized circle on the furthest court. Coach Pono walked over to the lady and her son. Coach Charlie followed, dragging.

"Hi, Coach," she said with a big smile. "This little guy hiding behind me is my son, Casey." She stepped aside so he could be seen.

"We heard about your team from Coach Engleman at Maryknoll and he told us to come on over tonight."

The little guy stepped forward and said, "Hi, I'm Casey Takahashi," then stepped right back to his hiding spot behind his mom.

"You said you were from Maryknoll?" asked Coach Pono.

"Yes," the mom replied. "Casey is in the 11th grade. Skylan Engleman plays on the varsity team," she said pointing to Skylan, a few yards away. "Casey played on the JV last season."

"Thanks for bringing him and thanks for coming, Casey. He is more than welcome to try out. We'll be done in an hour and a half."

Coach Pono headed back toward his group and Casey followed slowly.

"Everyone, this is Casey Takahashi," Coach Pono announced. "He'll be trying out with us today."

"Hi, guys. Hi, Skylan," Casey smiled, still standing rather nervously.

Coach Pono interjected, "Let's get going with *Tennis*. Skylan, explain it for Casey."

The second try at *Tennis* was as bad as the first. The second day of *Partner Setting, Partner Passing, Freeball Passing,* and *Shoulders* wasn't good either. Neither were the introductions of three more drills. A *One-Contact* ball-control rally could not go more than five or six touches before the ball hit the floor. Asking a player to open up during *Three-Man Pepper* might as well have been speaking Hungarian. Coach Charlie didn't even allow the guys to progress into *Quick Hitter Timing.* The new guys had enough trouble tossing the ball to themselves, standing on the ground, and snapping the ball to the one-box or five-box. Most standing-attacks didn't even make it over the net. Poor Skylan. With Tui and Micah being involved only in verbal participation, it was the first time in his life that he, the Libero, was the best hitter on the court.

After the training, Casey Takahashi and his mom accepted Coach Pono's offer to join the team, on the spot.

"This is where he wants to be," she said. "We were just hoping that you would have a place for him."

Perhaps in the past, things would have been different. Coach Pono didn't have much of a choice anymore. If a guy was of-age, walked into the gym to try out, and seemed like he would work hard and wanted to learn, then so be it. Coach Pono would take him. That didn't mean things were going to be how they used to be, ever again. It just meant he was staying true to Ka Ulukoa's Mission Statement:

"Ka Ulukoa is focused on preparing young athletes for the next level of competition and life, regardless of their financial status, by helping them experience personal growth through training and competition."

Coach Charlie appeared to always find peace in watching the growth of the game, as well as in his time away from the game. After watching poor volleyball and being directly involved, the only thing that could bring peace to Coach Pono's mind was his family. The time he spent with his wife and watching his kids perform was his escape. So those moments were cherished, watching his girls and attending Micah's playoff football games with Punahou – and prayer. It was all that could relax his mind.

Skylan, Preston, Kainoa, Kahiau, Trent, and Casey all showed up for Tuesday training. Tui and Micah came late in street clothes after their football practice. Coach Pono spent the weekend reiterating that he wanted Micah to say more.

"You can help more," he told him. "We have to have more leadership from you, especially when you aren't training."

Micah replied bitterly, "I am helping, Dad. I have been shagging balls and talking to the new guys about their technique."

"You can do more, Micah," Coach Pono astutely told his son. "You have to make them understand the culture of how we do things on our team."

Micah really had trouble understanding what more he could do.

The new guys improved their movements in training. In turn, the results improved as well.

"Baby steps," Coach Charlie said to Coach Pono as he could see him becoming frustrated that easy freeball tosses weren't being passed and set on the partner's forehead.

The guys did a little better with hitting the tosses to themselves over the net. Coach Pono and Coach Charlie added on at practice. They taught *Partner Serving* and cautiously chose *back row Three-on-Three*, with three contacts, as the last drill for the training. It wasn't the inconsistent volleyball that sent Coach Pono's patience over the edge — no — those fast-ending rallies and lack of control were only what brought him upon the edge. The flashbacks of Adrian Faitalia not diving for a single ball during his first days at Ka Ulukoa were what sent Coach Pono beyond. Specifically, having those flashbacks while watching Trent Thompson in *back row Three-on-Three*. Coach Pono was on him.

"Get your butt on the frickin' ground and dive!" he scolded him, hard. "Don't even start that lazy crap in this gym. If the ball hits the floor, you dive!"

That was a first for the new guys, hearing Coach Pono at maximum volume. The older guys hadn't heard it in so long either, with the exception of Micah's rascal activities off the court. That night, Coach Pono lay down in bed next to his wife, able to fall asleep only by the comfort of her stroke on his back.

The guys had their fourth training of the season on Thursday. The introduction was more of the same. Although they were only four practices in, it was interesting that the learning curve happened more slowly than it did back at the start to Ka Ulukoa. Yes, the players were different and the scenario was different, not having Tui and Micah in practice to help Skylan demonstrate the proper way. But four days was typically an eternity in the system in order to see undeniable improvement in the physical play. Watching this volleyball in comparison to the growth at 12 & Under was like watching a 60-year-old man try to become bilingual, versus a toddler being raised with two different languages by his parents. This road of learning was just not as smooth. That feeling was unsettling, considering that the opponents were much more developed now than at 12 & Under, in every facet of their game.

Trent continued unfocused and confused. Preston remained athletic, but short, and raw. Kainoa seemed tentative. Kahiau stayed nervous. Casey kept quiet. Skylan's trouble was trying not to get bored with the pace. Screeching through sloppy bouts of partner ball-control drills, inconsistent passing of freeballs, unpredictable attacks over the net, and misdirected serving attempts, the team stumbled, almost literally, into their back row drills.

The timid overall play, and Trent Thompson's indecision to maximize his effort in Three-on-Three, again, yanked at Coach Pono's patience and stopped him from progressing the three contacts cooperative drill into two contacts. Coach Pono sent the boys to water, and called no one over to take serve-receive passing reps. Tui could sense his coaches' frustration growing and could imagine Coach Charlie's exhaustion from hearing his own voice repeat the same message. So, Tui walked over in his sockless flip-flops and put his arm around Trent Thompson, who clearly had no understanding of the unacceptable atmosphere he was helping create.

"Listen, Trent. Things aren't done here like at Punahou" (Mind you, Trent hadn't even shared the gym with Tui in a varsity practice). "You've got to be more focused here —" he continued, as Trent was about to interrupt with a relaxed statement. "No Trent — seriously — you aren't getting it. If Coach Charlie tells you to do something, you do it. If he tells you to dig with your face, then you do it. If he tells you to hit the ball under the net, then you hit it under the net."

Tui released his arm from his two-week-old teammate and walked away from the water fountain.

Punahou Football advanced to the state finals and lost to Kahuku High School for the second year in a row. The loss was disappointing, but Tui and Micah both moved past it rather quickly. Tui played a good season and accomplished a big goal, maybe the biggest, of choosing a university for his future. Micah had no choice but to move past his inaugural season of high school football. On Monday, his basketball team was holding makeup tryouts for fall sport athletes and by Tuesday he was back in the Punahou gym with his varsity team.

The arrival of the last week in November was a big week for Ka Ulukoa as well. The team was through 10 practices and five weeks of training together, and the end of football prompted Coach Pono to add Sunday practices to the schedule. The fall season was enervating for Micah, who was managing the wear and tear of a scrawny Safety on the football field, also having to attend evening practices at Ka Ulukoa and transform into a technical instructor, just to return home to a pile of schoolwork. Likewise for Tui, who was responsible for the entire Punahou Football playbook, club practice, and school. At least for Tui, the winter allowed a few windows to spend time with family and watch his siblings grow up around him. Making himself appealing was no longer a necessity. College was lined up already. His only obligation was maintaining, athletically and academically.

Coach Pono and Coach Charlie were refreshed to have Tui and Micah back in training. Their presence had been beneficial during the previous five weeks, but there was no substitute for the new guys getting to watch things be done the right way. That was rehabilitating, but the coaches knew, and the older guys too, that they would only be as strong as their weakest link. Unfortunately, right then, the weakest link could be pulled out of a hat with a healthy number of options inside.

The coaches paired the older guys with the new guys during the ball-control drills. That helped from a time standpoint, since minutes didn't have to tick off the clock while the new guys chased their shanked pass or mishandled set. With Micah back, they could finally progress Coach Charlie's introduction of how he wanted the approaches done, into *Quick Hitter Timing* with the team's Setter. *Back row Three-on-Three* improved, mixing up Skylan, Tui, and Micah on opposite sides of the net. But there were only so many sprayed balls they could save and so many attacks they could hit right into a new guy's lap, while still focusing on doing their job and improving their own game. Tui, Skylan, Kahiau, Casey, and Trent rotated in, taking the passing reps at water breaks. Meanwhile, Coach Charlie usually took Preston and Kainoa off to the side to practice their transition footwork. Most of the time, Micah and whichever two of the five serve-receive passers were off, were the only ones getting water. They made it into *Primary Passing* and *Starting Six Transition* for the first time with the new guys. Tui, Skylan, and Micah were interested to see how the coaches foresaw their new team lining up the rotations.

Skylan walked on as the Libero, playing back row for Preston and Kainoa, who lined up as the Middles. Micah stepped on as the Setter. As he always did, Tui played the OH1, Outside Hitter position that followed the Setter in the rotation. Coach Pono put Trent on the right side, as the Opposite of Micah. Then he asked Kahiau and Casey to split time in the OH2, Outside Hitter position that followed the Opposite in the rotation, the position where Evan Enriques had always played. The pace was slow. The play was sloppy. Micah gave as many sets as he could to the new guys, but there were few opportunities unless Tui and Skylan were the ones passing the ball (not taking into account the off players even making their serves into the court).

For two weeks, over the next six trainings, the older guys gave what they could to their new teammates. Any passing and defensive advice that Skylan could provide, whatever visual aids that Tui could perform, every ounce of energy that Micah brought after his basketball practice, they gave. Regardless of the result at the end of each training, they all gave. The first semester of school came to a close. Fortunately, the news guys didn't have trouble keeping their academic end of the bargain. Coach Pono and Coach Charlie wished they had more time, but they prepared to play the hand they were dealt. The SCVA Invitational was just three weeks away. The first week would have to be without Tui. In a short 48 hours, he was off to meet Evan in San Diego for their re-invitation to the USA Volleyball Boys' Youth Holiday Camp.

Chapter 21 - The Shirts

Tui was almost as excited to spend a few days with Evan as he was about playing some competitive volleyball with the top-level boys in their age category.

Evan greeted his teammate, "Tui! I heard you committed to UH, Braddah! Big Mahalos, Hawaiian."

"Ha!" Tui chuckled surprised. "Thanks, man. Thanks. Glad to get it over with."

Evan divulged, "I'm going to a couple schools when we get to Anaheim. My dad is coming down. You gotta come with me."

"Unofficials or what?" asked Tui. "Yeah, for sure I'll cruise, as long as Coach Pono is cool."

"Rajah dat!" Evan said, satisfied. "How's things on the island? I mean, with club and all that."

"You know Keenan 'dem left right? All new guys now. Brah, only me, Micah, and Sky Man stay as returners — and you."

"Yeah, Tui, I heard. It's cool you guys did something, though," Evan said luminously.

"For sure," Tui replied. "You'll see when we get back from Mainland, though. Hope we don't catch rubs at the qualifier."

The USA Boys' Youth Holiday Camp named three Most Valuable Players at the duration of the camp. Evan and Tui were two of them. They received no actual trophy or prize for the honor, rather they both took home light blue USA Volleyball cotton t-shirts as parting gifts.

Micah snatched up Evan for a big hug when he and Tui walked through the doors of the baggage claim at Honolulu Airport.

"No hug for me?" Tui asked Micah lightheartedly.

"Nope, you are old news," Micah teased.

Auntie Maile was waiting at the Ma'a's house, talking to Lisa, when Pono and the guys arrived.

"Hey there, Evan," she said.

Evan smiled at her and dropped his bags to reach in for a hug.

"Man — ignored again. I get no love," Tui said forlornly.

"Hush, Tui," Auntie Maile snapped. "We see you all the time."

Lisa tittered quietly underneath the sound of Auntie Maile's self-induced chuckle.

"Try get beat in a game of Ping-Pong real quick?" asked Micah.

"Maybe if I were asleep you could win, Ficus," Evan sagely replied.

Tui looked over at his mom and raised his eyebrows, crafting her the decision maker in whether he could join. She raised her eyebrows back at him.

"Half an hour," she said sternly. "Be back and ready to go in a half hour."

The three of them raced downstairs before she could change her mind.

After Evan gave a warm greeting to Coach Charlie and Skylan at the next training, Coach Pono called for introductions from his new teammates. It was a short time before he'd be standing on the court in a tournament with some of them.

"I'm Preston."

"I'm Kainoa."

"Sup? I'm Trent."

"Kahiau —"

"I'm Casey."

"Howzit, guys? I'm Evan Enriques." He was going to say something more, but realized they were looking at him as if his name were common knowledge.

Coach Pono chimed in, "Okay, let's go over *Six-Man Base Defense* then get going with jog and stretching."

Evan's flow returned without delay.

"Ahh. I've missed the *One-Arm Digging*," Evan said during a water break.

He partnered with Tui all the way through the partner drills; consequently, he hadn't formed an opinion on his teammates' skills yet. Evan brought his competition with Tui from the Holiday Camp straight to Ka Ulukoa training, playing an unannounced game of *Follow the Leader*, copying Tui's attack pattern to the one- and five-boxes during *Quick Hitter Timing*.

Tui took notice, then pulled out a strand from his long ponytail and held it up to check the nonexistent wind in the gym. Then he smacked his first swing perfectly on the five-box and rolled the second crisply off of his hand and short to the 10-foot line. Evan copied the routine, impressively.

Tui flashed Evan a smile, saying kiddingly, "You think you are cool?"

Evan grinned back.

Three contact, *back row Three-on-Three* was enhanced with Evan in the gym, but the older guys knew that it was best for them not to hit only to each other, and instead snap the ball around to different guys, thus exposing the problem. The team advanced beyond their average of five or six contacts without the ball hitting the floor, but only to a lackluster betterment of eight or nine, which was nothing in comparison to their old ability of 90 or more touches without a ball dropping (equating to a minimum of 30 rallies over the net).

In contrast, *Primary Passing* was extremely improved, simply because the serves were more consistent and a tad more challenging. It was that way until Evan and Tui were switched onto the serving side and Skylan was in a serve-receive passing line with Casey, side-by-side with Kahiau. Just about every serve that loomed near the right two-thirds of the court, hit the court, before Micah'd had a chance to even consider setting it. It seemed as if the effort was finally there, perhaps even the focus, the skills just weren't.

Auntie Maile brought the guys their bags full of gear after practice. Each guy had a black backpack, black warm-up pants, a black warm-up jacket, black shorts, two black jerseys with the number that each guy asked for printed boldly in white, and instructions of what to bring for Auntie Maile's Breakfast of Champions. Skylan and Casey each got two red jerseys as the Liberos. As for everyone else, one of the two jerseys had a special surprise — definitely not that it was red. Instead, it had a small white stripe on the side, and it was sleeveless.

The flight to California was easy, as was the travel to the hotel. The new guys barely said anything and the older guys hardly noticed the difference in sounds of the vans without Keenan Meyer's mix-CDs. The house was the same as they'd left it and there were no arguments over who was taking what room. The new guys stood back and let the returners have their choice.

"How's that pool feel?" asked Preston.

"Noooo! Don't do it!" Skylan protectively drug out as he grabbed Preston's arm.

"Frickin' freezing, Brah," added Micah. "No good dat kine."

Auntie Maile stayed up, preparing as usual. Charlie Jenkins was away from the team, relaxing at his hotel, doing Jedi mind tricks, Micah would imagine. Coach Pono was awake as well, longer than he normally was in Anaheim. The tournament consumed his thoughts. He pondered how his guys would fair at the tournament and how he'd be most effective as their coach. Eventually, he fell asleep, after a call to his wife and daughters.

Guy Enriques picked up Evan early the next morning for his

first college visit. The University of California at Santa Barbara (UCSB) was a long distance, with two hours of driving each way. The guys had evening practice, but Tui went along at Coach Pono's approval. Evan and Guy agreed with the assistant coach of Pepperdine University that they could stop through oceanfront Malibu for a visit on the way back to Anaheim. Both campuses were aesthetically pleasing, covered with white buildings with glass windows, whose rooms overlooked the ocean that each university sat beside. Tui was already committed to the University of Hawai'i, but apparently it hadn't been widely broadcasted, as neither coaching staff mentioned it upon his arrival of unexpected companionship to Evan.

They made it through their day and headed back toward Anaheim. But not without some funny moments, first, like Guy Enriques' befuddled response after the assistant at *Pepper*dine told the boys that the head coach hadn't yet seen either of them play. That bulletin was a bummer since the guys had prepared some questions.

But, that disappointment was quickly old news after Guy's panicked response (fearing a lack of interest) of, "B-b-but they got the shirts!" referring, of course, to the random light blue cotton t-shirts that the boys were awarded at the USA Volleyball Boys' Youth Holiday Camp.

Evan and Tui couldn't help but drown their faces in their hands and nearly suffocate from laughter.

Still busting up from Guy's comment, Evan asked Tui in the parking lot, "Do you think he's gonna say that to every coach?"

Tui cracked up again and said, "I hope so. Treating those shirts like they are royal garments. Frickin' comedy."

Coach Pono wasn't intrigued by hearing any comical moments as Evan and Tui arrived late to the American Sports Center for their first pre-tournament training with the new team.

"You guys are seriously frickin' late?" he exclaimed. Shuddering in fury, he breathed deeply and he quieted his tone. "You guys have to be leaders right now. This isn't good for the guys to see." Coach Pono backed off, realizing that time was being wasted and there was nothing to be done after the fact.

The practice went on as usual. Coach Charlie watched intensely from the side with his arms folded. Coach Pono allowed the guys to get their repetitions without saying too much. Now that they were near the start of the tournament, he didn't want his comments to be result-oriented. If they sprayed a pass or missed a dig or misdirected an attack, he was okay. As long as the motions looked good, then he withdrew his voice for them to get comfortable.

The rest of the evening was uneventful. The guys ate Auntie Maile's pasta dinner and pulled out a miniature ball for an attempt at Mini-ball, which just wasn't the same. The new guys spoke a little more, but not enough to alert the media.

Ka Ulukoa held their training in the morning. Afterwards, Guy picked up Evan again. Coach Pono hesitantly allowed Tui to tag along. Those were the last of Evan's visits before the qualifier began. They attended the University of Southern California first, and then onto USC's rival school, the University of California at Los Angeles (UCLA). Evan and Tui were toured around two of the most historical athletic universities in California record, both with a healthy history of athletes from Hawai'i who chose them as their Mainland homes. Plus, they got to relive Guy's, "But they got the shirts," comment, twice, each time with a different lead up. Everyone, including Coach Pono and Auntie Maile, sat in the main room the night before the tournament. They spoke about anything unrelated to volleyball, since the tournament would provide quite enough of that.

The first day wasn't bad. The new guys got their feet wet with the style of the tournament and the warm-up protocols. The older guys managed the customary rust from the newbies and were spared having to perform very many spectacular plays to survive day one with a clean match record. Going 3-0 in matches on day one hadn't ever been a difficult task for Ka Ulukoa, but 3-0 in matches was much less difficult at the qualifier than Junior Olympics, mainly because the best teams from the eastern and northern coasts of the USA and Puerto Rico qualified near their homes, and didn't bother attending SCVA's three-day Invitational. Ka Ulukoa's high seed prevented them from having to play any, even medium-level talented, teams from Southern California on day one.

The second day was a slight adjustment. Having what was still the best Outside Hitting duo in their age group, and also having Micah and Skylan, was enough to wash out the disadvantage that Preston and Kainoa were facing in the Middle. Trent didn't do too much damage as an Opposite. After all, Micah didn't have to set him. Coach Pono found slots to sub Casey and Kahiau in to serve, or for brief defensive stints.

The vibe in the house was good that evening. Auntie Maile shared jokes with the guys from throughout the day. Coach Pono was happy about the contributions from his leaders and his new role players. Maybe they would make it. If so, day three was going to be a tight fit. Auntie Maile had to reserve a plane flight that left Los Angeles at 4pm the same day. The finals were scheduled for one-o-clock in the afternoon.

The team pulled up to the ASC on Monday morning and Micah got the chance to see his favorite parking lady, bright-eyed and cheerful. Unluckily, he didn't have any bags of nuts to give her. She insisted that his big smile at 7am was quite enough. Dressed in all black warm-up outfits, the guys' feet dropped from the van onto the pavement to walk inside with their water jugs hanging from their arms.

Skylan walked beside Auntie Maile and said, "You know, Auntie Maile, I hear these kids talking in the gym all the time, about how we aren't going to qualify now, with this new team. I think we have done okay."

Auntie Maile slowed her walk to put a few yards between the two of them and the others.

"You guys have played well. Ignore those outside voices. I'll be crushed if you lose an ounce of confidence."

Auntie Maile was right. The team had played well. They had a slightly different style, coming into the center and grabbing each other's backs in a circle after each play, and the older guys celebrated harder when a new guy made an impressive play. Maybe those things added two or three measly burnt calories to each match. Who cared about that? They made it to the match for qualification to the Junior Olympics Open Division and no team had exposed them.

Chapter 22 - Insomnia

A Ka Ulukoa trend that stayed alive was no one asking about future matchups. By that time, the guys weren't oblivious to who the best teams were or against whom they were predicted to play, but they all knew better than to ask, or simply didn't give it attention. When the guys stepped on for warmup in their match to qualify, and saw Coast 17-1s (previously Shorebreak 16s) across the net, it was as fresh to them as it was warming up across from the first team of the tournament. Warmups were normal. *Partner Setting* and *Partner Passing* were good. *One-Contact* was sloppy, but resembled the Ka Ulukoa of old, enough. The first round of *Quick Hitter Timing* had a few more swings clip the tape or sail out of bounds than desired, but the second round looked clean enough to avoid laughter from the large crowd growing on Court B4.

The teams stayed even through 3-3. A few Coast hitting errors on the D-attack put Ka Ulukoa ahead 8-5, until Ka Ulukoa's inability to sideout brought Coast back to 10-9. One real point in transition, an ace by Tui, a one-on-one stuff by Evan Enriques, and another ace by Tui surged the Hawaiians to 14-9. Tui missing a short serve in the net lifted the San Diegans' crushed spirits.

Again, though, Ka Ulukoa's inconsistent play with newbie Kainoa and newbie Trent as the next servers, brought Coast back to 15-14. Evan made his way around to the service line and his consistency was without contest. A sweet solo-stuff-block by Preston on the 6'6" Coast Middle, who had previously had his way every time he got set, Evan's crafty defensive saves, and a few more Coast hitting errors allowed Ka Ulukoa to cruise on a ten to three run and a 25-17 win.

Coast subbed in a new OH2 and moved their left-handed, 10th-grade OH2, Kysen Olsen, to Opposite. The length between his chin and shoulders gave him the necessary inches to reach his 6'4" height. The hope was clearly to get him more sets, playing on the right side. The kid was springy and could bounce balls with the best 11th graders in the gym, but his game was incomplete. The substitution was to no avail. Tui, Evan, and Micah could pick out the new Outside Hitter with their float-serves, blindfolded. Coast trying to change into a two-person passing system was even less effective. They passed poorly, to say the least. Kysen Olsen saw six paltry attack attempts in a set to 25. Ka Ulukoa was officially qualified and plugged into the semifinals.

Qualifying had always been the goal at the SCVA Invitational, but not a goal the team had seriously assessed in years. Yet still, the older guys didn't gain a feeling of relief or surprise to be qualified. Somehow, it felt like all the others. It was as if standing there, with the reality of being qualified, held no change in value compared to seasons before. The new guys were automatically grandfathered into that status too, and everything that came with it: the whispers, the base of supporters, the base of adversaries, and, of course, the flawless record. They now had the experience of being humbly qualified.

At 11am, Ka Ulukoa took the court for warmup, sporting their sleek, black sleeveless jerseys for the first time. Skylan got a sleeveless version of his red Libero uniform to show off his childlike biceps. Minutes later, during the end of their stretching and initial repetitions of *Partner Setting*, Southern California Volleyball Club's 17-Quicksilver squad took the opposing bench. They sported some clean-looking sleeveless tops as well, white jerseys over white shorts, feeding heavily into the stereotypical look of a Southern California beach-goer in the 21st century. With most of the teams out and the majority of their recruiting done, college coaches flooded the seats around Court B2.

After unsatisfying individual 15 & Under seasons, SCVC 17-Quicksilver picked up three important pieces to their roster during 16 & Under. Being in their second full season together, they developed into a high level California club, forming a strong rivalry with their South Bay, Southern California neighbors, Manhattan Beach Surf. SCVC also boasted the majority of their roster from California's top two powerhouse high schools, Mira Costa and the all-boys, Loyola High School. They were led by 6'1" Outside Hitter, Vinny Pizutti, the top-rated beach player in Southern California in his age group. Since the 16 & Under campaign, the team's only new addition to the starting lineup was a 6'7" Middle with a nasty jump-serve that didn't always topspin, Daniel Vaziri. The rest of their starting lineup was split in half by Loyola and Mira Costa players. The 6'6" Opposite, Connor Inlow, and two Liberos who split time, Billy Kopenhefer and Matt Jones, were all Mira Costa 11th graders. The 11th-grade products of Loyola were 6'6" Middle, Chase Corbett, 6'5" Outside Hitter, Bobby Nolan, and their 5'10" Setter, Ian Schwan. The team was big and physical, however, no bigger or more physical than Evan, Tui, Micah, and Skylan had ever scrubbed before.

SCVC's head coach, Jeff Alzina, matched his team up really well against Ka Ulukoa, about as well as anyone could have. Similar to most club teams, SCVC's biggest blockers were their Middles. Both Middles just happened to be highly above average in size. Chase Corbett stood at the net with jet-black hair, and a pale white face accompanied by rosy-red cheeks. His head attached to a stacked upper body, like a Navy Seal fresh out of training camp. Daniel Vaziri was a bit more full in the mid section, but strong and beefy just the same. His beige skin outlined his hairless baby-face. Unlike most club teams, SCVC's next biggest blocker was on the right side, which meant Evan and Tui would spend at least half of their front row attacks against 6'6" Connor Inlow's lanky arms.

SCVC had a clever game plan, running their Middles on Gap-attacks between Ka Ulukoa's right sides and Middle Blockers, thus keeping Evan and Tui uninvolved on the block. Evan and Tui were still effective though, digging balls from middle-back, area-six. On defense, Preston and Kainoa were only responsible for stepping over and commit blocking on the SCVC Quick Attack during every perfect pass. They slowed down SCVC's Gap-attack just enough with soft-blocks for Ka Ulukoa to dig and get transition sets to Evan and Tui. As always, they stroked the one- and five-box, and mixed in tips for kills. SCVC had no answer. Ka Ulukoa took the first set convincingly, with more antics and back-talk through the net than ever before.

The Hawaiians began their coast in the second set as well. Tui opened the second set in serve receive with a routine-looking tool off the block for a kill. Micah went back and topspin-jump-served an ace, and then followed it with another tough serve causing an overpass and an easy kill for Tui. SCVC finally sided-out on Micah's third serve with a cross-court kill by Pizutti from the right, 3-1.

After a Pizutti serve trickled over the net-tape for an ace, followed by a service error, Ka Ulukoa stayed ahead 4-2. SCVC scored on Tui's jump-float with a cross-court kill from Inlow on the Red-attack.

Daniel Vaziri nailed his tough sidespin-jump-serve. Skylan handled it well, but Trent's fluffy swing on the Red-attack turned an easy dig into a transition kill for Inlow. After another tough Vaziri serve, Tui's roll-shot on the Pipe-attack was dug up by Vaziri and Schwan set overhead to Inlow again, who took the kill down the line, and the lead, 4-5. Vaziri served again the next play, hard and in. Skylan passed it on a dime and Micah set Tui on the C-attack. He blasted an untouched kill to the five-box to even the score, 5-5.

That was enough to spark Ka Ulukoa. Behind a clean blocking scheme on SCVC's Gap-attack, a few sweet digs by Tui in the back row, and crafty wrist-work from Evan Enriques' in transition, Skylan held serve for the Hawaiians all the way to a 10-5 lead. Head coach, Jeff Alzina called for time.

"Low and tight," Coach Pono said in the timeout as his boys drank from their jugs. "No reaching. Let them swing wild and we stay here," he said, showing his open palms near his face.

Skylan served again. Schwan set Corbett on the Gap-attack, which he hit cross-court. Skylan dug it straight up (Big Circle) — Micah ran over to bump-set Evan, who chopped the ball near the one-box — Pizutti stepped over from area-six and dug it — Schwan gave the Go-set outside to Nolan — and 'Pop' — 30 feet out of bounds, his third *spatch-hit on Skylan's serving run alone. Alzina was fed up and subbed in a 6'1", dirty-blonde haired, chipper-looking, Loyola High School 10th grader at OH2, Matt Reilly.

Ahead 11-5, Skylan went right at Reilly with his serve. Reilly passed it well enough for Schwan to set Corbett on the Gap-attack for a kill, 11-6. They traded a few points until SCVC sided-out for 13-9.

Billy Kopenhefer ran on to switch with Matt Jones at Libero and serve in Corbett's place. Kopenhefer served his first, and scored. He served again. This time Tui put his Go-set from Micah to the floor with a convincing kill. He flipped his bushy ponytail and let out a load roar, 14-10.

SCVC and Ka Ulukoa exchanged points until Tui left the front row to serve at 16-12. Coach Charlie stood at the back of the bench in his blue jeans and black Ka Ulukoa warm-up jacket. His face was calm, per usual. His hands were plastered to the insides of his pockets as he watched. Tui hit his jump-float in Matt Reilly's direction. The serve knuckled through the air crisply with no spin until it sprayed from Reilly's arms. Ian Schwan chased and dove to save it — SCVC popped over a freeball for Ka Ulukoa — Micah set Tui in transition — he tipped the Pipe-attack short to area-four — Kopenhefer dug it up for Schwan to set Reilly in transition — stuff-block by Trent and Kainoa! It was 17-12 and the Ka Ulukoa boys power-walked in and wrapped shoulders for a tight squeeze of excitement in the team huddle.

Tui jump-floated short the next play. Vaziri stepped in and passed it up, very tight to the net. Schwan, who was back row, jumped up with his hand much higher than the net-tape and dumped the ball over to the center of Ka Ulukoa's floor. It was a funny-looking play, because Ka Ulukoa was rarely caught standing flat-footed on defense. There had to have been something illegal — there was. Micah dropped to a knee from area-one and grabbed the ball with a look of confusion on his face as he examined Schwan and SCVC's inconspicuous reaction. He quickly realized the foul and signaled to the referee that Schwan was back row and dumped the ball illegally. He was clearly above the net, to the height of his elbow, which was the only way a 5'10" Setter could aggressively jam the ball to the opponent's 10-foot line. But the ref claimed Schwan's hand was below the net and awarded SCVC the point. Micah said nothing more. The scorekeeper waited to flip the score to 18-12 in Ka Ulukoa's favor, but flipped it to 17-13 instead.

Vaziri cracked his tough sidespin jump serve, which Skylan handled nicely. Tui hit Micah's C-set to the one-box — Pizutti dove over and dug it — Schwan set overhead to Inlow, who hit the ball high and flat off the top of the block — Skylan turned from area-five and chased it beyond his own end line to save it — Micah set and Tui stroked the Pipe-attack over the net — SCVC dug — Red-set — Inlow waffled his second attempt out of bounds. It was 18-13 and Alzina called for his last timeout of the set.

Coach Pono delivered the same message from his knee while the boys drank and Coach Charlie stood over his shoulder listening.

"Just stay low and tight with your block," directing his message to the entire team. "Let them swing wild, and we are here," again holding his hands with fingers spread near his face.

SCVC regrouped and sided-out. Ka Ulukoa did the same: 18-14, 19-14, 19-15, 20-15, 20-16 they went.

Reilly served his jump-float cross-court. Evan stayed patient on his first attack and snapped the ball into the block — he covered himself — Micah set him again on the transition Go-attack — Corbett closed his swing-block to Schwan's shoulders and got over the net, big, to stuff-block Evan's five-box attempt straight down. A long rally ensued on Reilly's subsequent serve, and Corbett eventually got big over the net again and housed another swing from Evan Enriques. The SCVC fans were fired up, as was Pizutti, who ran over and jumped to bump chests with the rosy-cheeked Corbett. Coach Pono felt the need to give a quick reminder to his guys on mental toughness as this set drew longer. With a 20-18 lead, he called a timeout.

Reilly jump-floated again, Evan handled the serve well and Micah set him on the inside Lob-attack. Evan drove it home toward the five-box for a kill. Evan nodded his head in confidence to his teammates and then walked back to serve.

He knuckled his jump-float at Reilly's passing seam. Schwan set Inlow on the D-attack. Kainoa committed with the Gap-attack, so Inlow was one-on-one with Tui. Evan dug the cross-court swing, but sprayed it a bit outside of the court, so Micah ran to save it and his team popped a freeball over. Inlow took the easy ball with his hands and Schwan rose up, this time from the front row, and jammed a Dump-attack — into the net. Micah was ready for it, but threw up his arms to celebrate as he watched the good idea result so badly, 22-18.

Evan served again. Pizutti took the Go-set and got housed by Micah and Preston, but Matt Jones was in a nice spot to cover it. Micah and Preston chose not to block on Schwan's questionably located transition set to Pizutti. He ripped it for a kill and hugged his Libero for saving his butt on his first swing earlier in the rally, 22-19.

Kopenhefer jogged on to serve after the sideout. Tui passed from area-five and then ran from his far left passing position to hit an X-3 behind Micah on the right half of the court. His footwork was impressive, however Kopenhefer dove in with his hand spread flat on the floor under the ball and Pancake-dug Tui's short roll-shot. The ball lifted up to the net, but SCVC touched the net illegally on the joust, 23-19.

Preston standing-float-served for the Hawaiians. It took Pizutti three swings in the rally, but he eventually scored, 23-20.

Schwan jump-float-served — good pass — good set — Tui spatched it out of bounds, 30 feet past the five-box, 23-21.

Schwan served again — good pass — Micah's set lost a little bit of tempo, but was hittable all the same; again, Tui hit out, 23-22.

Again, Schwan served. The bottom fell out of his jump-float and Skylan dove in late to pass it — overpass — Pizutti jumped up at the net and smashed it down, 23-23.

Timeout Ka Ulukoa, and the audience's loud murmurs turned to clear comments about Ka Ulukoa's record.

The game wasn't over, and even if it had been, an SCVC win wouldn't have meant they won the match. A deuce game made the savvy audience forget that Ka Ulukoa hadn't lost, even a three-set-match, since playing Borinquen Coqui at 12 & Under.

That didn't stop an SCVC camera-dad from yelling, "If you can win the set then you will win the match! Win the set! Win the match!"

Laughable — the core players were too skilled, too smart, too experienced. They were too good. Inside the timeout Coach Pono spoke of only the play at hand.

"Pass and sideout," he said calmly. "Everybody pass. Everybody sideout."

SCVC earned the fans a shot at their wish. Southern California scored the next two points and pushed the Hawaiians to their first third set since the previous season's qualifier.

Ka Ulukoa served first in rotation one. SCVC also started in rotation one. Rather than his usual topspin-jump-serve, Micah opened the set with his jump-float. Reilly passed it on a dime and Schwan set Pizutti on the Red-attack — cross-court kill.

Pizutti served his jump-float as well, going away from his typical topspin-serve. Tui took the Red-set from Micah and cracked it to the one-box. Pizutti dug it chaotically and SCVC gave an easy overhand snap to the Hawaiians. Evan stepped in from area-six to dig the freeball-like snap — overpass — SCVC kill. *That was something ya don't see everyday*, thought Skylan. No matter, Pizutti served again, a long rally developed and Tui blasted a swing to tool off of Vaziri's scattered blocking hands, 1-2.

Tui walked back to serve with the ball. He reached to pull up his sleeve, but realized there was no fabric to be pulled. Reilly passed the jump-float — Inlow took the Red-set — Tui dug it with his hands — Evan chopped Micah's set toward the one-box — Pizutti dug — Vaziri tipped Schwan's Gap-set — Evan scooped it from left-front area-four and got the Go-set in transition — tool for the kill, 2-2.

Vaziri killed the next Front-1-attack on Tui's serve. Then Vaziri strongly contacted his sidespin serve toward Tui in area-one, causing a haphazard out-of-system pass. Micah ran to bump-set the Pipe — Tui chopped it in bounds — Inlow got the Red-set in transition and killed it in the seam, 2-4. SCVC's fans came alive, the gym had a loud buzz, and more spectators rushed over to sneak a peak. Vaziri missed his next, 3-4.

Skylan jump-floated to Reilly, a long rally arose, Kopenhefer dove in for a Pancake-dig on Evan's roll — Reilly took the transition set on the left and hit it hard toward area-five — Skylan stepped in aggressively and hand-dug it — Tui chased, but it had gone too far backwards — kill for Reilly, 3-5 SCVC.

Inlow jump-floated — good pass — Micah set Preston — Corbett had already bailed from area-three to go block Evan. With a wide-open net, Preston crushed the Front-1... right into the middle of the net. SCVC was stoked, 3-6! Micah grabbed the ball to roll it under the net to SCVC's end line, and then regroup his team. Evan passed Inlow's second serve well, and took the Go-set from Micah. Although Schwan and Corbett were already camping out on him, Evan found the seam for the kill, 4-6.

Trent walked back to jump-float. He generally just hit his plain vanilla serve toward the middle of the court. Matt Jones passed it and Schwan set the Gap-attack. Corbett tipped the far away set, out of bounds, 5-6 SCVC. Trent's next soft jump-float landed in the middle of the net. SCVC regained their confidence. Trent's head dropped a bit, but the rest of the guys from Hawai'i maintained their level emotions and reset into serve receive.

Matt Reilly jump-float-served. Evan passed and faked the swing against the waiting two-person block on the Go-attack, and instead, his tip peaked over the block and gently fell to the floor for a point. He confidently nodded his head, again, at his team, and gave Micah an aggressive two-hand slap on the hands before going to serve, 6-7 SCVC. Coach Pono twirled his finger and lifted his arms above his head.

"Next! Next!" he shouted to his guys. "Big Circle! Every body right here, Big Circle!"

A long rally came on Evan's serve, and Matt Jones flew in for another flat-hand Pancake-dig. Pizutti snapped Schwan's Go-set down the line, and it bounced off of Trent Thompson's arms and into the bench. It was 6-8, and Pizutti skipped merrily into the side change. The fans were so engaged, no one moved from the seats as the match continued.

After both benches of players and coaches had settled on their opposite sides, Kopenhefer exchanged with Corbett to start the play. From area-five, Tui passed the serve well, and Micah set Evan on the C-attack. He attacked the big seam in the block, taking aim at the five-box. His swing sailed a few inches long. As the line judge raised his flag, Evan examined the spot through the net, looking up and down as if he were reliving a swing that felt good and in. His team was playing good volleyball; they'd just missed a few plays. That was no reason for Coach Pono to call for time. Tui received Kopenhefer's jump-float again. It took him getting set twice in the rally, but Tui hammered the ball to the floor at the one-box, 7-9.

Preston served his standing-float and Pizutti smacked a Go-attack cross-court to area-five that bounced off of Preston's extended right arm, making him stutter-step after the kill. Pizutti joyfully circled his side of the court, 7-10. SCVC closed in toward 15 points.

Schwan hit another bottom-out jump-float and Skylan dove to pass it. This time, it was perfect. Micah dished the Go-set out to Tui and he blasted it toward the one-box off of Inlow's arm, and down for the tool. Tui snarled back with his chest puffed up and a loud yell to his teammates, 8-10.

At the service line, Micah flipped his wrist to toss up his topspin-jump-serve. It tailed left toward Pizutti in area-one. Pizutti passed it, and Kainoa, as always, committed with the Quick Attack. He made a nice soft-block on the ball, SCVC covered it — Inlow took the overhead Red-set from Schwan and hit it hard toward area-six — Evan lipped the swing with his platform — Micah ran in to set, and then tried his sneaky set-over on two — Inlow scooped it up from area-two with one hand and the ball hung tight to the net. Pizutti jumped up from area-four and shoved the ball down on Ka Ulukoa's side, but the referee whistled him for illegally reaching over the net, 9-10. This is when teams were historically flooded with the unsettling feeling of Ka Ulukoa's resolve. Regardless of what the score was, or who the player was, the feeling was inescapable.

Micah tossed up another topspin-jump-serve — Pizutti passed — Schwan set — Inlow approached for the Red-attack, again. Once more he hit it hard at area-six past Tui's solo-block. Evan step-dug it with two arms, but 20 feet back and out of Skylan's diving reach, 9-11.

Pizutti decided to stick with his jump-float-serve. Good pass — Tui got set on the Red-attack in rotation one and hammered it toward the one-box — the ball popped up off of Schwan's foot! SCVC scrambled and gave a freeball back to the Hawaiians — Tui got set again and cracked it down the line at the five-box for a kill, 10-11.

Tui rotated back to the service line. Pizutti shuffled to Tui's jump-float and was forced off of his feet to pass it (there was no Pipe-attack). Schwan set back to Inlow and he throttled it toward area-one — Tui stepped in front and dug the heater — it hung in the air for a while and sailed over the net toward SCVC's bench.
Connor Inlow yelled, "Outtttt!" as he was the closest to the descending ball.

It fell on the sideline — just in bounds. Tui screamed louder than ever and turned around to his end line to give a giant fist pump. Micah dropped to a knee and gave a massive fist pump as well, before falling flat on his chest and screaming in excitement. Evan, Kainoa, Trent, and Skylan ran over and huddled with their teammates. Connor Inlow buried his face in his hands. The score was 11-11.

Reilly passed Tui's next serve then took the Go-set. Reilly whacked it cross-court — Tui was sucked into the court a bit too far and Reilly's hit shanked off his arms and out, 11-12.

Vaziri jump served tough — Tui passed it medium (away from the net and toward the center) — Evan tipped the Go-set — dig — Inlow got set in transition — kill to area-six, off of Tui's hands, 11-13.

Vaziri hammered his second serve. Evan passed his heater with an emergency one-arm stab. Ka Ulukoa gave a freeball — Reilly took the Go-set in transition and tooled off of Trent's arms, 11-14.

The SCVC crowd was in frenzy. Coach Charlie stood quietly with his hands on his hips, observing. Vaziri railed his third serve even harder than the two prior, but waffled it 40 feet out of bounds.

With SCVC ahead 12-14, Skylan served his jump-float to Matt Reilly. Vinny Pizutti sprinted in front of Reilly to receive it. Schwan set overhead to Inlow and he struck it solid to area-six. Tui stepped in from area-six, to a defensive position even more shallow than where he started. The ball ricocheted off of Tui's hands and out.

Game over: 12-15.

Chapter 23 - The Decision

The SCVC 17-Quicksilver starters leaped in celebration. The bench stormed the court in ecstasy. Their second-string Middle Blocker ran from the sideline and cheerfully tackled Vaziri to the ground. Pizutti ran circles around the court, bounding with his hands in the air. History was created instantly for Southern California. It was as if that semifinals victory in the qualifier was a World Series Victory in Major League Baseball.

Ka Ulukoa's five-year-standing undefeated record was snapped. Following an incredibly emotional performance with a heartbreaking ending, the Hawaiians were normal. Kainoa, Casey, Kahiau, Coach Charlie, and Coach Pono joined the team on the court and Tui clapped his hands together just once as the team huddled. Coach Pono put his hand up, the team gave their respectful cheer to SCVC, and the guys approached the net. SCVC slowly pulled themselves away from their celebration to slap hands with Ka Ulukoa. No one had to deliver any messages about being classy; the team from Hawai'i didn't know anything different.

That was until hand slaps were done and Tui passed an opponent's parent, who said boastfully, "It's okay. Maybe next time."

Tui abrasively lashed out, "Wait until JOs! Try saying that to me at JOs!"

He immediately felt disgust in himself and took a seat on the bench to reminisce about the match. Subconsciously, he thought the loss of the old core players would call for him to do more. His intention was to compensate for that loss. Instead, his stares through the net, his flexing, his obnoxious celebrations, and his approval of his teammates' actions against character caused an unnecessary overdoing. Then finally, his frustrated outburst toward a cheeky spectator was his life's furthest example from tasteful. Acting as his team's protector was no excuse.

He walked over to Auntie Maile and she said only, "Move on, Tui."

Her son replied solemnly, "Mom, you've always told me to win with grace and lose with humility. I'm not frustrated — well, not just the loss — more so about the way that we got out of character."

Maile didn't say anything back. She maintained eye contact with him and soaked in his words.

He continued, "After they won, seeing those parents run on the court, and people going crazy... That isn't the way to win. You wouldn't have done that."

Again she kept quiet, just raising her eyebrows once and nodding to acknowledge that she was listening.

Coach Pono stood with Coach Charlie after the court cleared. "What do you think?" he asked, half-rhetorically.

"Who knows? Maybe it's a good thing," said Coach Charlie.

There was minimal time to *take in* what had just occurred. The team collected their glass 3rd-place trophy and Bronze Medals, and then moved outside to load up the vans, headed toward the airport.

The drive was rather quiet. Evan figured it was realistic for his team to lose one day. He just thought to himself that the first time his team lost would result in tears from his eyes. It didn't. The flight to Oahu was absent of its typical warm feeling. Auntie Maile spent years with the team. She felt the need to be comforting, but understood there were no words. After being bid wishes for safe travels by his coaches and teammates, Evan departed with his dad on through to the Big Island.

Skylan walked in for a hug from his mom as his team exited the baggage claim of Honolulu Airport. Along with most of the volleyball fans in Hawai'i, Arlene heard about the devastating result of the guys' semifinal match in Anaheim.

"Look on the bright side, Skylan," she said soothingly, "At least you guys qualified."

"You know, Mom," he said softly, "I heard all these kids talking at the gym about how we wouldn't qualify with our new players and how our streak was going to end. I never even thought it could happen until we played in that match. It was like we changed."

Arlene felt for her son. "Just learn from it, Sweetheart."

"Nothing we can do about it right now. Just have to get ready for high school season."

Micah resumed practices with his basketball team, while the other guys prepared for the coming high school volleyball season. Punahou was invited back to the Best of the West Tournament in San Diego. Skylan was surprised to hear that Maryknoll was extended an invitation as well. It was also the first season that his younger brother, Seyj, was with him at school, as a 9th-grade high school student.

Two weeks removed from the SCVA Invitational, Skylan found three letters waiting for him on the doormat.

The first had a header that read: *University of Southern California*
The second had the emblem: *University of California, Los Angeles*
The third read: *Grand Canyon University, Phoenix, Arizona*

All three were letters from the colleges, showing their interest in Skylan's skills at the qualifier. That was purposeful for his process. His mom was ecstatic coming home to her oldest son's news. Skylan had never been more motivated to play volleyball in his life.

Along with his older brother, Seyj was chosen to the varsity team at Maryknoll. Maryknoll was still dry on talent, headed by mostly raw athletes converted from basketball. The coach told Skylan that he wanted him to start setting in high school, so that he would have more control on the outcome of games. He hadn't run an offense since 12 & Under with Ka Ulukoa, but he didn't imagine it would be too much trouble, taking into account his recent confidence boost and the usual middle-of-the-road results from his high school team. Early on, Skylan showed a short temper with his younger brother. Seyj was asked to hit as an Opposite and Skylan didn't want to hear any nonsense about set adjustments or corrections.

"It's not that hard to hit in bounds!" shouted Skylan. "Stop tipping so much! You can't dig that easy ball?! Go straight over and stop getting tooled."

There was no escape for the 9th grader from his brother's high expectation, that flirted with unrealistic.

Micah returned from basketball just in time to join Tui, and Punahou's newest varsity team member, Trent Thompson, and travel to the Best of the West in San Diego. The pool play was designed so that Punahou played their last match of the day against Skylan's school team. Both teams weren't excited about flying all the way to California to play against a team that was in their league, but nonetheless, it was a fun exchange between old friends. Micah's tempo-sets to Tui, along with a decent group of role players around them, made Punahou too much for Maryknoll to keep up with. Trent Thompson was on the bench as the second-string Opposite. Tui gave Trent something to celebrate though, as he sent a rocket down the line that bounced up between Skylan's legs, causing an eight-minute delay. After the match, Tui slapped hands with the Maryknoll players, stopping at Skylan and flipping a backhand near his groin.

"You alright, Sky Man?" Tui asked humorously. "It's like you have a magnet down there."

"Oh, you think you're funny," Skylan scoffed, slapping his hand and moving on through the line.

On the second day, Punahou hung out in the bleachers during their off time and watched Maryknoll play against Loyola High School.

Shockingly, Maryknoll took a set from the California powerhouse. However, Loyola won the match after a tight third set. Three of the starters from SCVC 17-Quicksilver were in uniform for Loyola. The Hawaiians were anything but interested in seeing them.

Back on the island, Tui got an email and called Evan.

"Evan Enriques! Brah, did you get that email too?"

"Yes. I just saw it when I got home from school."

The email was an invitation. For the second year in a row, USA Volleyball invited both Evan and Tui to join the indoor USA Boys' Junior National Team for the upcoming summer's international competition in Mexico.

"It's during the same time as JOs. What are you going to do?" Tui asked.

"Probably just take some time to think. It says we have until May 12th to let them know."

"Yeah — March just started so that gives us like — some weeks at least."

Tui always wanted to experience playing with USA Volleyball. But during the years of late-July Select age group camps, by the time he got involved with High Performance tryouts, summer football interfered with playing. Once the previous season brought the invitation to join the USA BJNT, it was chasing perfection with Ka Ulukoa in early July that disallowed his acceptance to USA.

One day passed and Tui called to consult with Coach Pono. A few more days passed and Evan did the same. Evan told him about the invitation and told him that he was considering it. He asked Coach Pono for his thoughts.

Coach Pono said, "Tui called me too, and told me you guys are considering. If you guys both decide to go then we won't put a team together for JOs. We wouldn't have the players to go. It's up to you guys, though. It's a good opportunity."

Evan thought on it for a while that night. He called Tui and agreed that they would meet to sort things out in two weeks when Evan's high school team came for a tournament on Oahu. The invitation consumed their thoughts in the between time.

Punahou led the ILH in the standings and had their sights on a league title. Evan's team was cleaning up the competition in the BIIF league. Skylan's short temper with his brother scratched at the morale of his team, yet they were having their best results to date, holding down the 3rd-overall ranking in the ILH.

Finally Evan made it to Oahu. Kamehameha Hawai'i was eating

lunch at Zippy's, so Evan called Tui to meet him over there.

"Howzit, Evan?"

"All cool — Let's sit over there," he said, pointing to a two-person table in the corner outside.

Evan started, "Coach Pono said you guys talked. So what have you been thinking about?"

"I've always wanted to try and play USA stuff — just, football and club — you know?"

"I try and weigh out the options in my head. It always comes back to me so even."

Tui pulled his seat in closer.

"Individually, we didn't match up with anyone — with Koa — I mean — their Middles versus our Middles — their Outsides versus our Outsides. But as a team, we would always win. This qualifier was the first time that teams looked at us like we could be beat, and should be beat. You feel that at all?"

"I have an idea," Evan said, pulling out a sheet of paper. "Let's write down the pros and cons, for staying with Koa or leaving Koa, and going to USA or not going to USA."

"Shoots. Yeah, let's do that."

Ten minutes passed — then 15 minutes — and then 20 minutes before they let the pen that they were alternating settle.

"It looks way different on paper, huh?" asked Evan, partly sad that the list came out so lopsided.

Right then, both boys decided that they were going to accept the invitation from USA Volleyball.

Tui said jokingly, "My mom is going to beat me up."

"Just take the beating," Evan replied facetiously.

Tui gave his guy a handshake and a hug and parted from the restaurant.

Evan felt refreshed as he made it back to the Big Island. He told his parents about his talk with Tui a few days earlier, and realized that making a choice helped him fall asleep much faster. Tui's sleep patterns went unharmed. He felt at ease about the choice as well. Five days from his talk with Evan, Tui too, presented the idea to his parents. He sat with his mom in the kitchen and informed her of his choice.

"You can't leave your team," she said sternly.

Tui wasn't sure if that was a strongly stated unrequested opinion, or a command. He thought better of asking for clarification. Instead, he listened. Auntie Maile brought in a heap of exterior aspects, like his investment into the Ka Ulukoa team and the fact that he was already committed to college for football, as well as volleyball.

"Get a good night's sleep," she said to her son. Before he could even reply, she reiterated, "But you can't leave your team."

After returning home late from school, Tui placed a call to Evan.

"Hey — Evan."

"What's up, Tui?"

"I'm calling to let you know, I talked to my mom, and I changed my mind. I'm going to be staying with Ka Ulukoa for JOs."

Evan pulled the phone away from his ear and ran his fingers through his hair. Although, it wasn't his prerogative to add his influence any further.

He said, "Aw, man! Auntie Maile got to you, huh," trying to keep the mood light.

Tui knew his friend was disappointed. Maybe he was a little disappointed himself.

"Yeah, so that's it." Tui hesitated to ask, "Are you still going to go to USA?"

"Well, things are a little different now, so I will have to think about it. But probably, yes. I don't know."

"Sorry about that, Evan"

"No reason to be sorry, Tui. This stuff isn't easy."

Evan stayed on the fence while the high school season wound down. Skylan matured through the course of the season, taking a realistic view on the way he treated his younger sibling on the court. Maryknoll lost to Kamehameha Kapālama in the second round of the ILH to finish the season in 3rd place. Seyj Engleman got his arms tooled on the final play of the match and crumbled to the ground in disappointment. Skylan walked to his brother, picked him up off the ground, and gave him a big hug.

He whispered to him, "I'm proud of you, Seyj."

Arlene couldn't hear it from the stands, but she watched the encounter and it jerked a single tear from her eye. Punahou beat Kamehameha Kapālama for the ILH league title and moved to the State Tournament. Evan's team suffered a hiccup in the Big Island Finals, losing the match to Waiakea. Kamehameha Hawai'i still made the State Tournament, but with a lower seed that paired them with Punahou in the first round of States.

Evan wasn't playing his best volleyball. He worried that his mind was clouded by his unconfirmed decision about the USA invitation, and he feared that he couldn't play freely until he rid himself of the burden. Evan called Coach Pono.

"Coach Pono, it's Evan."

"Is everything alright?" Coach Pono asked. "What can I do for you?"

"I think I've made my decision," Evan said nervously. "Has Tui talked to you?"

"Yes, he called me two weeks ago. He is staying with the team for JOs."

Evan swallowed uneasily.

He said, "I've made the decision to try and go with the Junior National Team."

There was a long pause through the phone.

Then Coach Pono said, "You have to do what's best for you, no matter what. Do what's best for you."

Perhaps it was because the match was not the first time they'd faced off. Perhaps it was because the match wasn't a championship, but instead a first-round match. Regardless of the cause, Kamehameha Hawai'i against Punahou didn't have the same emotional pull from a year prior. Punahou beat Evan and Kamehameha Hawai'i in that first-round match on their way to claiming another Hawai'i State Title.

The club season drew nearer and rumors began to swirl that Evan Enriques would be absent from Junior Olympics because of USA. He exhausted his time. Just before the deadline, Evan delivered his email confirmation to USA Volleyball that he would be accepting the invitation to join the USA Volleyball Boys' Junior National Training Team in Colorado Springs.

Pono had Charlie over to his Kaneohe home. They sat on the patio in the backyard and looked out on the grass and the sand court. Pono explained to his friend, Evan and Tui's situation and how it played out.

He confided in Charlie, "It was tough enough with getting a new group at the beginning of the season, and now this, without Evan? I doubt we can do this, Charlie. It's been a great run, Coach."

Charlie rubbed his mustache and shrugged his shoulders.

"It's tough. We'll have to see."

Just then, Micah walked outside to the patio.

He said, "Hi, Coach Charlie. Hey, Dad. What are you guys talking about?"

"Getting ready for the season," Coach Pono said.

Coach Charlie just looked up at Micah from his seat.

Rapturously, Micah said, "I talked to Evan. He told me he isn't coming to Reno with us. But he said that he is still going to come train with us before he goes to Colorado Springs."

Coach Pono said seriously, "Micah, we are going to look at you taking on a bigger role. Be ready."

Micah gave his dad a smile and a thumbs-up. Charlie waited for him to walk back into the house before he dropped an intriguing comment on Pono.

"You know — they had Skylan doing the setting over at Maryknoll this season."

Pono turned his head and looked at his friend curiously. Charlie leaned back in his chair and looked out on the grassy mountains of Kaneohe.

By the return date for the Ka Ulukoa 17s, word had spread throughout Hawaiʻi (and parts in Western America) of Evan's preparation for absence from Junior Olympics. When Coach Pono confirmed its truth to the team, not one of the guys was hearing the news for the first time.

He said to the guys, "Evan will still come down to train with us, though, just for one week, to get ready for USA. He will be arriving in Oahu tomorrow. We will be making a few changes and some of you will be asked to take on a different role." Although he had specifics in mind, Coach Pono kept his eyes from directing toward individuals. "We will talk more once Evan arrives. Today, let's focus on getting back into it. *Tennis.*"

The training was basic, mainly revolving around restoring cleanliness and organization. They barely made it past *Three-Man Pepper* when Coach Pono called for his guys to take water. Coach Charlie pulled Preston and Kainoa to practice the fast two-step footwork for the transition Quick Attack. Coach Pono pulled out Micah to take some setting repetitions; he invited Skylan along for setting as well. After the water break, the guys did *Partner Serving*, and then Coach Pono called practice.

Trent spent the high school season training in practice, but on the bench in matches for Punahou. Casey and Kahiau did the same for their programs. Kainoa, who was only a 9th grader, wasn't even on varsity, yet, for Punahou. The return was rougher than it had ever been. It truly was like starting over.

Micah and Tui rode with Coach Pono to pick up Evan the next afternoon. Evan reached back, making a loud smacking noise when his hand contacted Micah's palm for a big handshake and a hug. Evan pretended to ignore Tui, who he hadn't seen since before changing his mind about USA, before smiling then walking back to him and giving him the same greeting as Micah. Those three boys greeted Micah's sisters at the house and they all filled the evening with laughs until it was time for Tui to return home. It was a disappointment that Evan would be visiting such a short time, making it only more important that they maximize their time together. The first stop in the morning: The Outrigger.

The team had training the next evening. Each boy took his turn greeting Evan and congratulating him on his Junior National Team invitation acceptance. Each boy gave his congratulations with a hint of fear in his voice as for what was to come for their Ka Ulukoa team. Coach Pono huddled the group.

"We are glad to have all of you back under the same roof. I will keep it brief. We have too much work to do." Only momentarily, Coach Charlie broke his poker face at that comment and smiled to its truth. "In Anaheim," Coach Pono continued, "that was the first time we let someone else dictate how we play."

The boys waited for him to say more, but he just sifted through them with his eyes.

And then he said, "Okay, warm up. Line Footwork. Then jog, and stretching."

The training was far from error-free, but the guys were centered. The training was so much more focused. Micah split the setting duties with Skylan in *Quick Hitter Timing*. That was exciting for him, because hadn't had a chance to hit in that drill before. *Primary Passing* had a different feel. It was odd for Tui to turn his head and not see Evan, who didn't begin on the receiving side. Skylan didn't begin on the receiving side either, which meant that he wasn't in the Libero position. Coach Pono lined up Tui in area-five, Trent in area-six, and Casey in area-one. Was this an experiment? Was he trying out Trent Thompson as an Outside Hitter? Was he putting Casey Takahashi in the Libero spot? No one was going to ask Coach Pono those questions, though. Coach Pono's order was law.

As a whole, the serve reception was quite bad. After some time, a few servers changed with passers. Kahiau went to pass and slipped his ball to Tui so he could serve. Evan made his way over to change with Tui. Skylan took over for Trent. Usually the team would add the hitting workup into *Primary Passing*, but Coach Pono kept it elementary for the day. He *did* add the hitting once the team reached the *Starting Six Transition*. The lineup was a bit unclear. Skylan set first and Micah was his Opposite. Then Micah set for a short time and Skylan was hitting as an Opposite for him. Coach Pono had both of them in the passing line when they weren't setting. Trent took some attacks on the left side and the right side. He also passed some rotations. Casey and Kahiau traded off at Libero. The only players with any normalcy in the drill were Tui as the OH1, Preston as the Middle nearest the Setter (M1), and Kainoa as the Middle closest to the Opposite (M2). The guys tried to act like it all made sense, but in reality they were very perplexed.

At Sunday practice, they persisted. The practice was the same. Although he just stood on the ground and didn't jump-set any balls, Skylan's setting was workable. Coach Charlie stayed with him at the net during the majority of his setting drills. *Back row Three-on-Three* was improving. *Primary Passing* and *Starting Six Transition* became clearer. It was a modified 6-2 offense that Coach Pono had in mind. That was interesting.

Tuesday came around and it was Evan's last practice with his guys. Everyone did their best to treat practice the same but there was an undeniable solemn feeling to the training, knowing that Evan was going to be leaving them, this time before the big dance. The guys endured, centered, and the training remained focus. There was something missing, though. Hard work wasn't enough to create a polished product, or even one that was presentable in Reno.

Skylan was in the 6-2 so that he could pass for the three rotations that he wasn't setting. However, Skylan wasn't a legitimate offensive threat the last time he hit inside a 6-2 offense at 12 & Under; so, now that he'd only grown to 5'8", nothing changed in that diagnosis. If anything, it would be worse now that the competition was so advanced and he had gone the last four seasons without attacking one ball in a tournament for Ka Ulukoa.

The issue was the same for Micah, just in reverse. He always trained doing everything in the Ka Ulukoa system, but all he knew in tournaments, since 12 & Under, was setting. He wasn't quite as small as Skylan, and maybe the team could get away with him passing for three rotations in the 6-2 offense, but who was going to pass while he was setting, if it couldn't be Skylan?

Trent wasn't ready for the responsibility of being an Outside Hitter on the team previously labeled as the best in the country. Tui couldn't pass the whole court alone. All of this was not to mention that the Middles and the new Liberos were in their first year of playing with Coach Pono and Coach Charlie's system. With the 6-2 offense, they were either going to be without an Opposite, or going to lose an OH2. They didn't have enough players. Without Evan, this is the way it was. The team left a completely focused, yet barley satisfactory performance, and bid Evan a farewell to Colorado Springs.

After dropping off Evan, Micah drove home with his father from the airport. The Ma'as never turned on the radio during a car ride. Pono believed in the family communicating. Pono was quieter than was typical.

Micah turned to his dad and said, "Dad, I'm hungry."

Pono kept his eyes on the road.

"You can eat when we get to the house, Micah."

"No, Dad, that's not what I mean."

Pono glanced over at his son's sober face.

Then he said, "I am too, Micah."

Micah came downstairs on Thursday morning. Evan Enriques wasn't there to accompany him. Pono was already in the kitchen.

"Micah, we are going to try you out at hitting, full-time," he said.

Micah hid his excitement, minding his expression so that his dad wouldn't think Micah took his message flippantly. He didn't ask any questions.

He said to his dad, "Okay," then walked to the refrigerator.

The only one who already knew the experiment that Coach Pono offered to Micah was Coach Charlie. The coaches hardly said anything about it at the start of Thursday's practice, just a comment to Skylan that he'd be spending more time with Coach Charlie for his setting. Training was facilitated as normal; the drills were the same; the order was the same. At the start of *Quick Hitter Timing*, Micah almost jogged into the Setter's spot, before realizing that wasn't his role for the day.

At the water break, Coach Pono had Micah take Tui's place so that he could watch his son pass some floats. In the *Primary Passing* workup, Skylan's setting was getting more consistent. His style was noncomplex, but with each day came fewer setting errors. The most they could ask for out of a Libero converting to the setting position was a hittable ball. Thus far, he was providing that.

Everyone was quite surprised, especially Tui and Skylan. Football and basketball had been good to Micah. He not only grew to about 6'1" from his 5'11" stature at the start of the fall, but he appeared to have a decent jump under him, as opposed to his narrowly credit-card-clearing hops all of his life. He was no Evan Enriques; though, the potential to be a half-decent attacker showed.

Evan settled himself in Colorado Springs. It only took the first few days for the USA coaches to change his duties. They moved him from an audition in the Libero position, to one at Outside Hitter. On June 19th, the USA Boys' Junior National Training Team was cut from a group of 22 to a 12-person roster that would travel to Mexico for the 2013 Federation of International Volleyball (FIVB) Boys' Youth World Championships, June 27th-July 7th. Wearing the jersey number 12, was Evan Enriques. He made the final roster. Evan's change in duty or the accomplishment of earning a spot on the BJNT didn't consume his thoughts. Nor was it what kept him awake at night. It was the least of his considerations. What kept him awake was his guilt. He felt responsible for Ka Ulukoa's inevitable demise. In Colorado Springs, he began to feel the things that Auntie Maile was emphasizing to Tui back in April.

On Oahu, the team was under two weeks from their departure to Junior Olympics. Coach Charlie added on to the system.

"We are going to change the *Freeball Passing*," he said. "Today, we are going to pass all the freeballs quick to the Setter, to throw off the blockers. Skylan stays down on his setting anyway."

The team didn't hesitate on Coach Charlie's order. After getting through Blocking Trips — making sure to review switch-blocking in preparation for JOs — warmup, *Partner Setting*, *Partner Passing*, and *One-Arm Digging*, the guys passed freeballs for 30 minutes, all of them low and quick, peaking no higher than the top of the 11-foot-high antennas. For 15 minutes, all platform. For 15 minutes, all hands. The hand passes rarely peaked higher than the top of the eight-foot net. Coach Charlie wanted the passes to be flatter and quicker.

They moved on through *Shoulders* and *One-Contact*. Coach Charlie added a timer onto *Three-Man Pepper* for short and concentrated rallies. Before *Quick Hitter Timing*, Coach Charlie added on again.

"We saw from the qualifier, teams are starting to close the one-box and five-box. We have to be prepared to adjust. We are going to practice hitting the sharp cross-court angle. Start with one-box and five-box."

His guys worked into the drill. Tui stroked his boxes with ease. Micah was still getting a feel for attacking, but understood what to do. Casey and Kahiau took a few swings from the left. Preston and Kainoa whiffed a couple and got solid contact on a couple. With no block up, Trent did fine, too. After two rounds each, Coach Charlie took an antenna from the court closest to theirs and weaved it onto their net, five or six feet inside of the regular antenna, symmetrical with the sideline.

"Okay," said Coach Charlie, "Hit inside of the second antenna to the sharp angle. If the set isn't there, hit to the one- or five-box."

Tui did fine, his ball only clipping the antenna a few times on its way to the floor where the 10-foot line met the sideline. Micah and Trent struggled on their Go-attacks, leaning in the air, over-rotating their bodies, and driving the ball into the top of the net and out or into the inside antenna that was simulating a Middle Blocker. Casey and Kahiau kept their tries to the one- and five-box. On Coach Charlie's order, Preston and Kainoa just kept their focus on transition footwork for their Quick Attacks. Coach Charlie paused them after two rounds.

"When the blockers go low and tight, we hit high to the one- and five-box. When they start to reach up high, we sneak under them to hit the sharp angle. Keep going."

A couple more rounds passed.

Coach Charlie said, "That's enough for today. More next training, move on."

Serving progressed with more focus on trying to get the newer guys to keep the ball in the court. *Back row Three-on-Three* (two contacts) and back row Four-on-Four (three contacts), without Evan, were back to a maximum of only eight or nine contacts before the cooperative rally ended. The coaches pulled guys out at water breaks for some individual passing and setting. Before adding in Hitters, the *Primary Passing* lineup was Kahiau, Tui, and Micah. Micah Ma'a as an OH2, passing and hitting? Was this rock bottom?

The passing away of Tui's grandfather, who had housed him and his family for the majority of his childhood, made for an even rougher training block. That man was gone and Tui moved to a painful place. The thing that was able to keep him level was the reminder of his mother's message.

You can't leave your team. Your investment into Ka Ulukoa stems longer than anything else you've done in your life.

Inside of their club facility, the guys continued their additions, training the quick freeball pass and plugging in the sharp angle attacks. With a quiet gym presence, the guys finished two more trainings before arriving on just one week until JOs.

On Tuesday, Coach Pono and Coach Charlie invited in a small group of players from the University of Hawai'i Men's Volleyball Team, just enough to conduct a scrimmage. The high school guys got licked. Coach Charlie gave the beating a name: *Healthy*. The coaches invited the UH players back to scrimmage on Thursday. He asked the guys to put their emphasis on the system and hardening the additions. The 17 & Under guys got beat again. *Healthy*. Irrespective to what they said to their guys, Coach Pono and Coach Charlie could see their newbies were taking on the role of a deer in headlights. Skylan was adjusting to a new position at a much higher level. Micah was stuck trying to find the rhythm that he always heard his dad referring to while talking to the Hitters. Micah had a never-ending list of questions for Tui about being an Outside Hitter.

Sunday was the last practice on the island before leaving to the Mainland.

The team was putting their shoes on when Coach Pono said, "Leave your flip-flops on. We are going across the street. Bring your bags."

The boys looked around unsure –- not even Micah knew what was happening. They followed.

Coach Pono told them all, "Order a small Acai Bowl to snack on and grab a seat."

The boys all gathered around a nearby grassy area and sat. Coach Pono dropped to a knee. Coach Charlie was the only one left standing. Coach Charlie pulled out one copy of *The Precious Present* from his bag. And then eight more copies followed. Coach Pono pulled out his own from his bag as Coach Charlie handed each boy the copy that he bought for him.

This is a kid's book. What are we doing here? Tui and Micah thought as they glanced at each other.

"Preston, will you read, please?" Coach Charlie asked.

"Sure — yes," Preston agreed.

Preston read, page-by-page. The guys slowly began to put down their Acai Bowl snacks and absorb the words that Preston was reciting. As Preston finished reading and closed the book, so did the others. Coach Charlie put up his hands in the shape of a square.

"This is *The Precious Present.*"

CHAPTER 24 - PLAYING IN THE DARK

The coaches, the guys, and Auntie Maile arrived at 10pm in Sacramento, California. There was no place for them to stay in Sacramento, so they took the two-hour drive to Reno, Nevada that same night. After a lengthy day of flying, the drive stretched itself out to feel just as long. Once they pulled into Reno, their pre-tournament team-talk was still on the agenda. There was no house for them to rent for the tournament. Auntie Maile had to resort to a hotel. They stayed in two separate one-bedroom suites. Coach Pono had Casey, Preston, Kainoa, and Trent with him. Auntie Maile had Skylan, Tui, Micah, and Kahiau in hers. After the meeting, Coach Charlie left to the Hilton to stay on his own.

They had a short night of sleep, and a hotel breakfast was uncomfortable. Auntie Maile had always done the cooking. Now the team was eating breakfast in a hotel lobby and there were random people walking around all over the room. Coach Pono walked the guys over to the Reno Convention Center to pick up their passes. He asked them to bring their bags along for morning training. The newbies' jaws dropped with the shock of someone's first time seeing the spectacular sight that is a full arena with 50 courts of competitive energy. Coach Pono paused on the traditional visit to Court 1.

Realizing that more than half of his team had no idea why he was stopping, he said, "This is where we want to end up, guys." Before moving on, he said to himself in a whisper, "This is where we've always ended up."

Coach Charlie was seated in a far away corner on the bench of the practice court, waiting. That morning of training, and the next, Coach Charlie said nothing. He only watched. Until, he spoke at the end of their second training, the last before the tournament.

"Limit your movement, and you'll get a greater gain."

That was all that he said before walking away from the team, heading for his hotel.

Coach Pono walked the guys back to the hotel to find Auntie Maile pacing in the hallway outside of their doors.

"Did you get my messages?" she frantically asked Coach Pono as he exited the elevator with the team behind him.

"Haven't looked at my phone. What's up?"

"I forgot, Kahiau only has a black jersey, and you said that he was playing as a Libero? He can't trade with Skylan either. Numbers have already been submitted to the Junior Olympics Committee."

She was clearly flustered.

"Okay. What can we do?" asked Coach Pono.

"I'm working on it. First thing though, we have to find a red polyester shirt somewhere."

"Alright."

Coach Pono walked into his room and laid his head down on the pillow. He thought to himself, *What else can go wrong?* Flat and quiet, he lay there, but restless, and unable to sleep.

Four hours later, Auntie Maile opened the door to her room and called her group out to the hallway. She then knocked on the door of Coach Pono's group.

Micah walked out of Auntie Maile's room and shouted, "Auntie! You are a miracle worker!"

Kahiau followed out behind with a big smile on his face. In her hands she held a shinny bright red shirt, long and wide, with the Ka Ulukoa emblem on the upper left breast and a large number eight in white. On the back was *Ka Ulukoa* centered in white, with another large number eight under it. The difference between Skylan and Casey's red Libero jerseys was unrecognizable.

Trent opened the door to Coach Pono's room and said, "Woah," with squinty eyes.

Coach Pono popped up behind Trent and opened the door wider to see the jersey.

"How'd you do it?" he asked, impressed.

"HA!" she chuckled. "I was lucky to find the shirt pretty quickly. It took a while, but I found a screen printer who said she could do it — at her house, though. She had a house full of cats, and I'm allergic to cats. Had to sit there for three hours, so you better appreciate it!" she said, playfully backhanding Kahiau near his chest.

The guys returned to their rooms from the hallway. Coach Pono returned to his room and lay back down.

Sure, the team appears to be acclimating to having to stay in a hotel. The newbies don't know anything different. And fine, we dodged a bullet with the jersey fiasco, he thought. But those things didn't make his team experienced all of a sudden. They didn't bring back Evan, or Keenan, or Noah, Austin, Adrian, or anyone. Those breaks didn't mean that the tournament field would crumble in front of them and not expose their weaknesses, the same way the UH group did — the same way that SCVC did. He placed his hands on his chest and whispered, "What are we going to do?"

The guys left the hotel without The Breakfast of Champions in their stomachs, but instead with stale cereal and overcooked oatmeal from the first-floor lobby. Coach Charlie met his group at the door of the convention center. Coach Pono approached Coach Charlie and allowed some distance between them and the guys.

Frustrated, he said to Charlie, "They gave us the 7th seed. Can you believe it? No respect."

The guys walked through the doors on day one and saw an ocean of teams filling the arena, many of them other 17 & Under teams beginning the first day of their tournament. Skylan noticed the looks. They weren't the same. The looks he felt were no longer the looks of fear — no longer the looks of envy. What he felt was the look of vulnerability. He felt like his team was walking through that arena exposed, walking to their court naked, with no place of refuge. Nonetheless, Ka Ulukoa settled onto their court.

The jog and stretching were normal. The four minutes of *Quick Hitter Timing* and serving were normal. Unfortunately, for what Ka Ulukoa had become without Evan, that normal play that was bound to transfer into the match, was ugly. Tui walked off of the court and took a glance at the hitting lines of their burly opponents, D1 Chicago.

It's going to be hard to take these guys, he thought.

Kahiau Machado didn't play well at Libero, shanking a bundle of average float serves and sending three attempts at a quick freeball pass over the net. Trent Thompson had a very slow start at Opposite, with no signs of his offensive or defensive game picking up pace. Casey Takahashi missed five of his six standing-float attempts as a serving substitute. Micah was in his first official match, ever, as an Outside Hitter. Ka Ulukoa struggled, but kept their heads above water and snuck out of the match in three sets.

Ka Ulukoa also took the next match against *949* 17s from San Clemente, California, in straight sets, and then, similar to the first match, they finished the third match two sets to one, in their favor. Ka Ulukoa's play didn't improve. Although they were the 7th seed, they were fortunate that day one still presented them three teams that were ranked lower than they were. It couldn't be blamed on nerves. The decision-making was bad. There was hardly any sense of responsibility. The Hawaiians survived the first day on the aggressiveness of Tui shuffling in front of guys at the end of the games to pass mediocre serves, and the happenstance that he was in the front row at the end of the games to get the sets from Skylan and put them to the floor.

Auntie Maile filled her departing words with enthusiasm for the guys. The newbies strolled out of the gym excited. They were back to their winning ways. Tui, Micah, and Skylan walked out of the gym worried, doing their best to shield the concern from their faces. Coach Charlie's expression was stoic, per usual. Coach Pono left the gym in fear of what was to come. Auntie Maile's pasta wasn't for dinner. The guys didn't share a room to interact all the time. They didn't play a good brand of volleyball. Nothing was the same.

Ka Ulukoa walked onto Court 9 on the second day for their first match against the pools' fourth seed, the team qualified from England, London Volleyball Club. They were of average Open Division skill. They had similar height to Ka Ulukoa, with slightly taller Middles. For a team from England, they knew Ka Ulukoa well, or perhaps they scouted them on the previous day. The London game plan was clear: to serve short to Micah and Tui (to take them out of having an approach) and hit the ball in Kahiau's direction in good situations, and the bad ones, too.

It probably would have been less embarrassing for the two of their players who topspin-jump-served to avoid it; Tui was practically yawning while passing their soft topspin-serves with his hands. For every one serve that Tui was receiving and making look easy, Casey had one error serving his standing-float. Trent's offense was existent, just usually negatively, in the fashion of being stuff-blocked or hitting out of bounds.

Each time his team made an error, Coach Pono yelled out, "Next! Next! Forget that, everybody sideout, everybody pass!"

Trent did make strides in defense, though, mimicking Tui and bursting in from area-one to overhand pass the short freeballs that came over, thus freeing up Tui for the transition Pipe-attack. Ka Ulukoa caught a miniature streak of points from London screwing up their own attempts at trick plays and giving Ka Ulukoa freeballs. The separation in score during the second set even managed to open up just briefly enough for Skylan to mix in a few standing-Front-1-sets to Preston and Kainoa.

A petite lady sitting next to Auntie Maile in the spectator chairs said, "Tui is so nice to Kainoa. You have a good boy. All of your kids are good."

It was Kainoa's mom. She had flown down from Hawai'i to watch the team play.

Auntie Maile flashed a smile accompanied by a chuckle, and then said seriously, "That's because they get cracks all the time if they're not."

Ka Ulukoa finished the match against London, two sets to zero.

After refereeing the next match, the Hawaiians returned to the court for their second match against the pools' third seed, Northern California Volleyball Club. Like London, NCVC 17s were a standard day two Open Division pool-play third seed, an average ball-control team, with one small and skilled Outside Hitter, as well as two big, somewhat raw Middles. Ka Ulukoa's scheme was to have Preston and Kainoa commit block on their Middles and be one-on-one at the pins. Luckily, the NCVC 17s Middles weren't as developed as they were big. They continuously tipped the ball over Preston and Kainoa's (rather tiny sized) block for Tui and Micah to scoop up from area-four and transition for points. Once the NCVC Setter began to set their skilled Outside Hitter, David Parker, he just hit the ball hard toward area-six, giving Tui and Micah good opportunities to dig him. Un-pretty, but Ka Ulukoa got the job done.

They took a long two-match break before playing their first opponent of the tournament ranked within the top eight, and the first seed in the pool. Auntie Maile had pulled together some snacks for the cooler the night before. The boys dug in. Anything was better than the hotel food prepared in mass production. Some took a nap. A couple played with a deck of cards.

The time had come for my High Line 17 Nike team. We had come upon our chance to face off against Ka Ulukoa. They were hurt without Evan; that was clear, but after watching them work in the two matches prior, I knew that this would be the toughest challenge we had ever faced, mentally. We were a long way from our scrimmages inside a small gym in Long Beach, California. I talked with my team in the huddle. My scouting chart was firmly exposed and I made sure that every eye was on it or me. I could hear them in front of my presentation, stroking the imaginary boxes — their hands hitting the ball clean and firm, time after time. I felt that we could beat them if we played our best volleyball, and I told my team that. Internally, I wasn't sure if we were ready. It was early in the tournament and we were not prepared to peak on the second day. The players lined up on the court. I looked over at Pono Ma'a and The Guru. 'This is it,' I thought.

Our Setter, Chandler Gibb, a skinny 6'1" boy, with his twig-like arms exposed through his red cutoff jersey and long flowing blonde hair, served, and a long rally ensued. 'Boom!' A nice crossover blocking move and our M2, Dominic Spencer, stuffed Tui, 1-0 us. We served again. Tui swung — big dig by our shaggy-haired Libero, Connor Freeman. Ka Ulukoa got the ball back — Pipe-set — another dig by our Libero — overhead Red-set to a clean kill by our Opposite, 2-0. Maybe we would rise to the occasion. We scored once more before they could sideout. Our blocking schemes were doing nice things for us, and if we could get an out-of-system set on the net in transition then we could find kills. It appeared that they had never seen anything like our All-American Outside Hitter, Storm Faagata, who was teeing off on open-net swings. We took an early 8-5 lead.

We passed well and we blocked well. I don't think that Micah had seen a player who could triple-block as aggressively as our second Outside Hitter, Brett Baldwin. I knew that if there was any team that would be difficult to crack, this one was at the top of the list. Tui was undeniable. He made a few highlight-reel digs and transitioned them out with successful Pipe-attacks. Before two blinks of an eye, the score was 8-9 in Ka Ulukoa's favor. We scrapped and they scrapped. It was a dogfight and I was impressed by my team's courage to stand up against them and play at a high level.

Coach Pono kept yelling. Anytime we would hit softly, "Easy!" Anytime that we scored, "Next! Next!" And anytime that we prepared to serve, "Pass! Pass!" No matter what part of the match we were in and no matter the scenario, the message was consistent. Ka Ulukoa took the lead 12-9. They had more ball control than we did, especially Tui, Micah, and Skylan. But we had much more size and power. They could make plays and we knew it.

Micah had such good court awareness, but Storm could bail us out with a step-close and a hard swing to the open spaces. We just had to limit our errors. We knotted it at 12. They took the lead. We knotted it at 15. They took the lead. It was 16-16 when my team's third-year captain, Ryan Bahadursingh, subbed into the match. He jump-floated a ball that took Tui out of the play, and after our Libero came up with a chaotic dig on Micah, our Setter popped the ball up in the center of the court and Ryan Bahadursingh step-closed hard out of the back row and crushed a Pipe-attack deep and down into Ka Ulukoa's court. 'Yes, that is the spark we need,' I thought... until the next play when Micah got set again and gently rolled it over our block to the ground for a kill. They bounced back just like that.

We hung in there, 20-18. We took the lead and Coach Pono called for time. That was a proud moment for a young coach. I said to my guys,

"They've got to go to four or 13 here" (referring to Tui and Micah). Out of the timeout we stuff-blocked Tui on a two-person commit block, 21-18 us.

Next play: cross-court dig on Tui, right up to the net, and a transition Front-1-attack for the kill, 22-18 us. Skylan set his Front-1-attack next. Then, another swing into the net, 24-18 us. They finally sided-out on a double-contact error by our Setter. He responded, with a gorgeous Go-Set that created an open net for our OH2. Kill, 25-19 us!

Now the belief had been confirmed. We could get those guys. However, I was clear. If there was any team that would be difficult to crack, this one was at the top of the list. The big note that I made to my team between sets was this:

"We played a good game of volleyball, but great is being able to sustain a high level over a long period of time. One thing we can add to help us is being more precise about serving number eight (Kahiau). He can give us a few more favorable situations."

In set two we did a better job there, but Tui and Micah began to pinch him. With Kahiau taking less and less court, it was our block that continued to take care of us. That, and this cool new set called The Drift that we added in for our Middles right before JOs. Ka Ulukoa's platform control and strategic offensive placement was taking us out-of-system consistently. But Storm Faagata was able to continuously step-close and kill high sets to keep us alive, punishing the ball off of Trent's arms and pegging Micah in his chest.

Things got tough when Ka Ulukoa pulled ahead 7-11 and I decided to call a timeout. We had stopped playing patiently and my guys were in a hurry to win, which made our focus sloppy. Storm Faagata sided-us-out on an inside Lob-attack, kill. They started to roll. I took my last timeout of the set at 9-15. I feared we were starting to look toward to a third set and my guys didn't realize, the way I did, how dangerous a third set with Ka Ulukoa 17-Mizuno was, regardless of whether or not they had Evan Enriques.

Again, Ka Ulukoa scored. I talked with my Setter between plays. The mentality had to change. We sided-out and pulled to 12-17. At 14-18, Coach Pono called a timeout. The excitement of that had faded. I just wanted my team to beat their team.

A few digs, a few stuff-blocks, and a few serves at Kahiau later, and we found ourselves tied at 18. Back and forth we went, 19-19, 20-20, 21-21, 22-22, and 23-23. We were going to do it. We were going to knock off the five-time defending champs.

Storm Faagata hit his topspin-jump-serve at Ka Ulukoa. It was a good pass and Micah took the Go-Set on the left side. He took a high swing *off our block for a kill, 23-24. Game point Ka Ulukoa. Casey Takahashi subbed in to serve. Standing-float to our Libero — good pass — Drift-set! Our M2 crushed it off of Tui's outstretched arm for the kill, 24 all.*

I subbed in our red-haired, left-handed, 6'0" second Setter, Cole Kendrick, to serve for our M2, as well as long and skinny, Hispanic, 6'6" Alex Albarran, for our Opposite. Alex Albarran was our second Opposite and overall best blocker. Cole Kendrick served a ball that clipped the tape and trickled over short. Trent was able to pass the let-serve. Skylan set Micah and he took a high and hard swing. The ball soft-blocked and became an easy freeball for us. We dug it and Go-set out to our OH2. One-against-one, he hammered it. Tui slid under from middle-back, area-six and dug it up — transition Ka Ulukoa kill for 24-25.

The next serve came from Trent. We passed and set our OH2 again. Tui dug him again, this time overhead with his hands. Skylan set Micah and he tooled, high and hard off of our block. Game!

Set three proved to be a dangerous situation, as Ka Ulukoa opened with a 0-4 advantage, then a 3-8 lead at the side switch, before cruising to a 6-15 win. I remember hearing Coach Pono every play ("Next! Next!"). Beyond that, all I remember was the final play of the match ("Everybody sideout. Everybody sideout."), and Coach Pono giving calm high-fives after their win ("Good mental toughness. Good mental toughness.")

The day was over for the Hawaiians. They made it through some real tests. In their history, they'd never dropped a set on day one or day two of any tournament. In this Junior Olympics, they did so on both. Yet, going into day three Power Pools, they still held their ground. They move up one seed to 6th, and they were still undefeated.

Coach Pono had individual meetings with the guys in his hotel room. The first was with his son, who said he felt like things were going, "Okay," and he was trying to get a rhythm as the games and matches progressed. That was definitely a statement heard growing up in a house with Pono Ma'a. Kahiau Machado was the last one he met with from Auntie Maile's suite. Kahiau entered his coach's room with a nervous smile on his face.

"So, how are you feeling about the tournament so far?" Pono started.

"Er — it's been fun so far. I have been a little nervous in the matches," Kahiau admitted.

"HA," Pono laughed without cruel intention. "I figured, after you came into the timeout against High Line and said, 'I think they found me.'"

Kahiau giggled shyly, then put his head down, embarrassed.

"Not to worry," said Coach Pono. "You're doing enough. Just stay focused on doing your job on the court, and we will see where we go." Kahiau nodded his head.

"Send in Casey on your way out, please."

Like Kahiau, Casey Takahashi walked into the room with an innocent smile on his face. Coach Pono asked Casey to grab a chair. Casey clasped his hands together and took a seat.

"How do you feel about the tournament thus far?"

Casey paused, and then said, "Well — er — I think we are doing okay. I mean... I am glad we are winning."
Coach Pono chose not to hold back.

"Listen, Casey, you can only contribute so much. So, if you come into the game and aren't focused enough to make a difference, then that is your fault." His tone was harsh.

Casey's lip quivered and his eyes became moist.

"You can go now, Casey."

The first match of the third day was Ultimate 17s, from Chicago. Auntie Maile was sitting with Kainoa's mom, talking story about how Tui had to return to Punahou Football Camp on Monday, the day after JOs ended. Charlie Wade passed in front of her sporting his green, flower-filled University of Hawai'i Men's Volleyball button-up.

"Good Morning," he said luminously.

She looked up, startled.

"Good Morning, Coach."

Ultimate hadn't shrunk since Ka Ulukoa saw them in the 16 & Under Open Division Quarterfinals. Luckily, their big game left-hander wasn't as sharp as he'd been one year ago, so Kahiau didn't have to dig many balls off the area-five line, which Coach Charlie asked him to be ready to do. Plus, Ka Ulukoa served just well enough to keep Ultimate away from the net and away from setting their massive Middles in serve receive; even Casey did his part at the service line. Ironically, for the few balls that the lefty did hit near the line, Casey happened to be playing defense and made some one-arm digs worthy of a highlight-reel inclusion. Two sets to none, Ka Ulukoa took down a team inside the top 12. An hour of rest and the Hawaiians would be getting warm for their last match of the day. Following an abnormal tournament start, the opponent dropped from 3rd- to the 4th- overall seed, Manhattan Beach Surf 17s.

It was good that Trent Thompson began to find the court in good offensive situations and keep the ball in play when the set wasn't ideal. He wasn't getting many kills, but he was no longer racking up the errors. MB Surf put together an interesting game plan. It was quite brilliant, actually. They knew, almost everyone knew, that Ka Ulukoa's Middles would commit block on their Middles, each and every decent or perfect pass. From the start of the match, they used that common knowledge, setting inside Lob-sets to Louis Richard and Hayden Boehle, leaving them one-on-one with Trent or Skylan's unimposing blocking hands. That wasn't even the brilliance. It was the execution. Richard and Bohehle would either hit the ball sharp to Kahiau's area, or they would tip the ball short, back toward the line near area-two, leaving Skylan and Trent to run after it, usually resulting in a kill. There was little that Tui or Micah could do from middle-back, area-six or left-front, area-four.

Manhattan Beach also had 6'7" Cole Paullin they could go to in the Middle. With him, it didn't matter too much if Preston and Kainoa commit blocked or not, he was hitting over the top. As he was at 16 & Under, the left-handed Jacob Tuioti-Mariner was still the rangiest Opposite in Southern California, maybe the country. Front row or back row, it didn't matter. Having him was like a National Football League (NFL) team having a seven-foot tall Tight End to throw bailout passes to. Anytime MB Surf got into a long rally with Ka Ulukoa and came away from the net, they could set Tuioti-Mariner and his power could finish it. After a Front-1-attack by Paullin for a clean kill, MB Surf won the first set, 21-25.

Set two had Skylan begin serving in Ka Ulukoa's customary rotation one. Ka Ulukoa had stayed away from having Tui and Micah switch blocking positions with Skylan against MB Surf, because Tuioti-Mariner was as effective on the back row D-attack as he was on the front row Red-attack. The Hawaiians had already lost a set, though, so why not make a change they'd trained before? So they did.

While Tuioti-Mariner was in the back row, Tui and Micah switched with Skylan and blocked on the right against Manhattan Beach's Richard and Boehle, leaving the 5'8" Skylan on the left to try his hand at slowing down the 6'4" and powerful, Tuioti-Mariner. Switch blocking didn't work well. MB Surf continued to used their inside Lob-attack. Tui's block was taking enough space to prevent Richard and Boehle from getting easy kills from sharp swings. However, if Tui and Micah chose to block, which was necessary, then there was nothing they could do about the short tip back to the line in area-two. Trent would have to get that.

Early in the tournament, teams were serving Micah; as they saw it, he was a Setter playing out of position and shouldn't be able to pass well. In addition to that, having him pass more would help take him out of the offense, seeing as Ka Ulukoa only had him and Tui getting sets. Micah was receiving serves quite well and confidently. Following High Line's example, some teams changed over to serving Kahiau. That strategy worked; therefore, as the tournament drew longer, Tui and Micah looked at each other and began to pinch Kahiau, basically creating a two-person serve receive. The only person ripping a topspin-jump-serve hard enough to require more than Tui and Micah's reception was Louis Richard. It was nice for Ka Ulukoa that he wasn't pinpointing it well enough or making it often enough to hit Kahiau's area, hence, Tui and Micah could manage it.

They were also fortunate that it appeared Tuioti-Mariner's extra weight, necessary for football season, didn't leave him as quickly as it had it the past, and that he wasn't as spectacular hitting on the left in rotation one as he was on the right, although his Setter insisted on setting him in rotation one nearly every time.

The score was 22-22. Ka Ulukoa held tight to the team seeded two positions higher, trying to keep themselves from being pushed off the edge, 23-23. The MB Surf Setter, Drew Pion, served a jump-float that clipped the tape, forcing Micah to dive in from area-six with an outstretched platform and pass it with the knuckles of his thumbs. The ball shot up tight to the net and Skylan jumped, barley creeping his right wrist above the net, and tried to save it. His attempt landed his arm in the net. Game and match point MB Surf, 23-24.

Coach Pono called for time. Very few words and a couple sips from their water jugs later, they set up on the court in rotation-six serve receive before MB Surf was off of their sideline from loudly whispering their scheme for their final play.

As Drew Pion loaded up to serve, a small girl stood up and yelled, "Come on, Drew! Just get it in!"

An MB Surf fan, assumed to be the girl's dad, cut it, "One more! Close it! Close it!"

Pion popped the serve into area-six and Micah platform-passed it easily. Tui's hand hit Skylan's Go-set and blasted off of the MB Surf Libero's chest and out, 24-24.

Skylan went to serve. Jump-float to Louis Richard in MB Surf's rotation one — decent pass — and then a left side Go-set to Tuioti-Mariner, which he hit around Trent and Kainoa — two feet out of bounds, 25-24. Ka Ulukoa coolly walked into the center and touched hands. MB Surf called for time.

After the break, Coach Pono stood on the sideline with his hands in the pockets of his jeans. Skylan hit a similar jump-float. The pass was pretty similar. Drew Pion gave the Red-set overhead to Richard — Tui shuffled out — one-on-one — cross-court swing... solo-bounce-block! Three straight points by the Hawaiians, Tui responsible for finishing two of them. MB Surf's chance wasn't over, but would have to wait for the third set.

Manhattan Beach went ahead 7-9 in the tiebreaker, and then — they cracked. Their opportunity to double-up on their Southern California neighbors' overtaking of the defending champs was fading. Tuioti-Mariner was visibly tired. The Manhattan Beach team with rock-solid ball control was missing their routine jump-float serves. On the contrary for Ka Ulukoa; carrying on from the start of the day's first match through the end of its last, Casey didn't miss a single serve. Coach Pono's message had apparently hit home for Casey. His teammates calmly followed suit and performed a consistent finish, 15-12 Ka Ulukoa. Maybe it was in the culture of Ka Ulukoa 17-Mizuno, but just like with High Line the previous day, if a team didn't close the book on that Hawaiian team in two sets, then the third bared its danger.

Coach Pono couldn't help but be happy with his team's resolve. Walking into the tournament crippled by Evan's departure, in the first season with the absence of Keenan, Noah, Austin, and Daniel, his guys advanced their seed and made the Open Division Quarterfinals, undefeated. Three-team Power Pools completed sooner than regular four-team pool-play pools, so the team left Coach Charlie to himself and walked to the hotel to pick up the vans. Coach Pono decided that his team would have lunch at Sonic. Tui grabbed onto Kainoa and pulled him in closer.

"Get over here, Youngin'. Nice job, Brutha." He called ahead, "You too, Casey. You really saved us today."

"What do you guys want?" Coach Pono called back, looking at Kainoa.

Kainoa thought it best to keep the order simple. No nonsense, changing the condiments and such.

"Er — I will have a number one, please."

"What do you want to drink?" Coach Pono asked impatiently.

"Lemonade? Yes, lemonade please."

"I'll have a number three with a strawberry milkshake," Micah yelled out.

"Ho Brah, that sounds good. Same, with a vanilla milkshake," shouted Preston.

"Number one with a chocolate milkshake for me," Tui ordered. It was easy to see the annoyed look growing on Coach Pono's face with how long it was taking to order in a drive thru.

"Dang," Kainoa whispered, almost silently, with his head down.

"What's up, Brah?" Tui asked.

"I wish I would have ordered a milkshake."

Tui chuckled and wrapped his arm around Kainoa.

"That's why you always order last," Tui said sagely, raising his eyebrows at his teammate.

Individual meetings finished up at the hotel. Coach Pono called Coach Charlie on the phone before bed.

"Hey Coach, you awake?"

"You hear me on this phone, don't you?" Coach Charlie said sarcastically.

"This tournament so far," he lowered his voice so the guys wouldn't hear, "pretty crazy, huh?"

"We told them to expect a struggle. It's been enough, so far," said Coach Charlie, very matter of fact.

"We've got this team from Arizona tomorrow morning, Club Red Never heard of them. They won a match and lost a match today, but they eliminated Balboa Bay from the tournament and took over the 5th seed. What do you think?"

"I think... we'll have to wait and see."

"Mhm —" Coach Pono murmured. "Okay, Coach."

"Okay, Coach," and Charlie hung up the phone

CHAPTER 25 - LITTLE RED BOX

The 17 Open Division Gold Bracket was scheduled to play at the same times. The quarterfinals were at 9am, the semifinals were scheduled for 11am, and the finals would take place on Center Court at 2pm. Included in the Gold Bracket were Nisotros (Puerto Rico), San Juan (Puerto Rico), Southern California Volleyball Club, Ka Ulukoa, Club Red, Manhattan Beach Surf, and Trujillo Volleyball Academy (Puerto Rico). It was a blessing for Ka Ulukoa that SCVC and Club Red combined on the second day to kick Balboa Bay out of the Gold Bracket. Balboa had, by far, the best spring season of any west coast club and was the favorite to win in Reno.

The guys got a nice draw into the quarterfinals of the tournament. The Club Red 17s were big in size, but not in experience. It was their first year playing in the Open Division at Junior Olympics and it showed. They played well and made big upsets in the tournament, like opening the tournament to take MB Surf's 3rd seed. In the same day, they had strings of bad volleyball, losing matches, like one against SCVC, and then rebounding to beat the originally 2nd-overall-ranked Balboa Bay in Power Pool. Before the match, Coach Pono and Coach Charlie made certain to reiterate that it would be a struggle, and any of the teams still involved could win. Club Red 17s was still involved.

Their Arizona group was fiery and intense, with a following of Arizona fans behind them cheering with opera-worthy pipes. Their squad was undoubtedly excited to be competing for their chance at the Gold Medal. It wasn't to be. Club Red wasn't yet skilled enough to hit Kahiau with their serves. Their Middles were large (6'8" and 6'6") and coordinated, but hadn't read blocked well enough to stick with the setting tempo of even Skylan, a Setter who stood with his feet flat on the ground while setting. Ka Ulukoa kept the service pressure on, missing just two serves the entire match, disallowing Club Red's passers to find any confident rhythm. The Hawaiians swept them in two sets and moved onto the semifinals. Ka Ulukoa had the rhythm.

Having five newbies joining in to secure their team a guaranteed try at an Open Division Medal in their first Junior Olympics wasn't too shabby of an accomplishment. The rest period wasn't long before the Hawaiians had to return to Court 3 and play in their half of the semifinals. The semifinal opponent didn't offer such a breezy task, as the 9am quarterfinal match had gifted them. Trujillo Volleyball Academy 17s of Puerto Rico were fresh from bouncing the 1st-seeded Nisotros from the Gold Bracket, and as it so happened, they'd met Ka Ulukoa in the final match of the first day.

Coach Pono's guys hadn't worn the sleeveless jerseys since Anaheim. They weren't prepared to change that for the semifinal. TVA hadn't been on any United States team's radar because they chose not to participate in qualifiers during seasons past. They were seeded improperly from the tournament's beginning, when they began as the 24th ranked team. They'd proved it in taking a set away from Ka Ulukoa on the first day, and they'd proved it by making it through every pool up through day four, before stripping the 1st seed of their ranking in the quarterfinal. They weren't inexperienced.

This was one of the rare Puerto Rican teams that kept their height comparable to the maturing Americans and was far more springy than any other team in the tournament. TVA kept it even with the defending champs up to 6-6. They used their explosive defenders and lightning-quick transition offense to hit the seams of Ka Ulukoa's defense and charge out ahead, 12-15. Coach Pono called for time.

Out of the pause, Coach Pono's guys played better volleyball. They started making digs at middle-back on fast sets, and Micah was using his short roll-shot over the TVA block, which landed in the center of the court more than a few times. Following a 17-17 timeout by TVA, Ka Ulukoa closed to the tune of 25-21; off of Skylan's dig, Micah ran in from area-six and scored the set point on a sneaky set-over on two.

He said with a smile, "See, Sky Man, that's how you do it."

Every play of the tournament, Trent was learning. He'd done enough up to that point. He was running into a brick wall, now. TVA found ways to get Tui on the ground in defense, which sometimes made Micah have to set from left-front, area-four. Skylan was not a consistent offensive option, so Trent was the only choice. Trent wasn't siding-out in long rallies, which gave TVA the space to pull ahead 6-8. Coach Pono noticed, and he talked with Coach Charlie.

Coach Charlie said, "Let's see."

Down 12-14, Coach Pono took a timeout. Nothing had changed in set two. However, he didn't panic his players.

"Keep passing. Keep siding-out. Everybody sideout," was his continuous message. Coach Pono glanced curiously at Coach Charlie.

"Let's see," Coach Charlie repeated.

Coach Pono's eyes opened no wider when Trent scored the next ball on a Red-attack off the block and out of play. Coach Pono's eyes *did* expand once Trent went to the service line and captured the next six points on a serving run composed of four digs, two out-of-system assists, three back row D-attack kills, and an ace, all by Trent Thompson — which gave Ka Ulukoa enough light to crack TVA and take the match in two sets. As he walked onto the court to slap hands, Coach Pono looked again at Coach Charlie.

Referring to the finals for which his team had just punched their ticket, Coach Charlie said, "Let's see."

Ka Ulukoa's match finished as the other semifinal's first set was winding down. Walking out into the hallway of the Reno Convention Center, Skylan passed the Court 2 semifinal of SCVC playing San Juan and watched Billy Kopenhefer running circles around the court of an incomplete match. It was a while until the 2pm final. A fraction of the guys chose to lie down. A portion of the guys pulled out cards to pass the time. Micah stuck his hand into Auntie Maile's cooler for some snacks.

A few minutes went by, and then Preston pulled out a gift from his backpack. Kahiau saw what he had and silently crawled over and sat up next to him. Tui raised his eyebrow and reached in his own backpack to pull out a similar prized possession, almost identical. Micah strayed from his handful of snacks and crawled over near Tui. Skylan pulled out one similar, then Kainoa, then Casey, and then Trent. Less than five minutes later, every guy had his cherished item in front of him. It wasn't a gift that they had received under the net from another team. It was *The Precious Present*, and their eyes were glued to its pages.

Coach Pono walked into the hallway from the arena and stopped in the doorway. For a brief moment, his breath escaped him. He approached his team and Skylan picked up his head.

"What's up, Coach Pono?" Skylan asked.

The rest of the team detached their eyes from the pages and looked upward to their coach.

"I was coming to see if you guys wanted to scout the other semifinal match."

Without a single turn of any neck for another teammate's agreement, together they said, "No."

"Okay," said Coach Pono, as he turned around and walked out.

The team placed their heads back into their books.

Coach Charlie sat in the spectator chairs inside of the arena, thinking about the fact that his team escaped the match against TVA setting only five Quick Attacks. His faith was strong — but realistic. He imagined that wouldn't be sufficient in the finals, against either of the teams that competed in front of him.

"They didn't want to come?" asked Coach Charlie, as Coach Pono sauntered back up to the chairs on Court 2.

Coach Pono proceeded to tell Coach Charlie exactly what he'd just witnessed from their players.

"I was taken aback," he said. "We have five guys that don't even start on varsity in high school. I thought they would want to watch, to calm their nerves." He choked up a bit. "But man — that was special. They are totally bought in, Coach."

Coach Charlie kept his eyes forward on the San Juan versus SCVC match, allowing Coach Pono his special moment.

At 12:45pm, Coach Pono walked back into the hallway with Coach Charlie trailing. He signaled Micah and Trent to awaken the few of their teammates who were asleep on the floor. The other semifinal ended a while before. Coach Pono and Coach Charlie stayed outside to talk story and let their guys be alone before the last match of the tournament. No boy asked who their opponent was, maybe because they knew instinctively. The team gathered themselves and arranged to walk in together.

Tui said to his mom, "Win or lose, I just want us to do it the right way."

At 1pm, Ka Ulukoa 17-Mizuno entered the arena.

SCVC 17-Quicksilver was already on Court 1 warming up. The net was strung up firmly on its eight-foot-high black poles. The court tiles were painted to give off the appearance of real hardwood. The court lines were pearl white and the beige hardwood colored court was surrounded by a bright blue outline. The Hawaiians put their bags down and noticed the buzz of conversation around the grandstands starting to get louder. By the time they made it through their stretching and *One-Contact*, the bleachers were starting to fill. In a rematch of the SCVA Invitational Semifinal, the freshly 1st-seeded Ka Ulukoa 17-Mizuno was hosting the 2nd seed, Southern California Volleyball Club 17-Quicksilver.

Ka Ulukoa won the coin flip and elected to receive. Each team utilized its four minutes. The players lined up for a long announcement of both rosters, followed by a presentation of the starters. Kahiau walked onto the court (before being waved in to replace Preston) to join Tui, Micah, Skylan, Trent, Kainoa, and Preston in an evenly shaped circle in the center of their half. Each guy stuck his right foot in and Micah prayed:

Dear God,
Thank you for bringing us here. Thank you for getting us this far in the
tournament. Thank you for The Precious Present and bless those less
fortunate than us. In your name we pray.
Amen

It was no surprise that Ka Ulukoa set up receiving in rotation six so that Skylan could rotate into being the first server. SCVC started in rotation one with Ian Schwan serving. Next up at right-front was Vinny Pizutti at OH1, followed by Chase Corbett at M2. Furthest from Schwan, at left-front, was Connor Inlow, positioned at Opposite. Their coach, Jeff Alzina, clearly paid attention to his squad's last meeting with the team from Hawai'i and started Matt Reilly at OH2. Nearest him was Daniel Vaziri at M1, and then Billy Kopenhefer jogged on to replace him as the Libero. Other than Kopenhefer's contrasting dark grey Libero jersey, they all wore their sleek white cutoffs, the same cutoffs they wore six months earlier while dethroning the champs of another qualifier championship. The whistle blew.

Ka Ulukoa started the first set with even passing seams; Tui, Micah, and Kahiau each took a third of the backcourt. Schwan served to Kahiau in area-one — Kahiau platform passed a beauty — Skylan stood straight-legged and flipped up a Front-1-set to Kainoa — he thumped it just beyond the 10-foot line in front of Kopenhefer, 1-0.

Casey loaded his standing-float at 3-2 — Pizutti passed it well — Inlow took the overhead Red-set from Schwan — Tui laid out in area-six to dig it — Skylan bump-set the tight dig from out of the net and Tui stepped in to snap the Pipe-attack over — Pizutti tensed up and shot his dig tight to the net — Schwan jumped up to Go-set with one hand, touching the dug ball with only his knuckles — the set flew wide, so Reilly leaned out and hit it the only place he could, outside the antenna. SCVC's error gave Ka Ulukoa their first real point, 4-2. Casey standing-floated again, and this time Reilly received it. A better looking Go-set to Reilly — Trent's block touched it, softening the ball for Tui to dig with his hands from area-six — Skylan stood flat-footed and flipped in a lightning-fast transition Front-1-set for Preston — Preston slopped it down to SCVC's court, 5-2. SCVC sided-out after another Casey Takahashi serve, this time passed by Kopenhefer, on a Gap-attack and tool by Vaziri.

After another good pass from Kahiau on Inlow's jump-float, Micah responded with a clean kill to the five-box, 6-3.

Pizutti passed Trent Thompson's serve forward along the net. Micah shuffled over in front of the Middle to block. Schwan launched a D-set overhead to Inlow, giving him an open net.

"Wait!" Coach Pono yelled out from the sideline.

Inlow flew in from the back row and swung — his swing clipped the top of the tape — Trent dug it — Go-set from Skylan — Micah turned it down the line toward the one-box... out!

The next play, Matt Reilly tossed up a topspin-jump-serve. The Hawaiians hadn't seen him use that in Anaheim — shank off of Micah's arms, 6-5 Ka Ulukoa.

"Ace from Reilly!" said the announcer.

Reilly topspin-jump-served again. Tui passed it with his hands, tight to the net — Skylan jousted at the net — then covered himself — Tui stepped in from middle-back and pushed a Go-set to Micah — smooth cut shot, sharp inside the block for a kill.

"Looks like we have ourselves a match!" the announcer added.

The teams traded a few. At 9-7, Schwan jump-floated short to Tui. Pipe-set to Micah. He ripped it and missed the five-box by inches, 9-8.

"Forget that! Pass! Pass!" Coach Pono shouted, tapping his fingers on his forearms.

Same serve from Schwan — same pass from Tui — Go-set — high and hard hit from Tui — soft block — Kopenhefer dig — Go-set — Pizutti swung sharp — out, 10-8. Pizutti waved his hand at Schwan, telling him to push the set out further. Coach Charlie watched on from the end of the bench and shook his head.

Skylan jump-floated Reilly in SCVC's rotation one. Schwan set Inlow on the left and he smashed the Go-attack cross-court off of Kahiau's arms and into the crowd, 10-9.

Apparently, Reilly and Pizutti had switched serving roles in the past months because Pizutti was still using his jump-float-serve. Tui passed it easily with his hands and approached for the Red-set from Skylan. He blasted it sharp, but Schwan's body was in front and lipped the ball — Kopenhefer bump-set to Reilly, who was still on the right from switch blocking with Inlow — he took a blast of his own — but, Skylan dug it — Micah strolled in from middle-back and set to Tui — he chopped the Red-attack cross-court, forcing Schwan to leap out on his chest with one arm to dig it — Kopenhefer bump-set Pizutti on the Pipe. The moment that Pizutti's cross body kill shanked off of Skylan's arms, Kopenhefer took off in laps around his half of the court. The set wasn't halfway over, 10-10. Pizutti served Tui again. Again, Skylan set Tui — he rolled it softly over the block — Schwan kept his feet to make the dig — Kopenhefer set the Pipe with his hands — Pizutti crushed it 20 feet out beyond the end line.

Ka Ulukoa didn't break away. SCVC couldn't gain their first lead. Preston served his standing-float at 16-14. Tui switch-blocked with Skylan while Inlow was in the back row. Schwan set Kopenhefer's pass to Corbett on a Gap-attack — Micah dug it in area-six off the touch by Tui and Kainoa — Skylan bump-set the Red for Tui — his swing rattled the block — down for a kill, 17-14. Head Coach, Jeff Alzina called his first timeout.

On the return, again, Schwan set Gap for Corbett off of Kopenhefer's pass. Tape-swing — Trent dug — tough bump-set — Tui freeball — passed up — Schwan set Inlow, back row D-attack, open net — Micah dug it from middle-back — Skylan faced Tui and set him the Red — tool, 18-14. Tui and Skylan were still switch-blocking when Preston served his third. Kopenhefer passed. Finally, Schwan figured it out. He set Corbett behind his head on the *Back-1-attack in (the much shorter) Skylan's blocking zone. Kill toward area-five, 18-15.

Ka Ulukoa sided-out and scored one more.

"Next! Next!" Coach Pono yelled, although his guys were undamaged at Corbett's frustrated bounce of a Front-1-attack, which made a loud thump, sending the capacity crowd into an uproar. The Hawaiians were in a nice flow.

Inlow prepared to switch block with Reilly, again, to defend better against the likely Red-set to Tui. Micah shanked Pizutti's jump-float and Skylan back pedaled rapidly to rescue it. His save rose straight up into a Red-set that Tui rammed to the one-box — Schwan stuck his palms together and played it overhead with a Tomahawk-dig — Kopenhefer set Reilly on a Red-attack, which sent Kopenhefer in circles around his court for the second time. This time Coach Pono was the observer who shook his head. He called for time.

"Let them take laps around the court and swing all over the place."

His guys drank and chuckled a bit at his imitations of a wild arm-swing.

"We stay here," he continued, showing his low and tight blocking hands, "And we pass," he said, tapping his fingers on his forearm.

The score came to 22-19 before Billy Kopenhefer followed an ace serve on Kahiau with a second serve in the middle of the net, 23-20.

Casey continued his streak of successfully made standing-float-serves. Pizutti passed — Preston stepped over and commit-blocked on the Quick Attack, as he did on every good pass, solo-stuff-blocking Vaziri's Gap-attack to the floor, hard. The crowd oohed at the thunderous block. To them, the set may have felt complete. Ka Ulukoa knew better. Inlow sided-out for SCVC on a Red-attack kill in front of Tui, 24-21. Inlow trotted back to serve. Kahiau passed his jump-float nicely. Skylan ran along the net and flipped up a Front-1-set to Preston, who killed it. Now it was over, 25-21.

Micah opened his palm wide to give each one of his guys a handshake and a hug before the start of set two. Skylan served his jump-float at Pizutti, who followed up a perfect pass with an inside Lob-attack, sharp, for a kill. SCVC took their first lead, 0-1.

They took the second point, too, after Schwan's jump-float developed into Tui being stuffed on the right by Pizutti and Corbett. Then, Schwan scrubbed his second serve in the middle of the net to score for the opponent.

Ka Ulukoa returned to push ahead 4-3. Kopenhefer passed Casey Takahashi's second serve with his hands. Red-set to Inlow, Tui stepped in from middle-back and dug it toward area-four. Micah landed from his block and opened up to bump-set Tui a Pipe. Tui snapped it — Schwan dug it — Kopenhefer set Reilly — he cracked it through the seam in Trent and Preston's block.

"Easy!" Coach Pono yelled as Tui slid in for another dig — Go-set for Micah — swing to the five-box — Pizutti dug it chaotically — Kopenhefer save — Schwan freeball over — Tui quick freeball pass, and Skylan set Trent on the D-attack... What? Why? Trent hit it out deep. Skylan must have been feeling very trusting. Pizutti joined Kopenhefer in a celebration lap.

Tied at four, Kopenhefer served Micah — good pass — Front-1-set to Preston — Pizutti dug — transition Pipe-set to Pizutti — easy tip — Tui scooped — Go-set Skylan — soft roll over the top of the block by Micah — kill. Micah rearranged his shorts and re-tucked his jersey. All of the Ka Ulukoa players wore their jerseys tucked in. Micah was the only one who constantly needed adjusting.

Trent jump-floated a ball that made Pizutti lay out on the court to pass. Overhead Red-set to Inlow — Micah loaded up and crossed his feet over — solo-stuff-block, which bounced back into Inlow's face before going down, 6-4.

Like Pizutti, Reilly left his topspin-jump-serve for a more consistent, yet easier to track, jump-float. At 7-6, Reilly targeted his serve to Micah's platform. A rally ensued, until Skylan used Micah's perfect dig to set Preston a Front-1, and he paint-brushed it out deep. Reilly served Micah again at 7-7. Go-set — Tui chopped it off the block — but Inlow dove to prevent the tool — Schwan set a Pipe off of Inlow's dig — Reilly hit wrist-away at Kahiau — his dig was low and fast, forcing Preston to freeball Skylan's bump-set — Pizutti dug it up, and Schwan, Dump-attack, kill. Kopenhefer circled, 7-8, SCVC in front. Micah platform-passed Reilly's third float-serve — Front-1-set to Preston — Pizutti soft-block — Schwan D-set — Tui soft-block — Skylan dug — Micah ran in from middle-back and fed Tui a Go-set — Tui took aim at the five-box — OUT! Jeff Alzina cheered his players on, 7-9.

A fourth serve to Micah, and another good pass — Go-set to Tui — he hit a play-in at Schwan and Vaziri's block for Kahiau to cover. Skylan bump-set — Tui jumped up with no approach and chopped it to the one-box. Inlow dug — Go-set — Tui slipped and fell — one-on-one with Skylan, Pizutti unloaded. Micah sprayed a dig into his bench. Tui hopped up and ran with Kahiau in pursuit. Tui leaned over the bench and clubbed the ball back for Micah to send over. Micah dangerously freeballed it short, the ball thinly clearing the net. Kopenhefer passed the tape-trickling freeball and Schwan set Pizutti, who finished the Go-set cross-court. Timeout Ka Ulukoa.

Coach Charlie didn't join. He stayed at the end of the bench and closed his eyes, visualizing what he'd seen in the match. Coach Pono allowed his guys to drink water and rest a moment. At a 7-10 SCVC lead, Micah took a fifth jump-float from Matt Reilly. Tui hit down the line on the Go-attack — he was blocked — Kahiau covered — bump-set by Trent — Tui snapped to the one-box — Inlow dug — Schwan Gap-set — Vaziri kill, and 7-11 was the score. The SCVC fans filled the arena with screams of rapture. Matt Reilly's sixth serve drifted to Kahiau. He passed it well. Tui took another Go-set from Skylan, and tipped it short over the block for a kill. He spun his finger in a circle like Coach Pono as he turned to his teammates.

"Let's go. Next play," he mouthed.

Tui readied himself to switch-block with Skylan as Preston served his standing-float. Kopenhefer popped it off his platform to Schwan. Micah did a Matrix-like movement to dig Vaziri's hammered

Back-1-attack over Kainoa's block. The dig shot up to the net and Tui jumped up from area-two and floated a second contact tip over Kopenhefer's head to the five-box for a kill, 9 serving 11. SCVC felt in control, though. They'd found a current and were riding with it.

Down 11-14, Tui jump-floated to SCVC's rotation one. Pizutti shuffled to get it on his platform — overhead Red-set to Pizutti — and a solo-stuff-block by Micah Ma'a, 12-14. Tui delivered the same serve — Front-1-set to Corbett — and a solo-stuff block by Kainoa, 13-14. Tui silently pumped his fist once and walked back to continue. Jump-float at Pizutti — Go-set to Inlow on the left — Trent Thompson crossed over and solo-stuffed it, only it landed six inches out of bounds — tool.

Pizutti trotted to serve, 13-15. A transition error by Pizutti and a transition tool by Micah led to a 15-15 tied score.

A medium pass by Kopenhefer on Casey's second standing-float led to a Red-set for Inlow — Sharp swing — lipped haphazardly by Skylan — one-arm save near the referee stand by Trent — and Tui freeballed over — Corbett knuckled Schwan's Back-1-set 15 feet out of bounds. The Hawaiians regained the lead. Jeff Alzina paced up and down his sideline before calling his first timeout.

A thought came to Coach Charlie and he approached his guys as they sat down to drink water.

"Skylan, Preston, Kainoa: your hits on the Quick Attack aren't getting us kills," he said, bluntly. "For the rest of the match, you guys get up fast and when Skylan sets you, get on top and throw the ball down to the floor. Straight down."

"Er — okay..." Skylan had some questions but chose not to ask them.

Preston and Kainoa shrugged their shoulders and walked back onto the court.

Casey made another standing-float which Pizutti passed up to Schwan. He flipped the ball back to Inlow — one-on-one with Micah — Inlow got dug by Tui at middle-back — Skylan bump-set a Go to Micah — snap to the five-box — Pizutti dug — transition set to Inlow — he crushed the Red-attack to the floor, 16 all.

Tui passed Kopenhefer's serve with his hands, Front-1-set to Preston and he threw it straight down. Inlow stared at the ball as it flew to the floor in front of him. SCVC players and the bench jumped up to demand a lift call from the ref. Inlow was still watching the spot where the ball fell. It was a kill, 17-16.

Trent jump-floated — Pizutti spray — Schwan save — Reilly

crush into the net, 18-16, and SCVC looked rattled. Pizutti corrected with a good pass. Schwan set the Red for Inlow. He hammered around Micah's solo-block — Tui stepped into the seam and dug it, but over the net and Reilly killed the overpass.

Tui gave Skylan a quick hand-pass off of Inlow's float. Go-set to Micah — short roll over the block — Pizutti dove in from middle-back and dug it back over the net — quick freeball dig by Tui — Preston jumped up quickly for the Front-1-attack and tapped it down. Once again, Inlow followed with his eyes as his body rested still, 19-17.

Micah topspin-jump-served and Pizutti passed it tight (opportunity to break the set open). Schwan jousted Tui, and won, 19-18.

"Ooh!" the crowd encouraged as the ball hit Ka Ulukoa's court.

Kahiau stepped in aggressively to take Reilly's jump-float with his hands. Go-set — Tui ripped it through the two-person block — Reilly dug it over toward his bench — Schwan backpedaled and set Inlow for a D-attack — Tui didn't block — Preston did — tool for Inlow, tied up at 19.

Reilly served a jump-float to Micah's platform — Go-set — short roll over the block by Tui — Pizutti scooped it from area-four — Dump-attack by Schwan — Micah slid in from middle-back to pop it up — Go-set — Tui hit to the five-box — Kopenhefer dug — Schwan Gap-set to Vaziri — kill off of Kahiau! SCVC regained the lead.

Each team earned a sideout, 20-21. Vaziri served a jump-float, allowing Kahiau to pass a gem. An exceedingly quick, flat-footed Front-1-set by Skylan was delivered to Kainoa, who tapped it over and down while Inlow watched it hit the court in front of him for a third time that set. The fans hung on the edge of their bleacher seats.

Skylan served a crisp ball that knuckled left into the seam between Pizutti and Reilly. Pizutti stumbled trying to track it, but passed it well. Tui, Kainoa, and Trent all jumped and triple-blocked Corbett's Front-1-attack. The block sped to the floor; however, Ian Schwan dove out with one arm to cover it, a few feet high. Billy Kopenhefer dropped down and bump-set his Setter's save. His attempt at a Red-set sailed over the net.

Tui followed it and calmly said, "Out," as the ball landed on his line and in. Kopenhefer took off on a lap, 21-22 SCVC.

Tui received Schwan's jump-float, as well as the Red-set from Skylan, and tipped it short over the block for a kill.

Tui, then, served Pizutti cross-court. Schwan gave the Front-

1-set to Corbett and he tipped it cross-body. The arena was silent for a brief moment as Skylan dove in to Pancake-dig Corbett's tip. Tui bolted in from middle-back and set Micah, who slapped the ball off of Pizutti and Corbett's tightly sealed block for a tool, 23-22. Jeff Alzina called his last timeout.

Out of the timeout, half the crowd broke into a chant, "SC! - VC! - SC! - VC!"

Tui jump-floated Pizutti, accurately. Pizutti got the Red-set from Schwan and blasted around Micah's solo block. Tui extended his left arm for a nice one-arm dig, but it sailed out of the end zone, 23-23.

Pizutti took his turn at the service line. Jump-float — Kahiau received it with his hands — Go-set — Micah aimed for the five-box, but tooled Corbett's left hand instead, 24-23. Match point.

Casey dribbled the ball at the service line, looking nervous enough to pee his pants. His standing-float sailed over the net and into Kopenhefer's platform. A Red-set to Inlow and a sharp kill took the set to extra points, 24-24.

Kopenhefer jump-floated short. Trent stepped in and passed it medium — Go-set to Micah — he took an identical swing to his last and tooled Vaziri's left hand, 25-24. Second match point.

Trent jump-floated — Pizutti passed — Inlow attacked Schwan's Red-set... and tooled Micah's reaching hands.

Coach Pono yelled, "Selfish! Selfish!"

Coach Charlie chuckled behind his mustache.

Inlow journeyed to the back row. Tui passed Inlow's jump-float to Skylan's forehead. Front-1-set to Preston — he threw it down — Inlow dove in for his first Quick-Attack-dig of the set — gorgeous Pipe-set from Schwan — and Pizutti fanned it wrist-away, 10 feet out of bounds to his right, 26-25.

Micah lifted his toss off his hand and drove his topspin-jump-serve deep. Pizutti lifted a leg up to pass it. Schwan ran along the net and set over the top of Vaziri to Reilly on the left. One-on-one with Skylan, he smacked it hard — soft-block — Micah dug from middle-back — the dig was perfect — and Skylan jumped... Set-over. All six SCVC players froze... Kill!

Trent, Preston, and Kainoa opened their arms for a group hug with Skylan. Tui sprinted over to Micah and launched him into the air with his arms. Coach Charlie put on his big black backpack and shook Coach Pono's hand, until Coach Pono pulled him in for a hug.

After coming through the line of hand slaps with SCVC, Coach Pono wrapped his son up in his arms and cradled his head. Auntie Maile passed through the pack of media and reporters onto the court to give her gratitude to Coach Pono and Coach Charlie. She then located her son, last, and bear hugged him like she'd never let go.

As the dust settled, the guys took a seat on their bench. Skylan thought about the emotion of winning that. He never thought it would be possible. It felt to him like winning 12 & Under all over again. Tui reminisced about 14 & Under, the year he fully committed to the belief in the system, that if any player got put on his team with Coach Pono and Coach Charlie's coaching, then they would be able to win a match. It was proven over the test of time. Micah sat and thought about what was for dinner.

Skylan and Kainoa were awarded their first All-Tournament Team achievements. Joining them was Micah Ma'a. Tui was named the Tournament MVP.

Coach Charlie brought the guys together and told them, "I was going to buy you all dinner regardless of winning or losing. You trained focused, and I am proud. Get to the hotel and put on whatever you've got. I'm taking you all out for a steak dinner."

The last ball dropping at Junior Olympics in a player's 11th-grade season granted NCAA programs a chance to talk face-to-face with players, away of their college campuses. College coaches swarmed the lot of unsigned players they'd kept their eyes on throughout the tournament. Ironically, Skylan's show of versatility propelled the interest of USC, UCLA, and Grand Canyon University into notable discussions about his future with their programs as a Libero.

Pono and Charlie branched off while Auntie Maile waited for the guys in the arena.

Pono smiled as he thought: *In Anaheim, the team played into SCVC's style and it was the death of their streak.*

Coach Charlie smiled back at Pono, with his own thought: *In Reno, SCVC changed into Ka Ulukoa's style. First Pizutti, then Reilly, and finally Vaziri, discarded their topspin-jump-serves to present Ka Ulukoa the serves they were accustomed to. They got careful. That ultimately allowed his team to keep a streak of theirs alive.*

"Wow, Coach, the feeling is sweet," Pono said as he walked with Charlie. "We reached the finals with a rag-tag team of five new players, and two of our three core guys played out of position."

"It's a proud time, Pono," Coach Charlie said, looking up with softness in his eyes. "It made sense why we spent so many years training complete players."

Pono's phone rang.

"Hello?"

"Hi, Coach Pono! Guy and Julie Enriques, here. We were following the tournament online and just saw the results! Big Mahalos and congrats! Evan is going to be so happy."

"Thanks for calling, Guy and Julie. Aloha!" Pono hung up the phone.

As he began to speak again to Charlie, his phone rang.

"It's Maile," said Pono. "Hey, Maile."

"Hey, Coach Pono. It's Sky. Will you put Coach Charlie on the phone?"

Pono handed the phone to Charlie.

"It's for you."

"Charlie, here."

"Oh, hey, Coach Charlie. It's Sky. I just wanted to tell you, the moment you introduced *The Precious Present* — that was the manual to winning — making the best play possible. Thank you."

"Aloha, Skylan."

Coach Charlie hung up the phone.

Chapter 26 - Without You

One week later, Pono sat with Lisa at the breakfast table during a sunny morning in Kaneohe. They were awaiting the arrival of Mike Among. To show his appreciation for taking over his guys' practices before JOs, Pono had invited Mike over for breakfast. All of Pono and Lisa's kids were gone from the house. It was a morning of relaxation.

"Howzit going, my man?" Mike asked as Pono opened the front door.

Pono smiled at his college teammate and pulled him inside.

"Hey there, Lisa," Mike said as he sat down at the table.

"Hell of a run you had up there in Reno, Pono."

"Much appreciation," said Pono. "Thanks for helping out with Mehana this season, too."

Mike cut in, "No seriously, Pono. Braddah, what you and Charlie did with the guys up there was special."

Coach Pono's expression faded a bit serious.

"You know, Mike — we were shooting past championships."

Lisa looked over from the stove and smiled at her husband's remarkable words to Mike. Mike could tell. *Pono has big picture stuff in mind for these players when he's chasing these championships*, Mike thought.

Three weeks passed and Evan returned to the Big Island after leaving Mexico and traveling straight to Oregon to coach camps with his dad. Around the same time, Skylan returned home with his mom from a week of USA High Performance with the Aloha Region Team. It was an opportunity for his college recruiters to watch him play Libero for a few days. Arlene wept as they left the tournament.

"Don't cry, Mom," Skylan pleaded. "After Reno, and then this, it's the first time in volleyball that I feel good enough. I'm content."

Skylan's dad had unsettling news for Arlene and his son upon their return.

"Er — Skylan, tuition has gone up too high at Maryknoll. So, you won't be attending there anymore."

"What? But Dad, it's my last year of high school."

Arlene added, "We waited until after your tournament to tell you. We set up summer school for you to prepare."

"Prepare for what?" Skylan asked angrily.

Dave said, "You'll be transferring to Moanalua High School."

Tui and Micah were a month deep into summer football practice at Punahou. The Punahou Football double-days kept the majority of Micah's time away from the beach. But anytime that he got a weekend away, he caught the bus straight down to The Outrigger. After losing in the state championship the past two seasons, Tui wanted his focus to be on the football field, leaving nothing to chance. Micah was in stride to start at Wide Receiver for his 11th-grade year, so Tui baited his attention to football too, claiming that he'd throw to Micah often.

Pono got volleyball back on his son's mind when he told him that Evan had just called and confirmed that he'd be coming back to Ka Ulukoa for the 18 & Under season. Micah was stoked, and he made sure that Tui knew right away.

Evan said during a phone conference, "Braddahs, I pass through Oahu during my recruiting trips in September. If you really love me, you'll come see me at the airport."

"Er — I guess we don't love you," Tui said sarcastically.

"Where are you visiting, anyway?" Micah asked.

"UH when I come to Oahu. USC, Stanford, and UCLA when I go to the Mainland."

Tui said, "We all gotta play together in college," insinuating that Evan should choose UH.

"We'll see!" Evan teased.

Each of them resumed school for his 12th-grade year in high school, other than Micah, who was beginning 11th grade. It was Tui and Micah at Punahou, Evan at Kamehameha Hawai'i, and Skylan at his new school, Moanalua. It was an exciting time for Evan, even after his first USA Volleyball experience internationally and before his college visits. Evan was entering his final year of high school with Emmett, Addie, and Avery by his side. Addie and Avery Enriques were accepted to the high school at Kamehameha Hawai'i, which meant Guy Enriques might have his hands full on the volleyball court. Rascals.

Skylan encountered a surprise at school when he ran into Austin Amian. Like Skylan, he was a student at Moanalua. Austin still played, yet chose not to bring up volleyball in his short conversation with his old teammate. The primary task on which Skylan concentrated was keeping a low profile, while still making new friends. He didn't want kids to think that he was into himself because of what he'd accomplished in extracurricular activities outside of school. He remembered the feeling from Maryknoll, and it was the last thing he wanted to manage during his closing year of high school.

Tui stayed true to his word at Punahou Football. He targeted his 11th-grade Wide Receiver more often than any other player. Micah made the most of it, too, pulling in more catches and touchdowns than anyone else on their squad. Punahou glided to a traditional unblemished start against their first four league opponents.

Evan departed the Big Island for the first of his four collegiate official visits. He crossed the Pacific Ocean to Los Angeles International Airport and took a ride straight over to USC's campus near downtown LA.

I was working as an assistant coach at USC and met Evan there on his visit. His official was overnight with two other players we had on campus. He had a lot of questions for me, concerning my college days at the University of California at Irvine. Our USC head coach really wanted this kid. I knew why. We offered him about 50 percent of a full-ride scholarship, which would have been high for a potential Outside Hitter who would likely end up playing Libero. It was high for a player of any position, actually, considering that NCAA Men's Volleyball Programs only had 4.5 scholarships in total.

Evan had more visits to take and cruised down the highway to UCLA in its own tucked away corner of LA, called Westwood. Like USC, it had a cherished history and a bitter crosstown rivalry. They had the most NCAA Men's Volleyball Championships in history, with 19. Most of those came over the 50-year career of head coach, Al Scats. He had retired a season earlier and UCLA had a new leader named John Speraw. Speraw's staff spoke and Evan logged the info in his mind during his two-day official visit. Both LA campuses were beautiful. Both programs were consistent title contenders. The most important information for Evan to leave UCLA with was how comparable the scholarship offer was to USC. He felt a duty to help take a financial load off of his parents.

After four days of official visits, Evan took a plane over to Northern California and drove to Palo Alto, the home of Stanford University. The culture was rich there and they had a long history of taking good care of volleyball players from Hawai'i. That was something Evan enjoyed. They were also title contenders and were unsure if Evan's role would be as an Outside Hitter, as a Libero, or both. Evan again took in the experience, while at the same time keeping his ears open for how the financial package would compare.

Two days later, the University of Hawai'i hosted him fourth. The staff showed him a lot that he'd already seen growing up, and the players he knew the majority of as well. By the end of the visit, he decided that his biggest attraction to UH was Tui being committed there. Although he did want to play with Tui and Micah in college, UH's highest appeal being his teammate's company was not enough influence. Evan put in a phone call to Tui at Honolulu Airport.

"Hello?" Tui answered.

"Braddah, I see you didn't come see me. I'm at the airport, leaving Oahu in an hour."

"Oh, you'll be fine. I know it's hard for you not to see me," Tui teased. "How'd they go, though? You're gonna pick UH, huh?" His voice was optimistic.

"Tui — HA! — Bad news for ya, Hawaiian. It's not gonna be UH." He waited for a reaction — nothing. "It's not gonna be UCLA either."

Evan decided that his route would lie between USC and Stanford.

The guys were settled into their school lives and summer break was a distant thought by the time Lee Lamb's tryout meeting for Ka Ulukoa rolled around that fall. Lee continued his praises from the Ka Ulukoa Luau about how well the club had grown, not just in the community, but also nationally. There was no tryout for Coach Pono and Coach Charlie's 18 & Under. Eight players stood from Lee Lamb's meeting and ventured to the furthest court. Skylan Engleman, Larry Tuileta Junior, Micah Ma'a, Trent Thompson, Preston Kamada, Kainoa Quindica, Kahiau Machado, and Casey Takahashi were all present. Without a word of hesitation to Coach Pono's usual offer of auditioning elsewhere, all eight committed.

Punahou Football kept their winning streak in league alive. They made a return appearance to the State Tournament; therefore, Tui and Micah stopped attending even the evening Ka Ulukoa trainings to shag balls. The two of them locked into football. Ka Ulukoa training stayed with five players regularly — four players if someone had senior pictures or a makeup assignment at school, to ensure graduating. The system didn't change. Skylan stayed in the Setter position and Coach Charlie worked with him on adding some speed into his sets and jump setting for better tempo. The five newbies, who were no longer Ka Ulukoa rookies, put their work into improving ball control and volleyball IQ.

Punahou Football reached the state championship, against Mililani High School. Tui and Micah played well in the championship on the University of Hawai'i at Manoa football field — well enough to break over the hump and win the trophy.

"That's what I'm talkin' about!" Micah yelled to Tui as they walked toward the bus to head back to school.

"Yeah, man! Great game, Tui! Way to lead us!" their teammates shouted, walking by patting his head and slapping his back.

Tui smiled. It was a good feeling to end the cycle of losing the last football game of the season. And then suddenly, Tui fainted and collapsed.

Chapter 27 - Only One

The head football coach burst through the commotion and ran to Tui's sprawled out body. A collection of Punahou parents hurried and called 9-1-1. An ambulance arrived and rushed him to the emergency room. Auntie Maile showed up in a panic with her eyes bloodshot from crying. She got the news on her speed over to the hospital. Tui's collapse on the grass outside of the bus was the result of a concussion he had suffered during the game. Tui was going to be out of athletic competition for at least a few weeks. Auntie Maile led her son out of the hospital and gave him a big hug at the door.

Tui said to his mom, "I think it's time for a change. I'm going to cut my hair."

In combination with starting Punahou Varsity Basketball, Micah was responsible for returning to participation in Ka Ulukoa trainings. While Evan was on the Big Island and Tui was recovering from his concussion, Micah executed his hitting attempts and serve receptions as an Outside Hitter. Coach Pono and Coach Charlie reintroduced the skills, briefly. By then, the players could run the drills like clockwork. Everyone awaited Tui and Evan's returns.

Evan made it back to town for the Christmas break, just as Tui was cleared to play. The team had a club practice the same night that Evan arrived to the airport and Micah decided to show off the vertical he'd been increasing, before his dad and Coach Charlie pushed him back into setting full-time. During *Quick Hitter Timing*, Micah approached in for a Go-set from Skylan and smashed it sharp cross-court, inside of the 10-foot line. He transitioned and approached in again for an inside Lob-set and bounced it straight down off the 10-foot line, almost up to the ceiling. Coach Pono's faced turned bright red as he walked toward the court to yank his son.

"WHAT THE FR —"

Very out of character, Coach Charlie chuckled and held back Coach Pono.

"Hang on. Maybe we could use some variety," Coach Charlie said, thoughtfully. "Micah is better being who he is. Give him a little leash."

Coach Pono reluctantly stayed back. Evan and Tui acted unimpressed. Trent and Preston didn't. None of them were brave enough to try the same in front of the coaches.

"That was some nice hitting in there, Ficus," Evan antagonized Micah on the car ride to Kaneohe.

Coach Pono held his tongue while the hairs on his neck stood up.

"I mean, really. I wish I could fly in and bounce like that," Evan instigated.

Micah shined a goofy closed-lip smile to Evan, thinking better of taking Evan's bait.

"Brah, Tui told me you decided no on UH," Micah remembered.

"Oh, yeah. How did your visits go, Evan?" asked Coach Pono.

"Pretty well, I would say. I think I got my choice down to USC or Stanford."

"Both good schools," said Coach Pono.

"Yeah, but we were all supposed to play together!" Micah said selfishly.

"By the way," Coach Pono cut in, "UH guys are going to come and scrimmage next week before the qualifier."

"Okay, shoots!" Evan and Micah shouted together.

Evan flowed right back into the system. As the time to scrimmage came the following week, the volleyball inside of the Ka Ulukoa facility took on the feel of being back to normal. The University of Hawai'i team was around the island over the holiday break to prepare for the NCAA season beginning in January. Everyone slapped hands and finished their warm-up time. UH lined up a star-studded group: 6'0" Joby Ramos at Setter, 6'5" All-American Brooke Sedore at Opposite, 6'7" All-American Taylor Averill at M1, 6'9" Davis Holt at M2, 6'7" Jace Olsen at OH2, 6'6" JP Marks at OH1, as well as 6'4" and 6'5" UH Outside Hitters, Kupono Fey and Scott Hartley, who slotted themselves as Liberos.

Unlike a season ago, the Ka Ulukoa players didn't show fear. They didn't back down in the least. Although the UH group won during all three of the sets that the teams played, Ka Ulukoa kept pace. In fact, it was quite comical how effective the quick freeball pass was against the college guys. It was amusing to watch Averill and Holt become confused about which direction to block and pop up and down at the net before Skylan touched the ball to set.

Pono said to Charlie on the way out, "Our guys looked good, Coach."

"Good thing. This will be the toughest year," Charlie replied.

Skylan waited to hear more from USC and UCLA. Meanwhile, he scheduled his official visit with Grand Canyon University before the start of the SCVA Invitational. So this time, it was Skylan who left the team two days early to fly to Arizona for his first official visit. GCU was an NCAA Division II school, prepared to make its jump into Division I before Skylan's freshman season. He enjoyed that GCU had a religious culture and a community of Polynesian students, even a minority from Hawai'i.

They liked Skylan's skill and development, a lot. They offered him within the first hour of stepping on campus. A 25 percent scholarship was the deal, 10 percent volleyball, and 15 percent academic. Skylan took the night to discuss it with his family and weigh his options. By the morning, Skylan was verbally committed. With blessings from his mother and best wishes from his father, Skylan flew to Orange County, California a happy student-athlete. *The only thing more relieving than committing will be when I sign in April,* he thought.

All of his teammates greeted him with excitement and hugs as Skylan gave them the news at the Anaheim house.

"Got it done, Brah? Congrats, Sky Man," Tui said seriously, giving Skylan a big hug.

"Yeah, boy! Big congratulations!" Evan hollered. "What they gonna have you doing? Passing dimes or setting butter?"

"I think I will play Libero," said Skylan. "But ya know — who knows?" He looked over at Coach Pono, who was still smiling brightly.

"What time are we going to the American Sports Center tonight, Dad?" Micah asked.

"We aren't playing at the Sports Center this tournament, guys. They have everyone over at the Anaheim Convention Center. But, 7pm. We'll get over there at 7pm."

"What? So you mean we aren't going to see our parking lady?" Micah stared at his dad with the look of a boy lost from his parents in the grocery store.

Auntie Maile chuckled, "I'm sure you'll live, Micah."

"No, I'm not sure I will," Micah replied dramatically.

The Anaheim Convention Center was chilly in the evening. The venue reminded the guys of Junior Olympics. Sixty tiled courts laid down on concrete, divided up into three large halls. In the two trainings that Ka Ulukoa held before the start of the tournament, Micah only took a few setting repetitions. If any problems arose, then Trent could sub in front row for Skylan and have Micah set in the back. But Micah proved himself as an offensive weapon in Reno, as did Skylan as a Setter, and with Evan back alongside the team, it was the perfect recipe to have

Micah pass and hit as an Opposite. He was feeling a new swagger to his game. That was illustrated by his bravery to show off his flashy offensive capabilities in front of his dad and Coach Charlie.

Walking out of the second evening of training, Micah wrapped his arms around Tui and Evan's shoulders and said, "We are going to *go off* on them if someone says something cocky." Then he smashed his fist into his palm.

"Right — just stick to your Kendama, Ficus," Evan insisted. "Where is your Kendama today, anyway?"

"Yeah, chill, Micah," Tui added. "And Brah, why are you always wearing pajamas?"

"Right he-" Micah detached himself from pulling out his Kendama to look down at his plaid checkered fleece pajama pants.

"Come on! I always wear these, fool. These are my thing, and super comfortable."

"Freakin' rascal, this guy," Tui said to Evan, flipping his thumb like a hitchhiker at Micah's pants.

The next morning, Skylan walked into the kitchen first. He smiled at the site of what was on the table.

"Oh man — Auntie Maile — I missed this!"

"I did, too, Sky. Go wake up your teammates so we aren't late. It's gonna be a headache to park over there at the convention center."

Skylan did what she asked and the guys slowly filed out into the kitchen to a table full of Auntie Maile's Breakfast of Champions. Skylan flew in from Arizona, so he'd almost forgotten that he gave Auntie Maile his rice and spam at the scrimmage against the UH players. The guys took their time with their breakfast. After what happened with the housing in Reno, they weren't sure how many more times they'd get to experience it. As they finished, they opened their backpacks to check for jerseys and shoes; they grabbed their water jugs, and left the house for day one.

Auntie Maile was right. It took an extra 20 minutes to find the parking structure to the Anaheim Convention Center, located across the street from Disneyland. Auntie Maile rolled down the window and Micah's attitude came back sharply when he saw a man wearing black sunglasses taking the cash to enter.

"We should have just walked from a couple blocks away like we did for training," Micah said bitterly.

"It would be hard with the cooler, Micah. Relax. Hi, sir. How much is it to park all day?"

The man said, "Twenty-five dollars, ma'am."

Auntie Maile began to feel the way Micah did.

"Twenty-five dollars? Does that come with lunch, too?"

"No ma'am, it doesn't," the man replied seriously.

"I was kidding," Auntie Maile said under her breath as she pulled out 50 dollars for her van and Pono's van behind her.

They pulled off and Micah said, "That guy looked like *An Agent* from *The Matrix*. Miiissster Aaannnderson," he joked.

His teammates chuckled at his comedy show. Auntie Maile slapped his leg to stop playing around.

Coach Charlie was sitting on the bench of their court as the team came in through the back door. He looked at his watch.

"The parking situation is ridiculous here," Coach Pono said. "Anyway, let's get going, guys. We play first."

Day one was smooth, like old times. Kawika and Erik Shoji were in town for the holidays, so they came to watch for a little while at Coach Charlie's request. Coach Pono was thankful to have some options for versatility on the court, which he hadn't had anytime recently. Having Evan back meant that he could play Micah on the left some games and put Tui on the right. He could sub Trent in at Opposite for Skylan and have Micah set while he was back row. The biggest advantage that Coach Pono added for his team after Evan's return was passing with four players. Tui, Evan, Micah, and Kahiau could all pass, so why not? It made the seams smaller and created less work for the hitters to approach after passing. Ka Ulukoa looked fierce. In fact, after they finished their last match of pool play, four young boys from another club came over to their court as Ka Ulukoa took off their shoes.

One said to the group, "Oh my gosh — it's you guys."

Micah broke his gaze from the Kendama in his hand and looked up to see if the boy realized the ridiculousness of his statement.

"Yes. It's us," he said kindly, "whatever that means," he added under his breath.

"And, oh man! It's you. But you cut your hair," another one said, talking to Tui.

"What's up, boys?" Tui asked nicely.

"And who are we?" Skylan asked, curiously.

"You guys are *The Black Death*," said the first boy. "If a team sees that they got you on their pool-play sheet, they already know they are going to lose."

"The WHAT?" Evan asked.

Micah and Skylan were already busting up laughing.

"I think he said, The Black Death." Tui struggled to hold back his laughter.

"Seriously, it's no joke," added the second boy.

Tui gathered himself. By now, Micah and Skylan were both on the floor, laughing.

"Er — uh — thanks, boys — I guess," Tui said. "Aloha."

Micah and Skylan nearly burst into tears of humor every five minutes on the way home because of what they'd just heard.

Already 3-0 from the first day, the Hawaiians walked into the convention center focused, trying for a repeat result on the second. Coach Pono was surprised to see that the third and fourth seeds in the pool didn't give his team much trouble; although, the second seed might. They were a familiar looking group.

My club team changed over to Southern California Volleyball Club as another 18 & Under team in the club, SCVC 18-QS. I scouted the Hawaiians' day one matches hard with my assistant. With Evan back, they were so flexible in their options. Tui lined up as the Opposite and Micah as the OH2 against us. We served first. Our best player, Storm Faagata was at the line. He hit a great serve right at their Libero, who we were targeting. Kahiau passed it decently and Skylan stepped under it to deliver a crisp set without an ounce of spin out to Tui. Tui slapped it high off of our block, 0-1 Ka Ulukoa.

Skylan stepped back to the service line behind area-one. He float served it straight down the line to Alex Albarran, our Opposite from the previous season who had just converted to a serve receiving Outside Hitter. Surprising at the time, Alex passed it perfectly to our Setter, redheaded Cole Kendrick, and we set our Middle on a Front-1. Kainoa commit blocked and stuffed it straight into the floor, 0-2 Ka Ulukoa. Skylan served again, targeting Alex. The served knuckled perfectly off of his hand, clipping the top of the net-tape and trickling over in front of our diving OH2, 0-3 Ka Ulukoa. Our new Libero, Erik Sikes, who'd challenged Evan for a spot on the USA Boys' Youth A1 Team a year prior, pushed our OH2 over to stand on the line. Again Sky served, targeting the same spot. The ball floated near Alex Albarran's right shoulder and our Libero tried to cut it off. He shuffled into a stumble, and sprayed the serve off of his arms over near the antenna in area-two. Our Setter, Cole Kendrick, got his hands on it and gave it to his only option, our newly positioned Opposite, with straight blonde hair and short arms for someone 6'3", Logan Atkinson.

Logan Atkinson hit it as hard as he could, straight away into Tui's solo-block which was awaiting him, 0-4 Ka Ulukoa. The Ka Ulukoa boys never changed their demeanor and Skylan never changed his routine as he served one point after another. Once again, he served the area-five line and our Libero was pushed so far over that he was able to take it. Perfect pass — we finally got the ball to our best player on the back row *Bic-attack (much quicker Pipe-set/attack) and scored, but not without Evan touching it.

Ka Ulukoa received serve with four passers now that they had Evan back, Tui, Kahiau, Evan, and Micah all taking their share of court. Our M2 was able to target Kahiau's sliver of court and we scored on an ace off of his platform. After that play, Kahiau's area of the court started to shrink smaller and smaller. They didn't even have to say anything out loud; Tui and Micah knew what to do. They had gone through this same process the season before at Junior Olympics. Evan knew well, too. He was coming off of a summer as a starting Outside Hitter for the USA BJNT. Although Tui passed our M2's serve right on Skylan's forehead, we were able to score the next point from a commit block on Kainoa. That was short lived.

Ka Ulukoa went on a ten to four run, putting on an absolute ball-control clinic. Digging our open-net back row Bic-attacks — hitting play-ins into our block to get easy, coverable balls back — watching our bad swings sail out of bounds — float-serve acing us in the corner — and there was no doubt that every one of those guys from Hawai'i was ready to set and cover.

To sideout in serve receive, Storm ripped a ball sharp cross-court past Evan's block for a kill. After the play, Skylan bent over and did a push-up on the tile. This is the same kid who, on one play, didn't dive for a ball against us at Junior Olympics (a ball that was highly improbable to dig) and then gently dropped to the floor to do a push-up, while his team was ahead by twelve points. No teammate or coach or parent told him to do it. That's just how these Ka Ulukoa guys were, different — disciplined.

Down 7-14 in the first set, we sided-out again and caught some momentum, winning a rally that changed sides of the net nine times, to put us at 10-14, followed by a high floating ace from our Setter, which landed on the line in area-one to reach 11-14. We scored once more before Ka Ulukoa sided-out to reach 12-15.

Preston hit his standing float serve at our Libero in area-six. Erik Sikes passed it on a dime. Overhead Red-set to our OH1 — cross-court swing — Micah one-arm dug it — Skylan set the back row Pipe to Evan — five-box roll-shot to our Libero — the ball was dug well to our Setter

— Front-1-attack from our M2 — off of Kainoa's hands — Micah dove and dug it — Skylan overhead set Evan, who'd wrapped around for the back row D-attack — our Libero stepped in on the tough swing to make a medium-dig — we overhead set a Red to Storm Faagata — Evan dug it with his hands — the back row D-attack from Micah rattled in our block — a quick cover by Kainoa turned into Skylan setting a high Go-set to Tui — Tui snapped the ball into our block and covered himself — Skylan set Tui again — a little harder this time, he hit into our block — Skylan covered — Micah stepped in to set — Tui got it a third time — my team yelled, "OUT!" as our defensive specialist, Connor Freeman, ducked the ball that Tui hit over our block and behind the end line, 13-15 Ka Ulukoa.

A few points went by, and then Micah topped my favorite swing of his from the season before. With Ka Ulukoa in front 13-17, Micah rose up in transition and hit a Go-attack clean over our Opposite and M2, which smacked the area-five corner where the end line and the sideline meet (five-box). It was beautiful. We had to have a change. I subbed our Opposite out for his replacement. We were hanging in there.

With Ka Ulukoa still ahead 15-19, I subbed in my fourth-year captain, Ryan Bahadursingh, to serve. From area-one, he served a line-drive to their area-five that forced a dive from Micah in order to pass it. Skylan bump-set overhead to Tui, who snapped it into Alex's solo-block, straight down. My team was ready to turn and celebrate as Tui dropped to a knee after his own swing and swiped the ball up with his left fist before it could touch the ground. Skylan dove in on the two-foot-high cover and popped up a set with his right fist — Tui set it over. Our serving sub, Ryan Bahadursingh, passed the freeball and we ran a Bic-set, so low that Storm Faagata was forced to tip it over. Skylan dug the tip to Tui, who was blocking on the right side in area-two. Tui gave Evan the back row Pipe-set — Evan snapped into our three-person block, landed, dove, and covered it with his left arm before rolling in a circle — Tui set the low covered ball to Micah on the left side. He ripped it off the top of our blockers' hands and it hung in the air, falling into the waiting hands of our Setter. An overhead dig to Ryan Bahadursingh transitioned to a side-set to our OH2 — one-on-one — Alex Albarran hit a hard driven swing down the line around Tui — Skylan dug it off of his chest — Evan stepped in to Red-set for Tui on the right side — Tui controlled the swing into our three-person block for Kainoa to cover — Skylan set the Go-attack for Micah, which he tooled off of our M1 out of bounds for the — wait... The ball clipped Micah's jersey on the way out, our point! Is that what we had to do to score against those guys?

We were trading points, closing in at 18-21. Connor Freeman

served for our OH2. This was our best defensive rotation. He targeted Kahiau in the serve receive line but Micah stepped in from area-one and passed it with his hands. Our M1 took a shuffle to his right toward Preston's Gap-attack and the more likely Go-attack to Evan. Skylan flipped Micah's pass back over his head for a Red that Micah was in a nice rhythm to attack. My defenders locked in for the blast off or around Storm Faagata's one-on-one block. Micah duplicated my favorite swing of his from the previous season, this time on the right side. He snapped the ball fast, just inside of Storm Faagata's arms, and it rolled right over the tape to the 10-foot line for the kill. Micah watched it hit the floor and calmly pointed at Skylan before touching hands and walking back to serve. I was admiring while I was trying to beat them.

Down 20-23, our Setter served an ace down the area-one sideline. The match was heating up and the chairs had filled in the crowd. There was only room to stand and watch from behind the seats. Cole Kendrick served again. Evan passed the line-drive serve — Skylan set Preston on the Front-1 — he hit it cross-body toward area-one — Cole Kendrick dug it off of his chest into the net. Landing from his block, Storm Faagata reacted quickly in right-front area-four to pop the ball back into the net. Our M2, Kyle Radecki, bumped the third contact at a sharp angle to get it over the net. His bump sat on the top of the tape for a moment as the crowd said, "OH!" It eventually trickled over to Ka Ulukoa's side and Skylan played it up. Micah entered from the back row to set and sneakily set it over on two, trying to score. Kyle Radecki reacted at the net and popped it straight up in the air. Storm Faagata ran in to joust against Preston for the 50/50 ball as it drifted back on Ka Ulukoa's side. Preston covered himself to Micah who was waiting to set Tui on the left side. Tui swung high off our blocker's hands and the ball fell over area-one for Cole Kendrick to dig. Erik Sikes overhead bump-set to Storm Faagata on left front. He snapped it low into the hands of Skylan and Preston. Kyle Radecki covered off of his shoulder, and our replacement Opposite stepped in and set Storm Faagata again. 'Boom!' He killed it one-on-one against Skylan to the floor, 22-23 Ka Ulukoa. Cole Kendrick served Evan, and Tui ripped Skylan's Go-set down the line for the kill, 22-24.

Set point Ka Ulukoa. Preston served Storm Faagata in area-one and Kyle Radecki killed the Front-1-set from our Setter, 23-24.

Set point again. Storm Faagata jump served and missed long by three feet.

In set two, we got hot early. After being down 2-4, we strung together a nice run of points; targeting Kahiau and taking some nice out-

of-system swings in transition, we went on top by four.

We traded points to stay ahead 10-6 after a pass and area-five corner hit by Storm Faagata.

We led 12-7 following Erik Sikes digging Preston's Front-1-attack tip and a successful Red-attack kill from our Opposite.

After the Bic-attack from Storm Faagata, we lead 13-8.

Evan answered, 13-9, and then served.

Good pass — we set the back row D-attack to our Opposite — no blockers were up and Logan Atkinson hammered it over the open-net — Kahiau dug it — the ball sailed across the court toward Coach Pono on the bench and Tui chased — he popped it up and Micah ran from area-six to send it over — Erik Sikes dug — Cole Kendrick set the Bic-attack to Storm Faagata and he hit it out, but off of Kainoa's hands, 14-9 us. We felt it. That was our chance to close the set and extend the match.

Logan Atkinson served his float and Micah passed in front of Kahiau — Skylan set over on two — Erik Sikes dove and popped it up with the Pancake-dig — Logan dove and touched it with his right arm — Erik Sikes, who was still on the ground, army crawled 12 inches to punch it over the net. (We were working really hard and playing well.) While Storm Faagata was flailing his arms in area-six to cheer the hard work of our team, the play wasn't over yet. Micah used Ka Ulukoa's infamous quick freeball pass to Skylan, who set up Tui for the Go-attack. Before our blockers got balanced, or Storm Faagata got his feet back on the ground, Tui smashed the ball into the area-five corner for the kill.

Coach Pono and The Guru's team stayed patient and within their system, while we became impatient and started to do more and tried to take the points terminally, rather than letting them come to us. We had played so well to that point, but Ka Ulukoa didn't stray their course. We lead 16-12 in the second set before the Hawaiians completed a thirteen to three run to close the match. I was so frustrated. We had prepared and we had studied. I had thought we were ready.

Ka Ulukoa's day was over. They were into the quarterfinals.

The guys hadn't played their toughest challenge. The quarterfinal match didn't provide that either. The hype was already two days old, even before Ka Ulukoa walked from the hallway back into the convention center for their 11:30am semifinal, which was staggered with Balboa Bay 18s versus Baja 18s' 10:30 am semifinal. Balboa Bay hadn't been the talk of the town in Southern California, as of late. Nor was the talk about SCVC 18-Quicksilver, or SCVC 18-QS, or MB Surf, or

Coast. Just the potential meeting of the two teams that were about to meet in that tournament was enough to lure spectators, who hadn't planned on attending the tournament, from their homes. Now that the potential had become a reality, the crowd assembled even before the warmup began. Anyone arriving on time was lucky to find a place to stand with a half-decent view of the court. Before the opponent secured their Junior Olympics 18 Open Division Bid in the quarterfinals, the semifinals match that was about to happen was seen as a once in a lifetime opportunity. Why?

It was the match that every California volleyball fanatic had anticipated for months. The next powerhouse team from the Mainland to take their shot at the historical Ka Ulukoa was The HBC 17-Black, who had spent the season playing up a division. They had just come off of winning their first 18 & Under tournament at the SCVA Holiday Classic three weeks prior.

The HBC 17s from Huntington Beach, California were an impressive group. Their Libero, Blake Diamond, had a smooth look to him. His jet-black hair was slicked back away from his forehead. His shiny silver uniform top had a hard contrast to everyone else's Oakland-Raiders-black jerseys. A 6'5" Polynesian Middle rose up from the bench with the biceps of an NFL (National Football League) linebacker and the mean mug of one, too. Kimball was the name — just Kimball. The HBC started a much smaller, 5'9" M2. He was also Polynesian, with a full-grown mustache. He was small, but had the ball control that may as well have slotted him in the Libero position, Wellington Afusia. At OH2, Blake Markland, was a 6'3" blonde-haired California boy from Manhattan Beach, with a *hit hard or go home* mentality. At Opposite, they started a 6'3" left-hander, also blonde, Ben Vaught. He was developed nicely from playing a good amount of Orange County beach volleyball.

However, he also had a gem of a Setter. They had Josh Tuaniga, the previous summer's USA Boys' Youth National Team Setter. He was a strong Samoan boy, about 6'2" with hands as big as Micah's. His weapons began before he touched the ball to set in a rally. His jump float serve scored the most aces of any float server in even the 18 & Under division. From anywhere away from the net he could push the ball, super fast, back into system, and he used his dominant left hand to attack on two, causing defenders all sorts of trouble.

The most important member of their team, standing beside Tuaniga, was fellow USA Boys' Youth National Team member, and the best high school Outside Hitter in the country (of any division), Torey James DeFalco. He stood 6'4" with a dark tan from the hours and miles he'd put on his body while playing on the beach. His arm-swing was initiated from a lightning-like shoulder, which absolutely punished his serves and spikes. He had the patience and court awareness of a veteran of the USA Men's National Team at only 17 years old. All season, every young boy in the gym made sure to stop by the HBC 17s warmup to see TJ DeFalco approach on open net Lob-sets from Tuaniga and bounce them to the tallest ceilings in California. The thump of his swing was easily recognized in any gym, even 20 or 30 courts away.

Evan and Tui thought it would be amusing to softly roll and stroke their swings to the one-box and five-box during the entire *Quick Hitter Timing* warm-up. As he kept setting them, Skylan noticed quickly and found it amusing, too. Micah wasn't as gracious to the volleyball. He had five seasons of pent-up smacks to take out on the ball, so he didn't hold back in his warmup.

The court was packed. Referees throughout the arena had "technical delays" and paused their matches as kids rushed off to stand on chairs to see over the heads capacitating Court 2. Both teams slapped hands without a single grin. Ka Ulukoa wrapped shoulders and touched the tips of their shoes in the huddle through Micah's prayer.

The HBC circled up in a huddle and took the attention of the entire gym, as they always did, chanting at the top of their lungs, "THE - H – B – C! THE – H – B – C!"

The HBC 17s were the bad boys of club volleyball. They'd earned their reputation, instilling intimidation into every opponent with their hard-hitting style and flashy defensive plays. They had earned their respect, winning 15 Open and 16 Open during the two previous Junior Olympics, without dropping a set. They just skipped over 17 & Under and qualified in the semifinals to earn their bid to the 18 & Under division for JOs in Houston. The HBC 17s were better than good.

Chapter 28 - Graduation

Although the winner was going to the finals of the SCVA Invitational to play against Balboa Bay 18s, who'd just finished the first semifinal, to the audience, this match was the finale. The fans got what they came for that day. Both teams stayed even early on as Ka Ulukoa executed their normal style and DeFalco made spectacular digs which translated to kills from Tuaniga's ability to create consistent one-on-one attacks for his Hitters. There was something interesting, though. The HBC 17s' matches were generally filled with chanting, taunting, victory laps, and loud celebrations in which their large following of fans participated. That was not so, in the match against Ka Ulukoa. Other than some claps when The HBC would sideout, the match was quiet and there was limited noise between points. Perhaps The HBC 17s were trying a new kind of focus to reach the new goal of beating the six-time Junior Olympics Champions.

Ka Ulukoa pulled out to a 13-6 lead. The HBC 17s stormed back to take the lead at 20-21 before Evan tied it at 21.

In serve receive, DeFalco took a sharp cross-court kill off of Tuaniga's fast Go-set, 21-22.

A tip from Evan transitioned to another dig and kill from DeFalco, 21-23. On the next play, The HBC soft-blocked Evan — DeFalco dug it, killed it, and threw his fist in the air, 21-24. TJ DeFalco was showing his worth. Coach Pono called a timeout.

I watched The Guru drop to his knee as the boys drank water. He flipped his right palm over his left fist to the east and to the west. I was locked in on him, so curious what he was saying.

His players looked at him confidently. Out of the break, Ka Ulukoa sided-out. At the service line, Micah hit his topspin-jump-serve. DeFalco got the Go-set and wiped the ball off of Evan's block — it stayed in bounds and The HBC Libero, Blake Diamond, covered it — DeFalco got the set again — Evan soft-blocked him one-on-one — Tui popped it up with his palm in Kahiau's direction — Kahiau set the Pipe for Tui — Tui got set too far behind the 10-foot line and just tried to stroke the ball into play — Tuaniga jumped up alone to block and the ball tooled off of his hands and out of the court. Tui smiled. It was still game point, 23-24, and Micah topspin-jump-served again. The HBC passed it well and Tuaniga set DeFalco on an inside Lob-attack. Evan shuffled too far out and couldn't block; the net was open. DeFalco lifted off the court tile...

and... scrubbed it — right into the middle of the net!

DeFalco grabbed the net. He couldn't believe it. No one in the arena could believe it. Micah changed to serving his jump-float. Ka Ulukoa dug DeFalco's next attack and transitioned out the next two points for the win. After Evan tooled the block to close the set, the Hawaiian boys hugged one another.

Ka Ulukoa held their momentum in set two, going ahead 5-2, and then 8-4.

The HBC tied the score at nine, but it wasn't long before Ka Ulukoa regained a lead of 16-13 and sided-their-way-out to a 25-22 win. Before that, they'd already secured their bid to Junior Olympics. Now exhausted, but happy, they'd achieved a trip to the finals.

First place in the SCVA Invitational was never the overarching goal for the Hawaiians. Although it was a reality more often than not, their true purpose was to achieve that Open Division bid to JOs. Achieving that purpose gave them the opportunity at the real overarching goal — the one they'd apprehended, not only six times, but 100 percent of the time. Six for six they were, like Michael Jordan's Chicago Bulls. Before it was all over, their eyes, and Coach Pono's eyes, locked in on seven.

Back at their homes on the island, Hawaiian cultural traditions brought a bundle of family responsibilities for a team of 12th graders who expected to have their easiest year of academics. The 11th-grade Micah had the most athletic responsibility, returning to Punahou Varsity Basketball immediately, while the others got two weeks off before the start of high school volleyball. Yet, in relation to the 12th graders, Micah, Kainoa, and Kahiau had spare time most often.

On Wednesday night, during the first week in February, Evan felt like he'd found his answer. Irrespective of Guy and Julie's insistence that Evan should pick his school with no concern of its financial burden on them, their son chose the offer with the largest overall scholarship. After the athletic, academic, and financial aid packages were put together, and after taking into consideration that it was in the top five of greatest academic institutions in American antiquity, Evan verbally committed to Stanford University, on 80 percent.

After the long process of telling his parents, and then his brothers, and then calling the staff at Stanford, Evan called his guys.

"Wait, Tui, I'm patching through Micah on a three-way call."

'Click.'

"Hello?" Micah answered.

"Tui. Ficus. MY BOYZ! Wanted to call and tell you guys, I just verbally committed to Stanford."

"Holy crap!" shouted Micah. "So big-time for you, Brah. Congrats!"

"Heck yeah, man." Tui added. "You're going to feel more free now, for sure."

"Oh, for sure," said Evan. "I already do. Yeah, I'm super excited."

"How much — I mean, what did they offer you?" Micah asked coolly.

"Ho, Brah. Tui, you hear his frickin' guy? Chill, Ficus, you'll find out."

Tui and Micah chuckled.

"Anyway," Evan continued, "I'll talk to you Hawaiians later. Gotta go help out my mom with graduation stuff. Oh yeah, you guys are both invited to come to my grad party in June, if you can make it."

"Shoots," said Micah, optimistic that he could attend.

"Shoots, thanks Evan," said Tui.

As Tui hung up the phone, his dad laid his hand on Tui's shoulder.

"Hey Tui, your mom and I are going to take you on a visit to USC. It's an unofficial, at the end of this week. Be ready."

Tui looked at his dad as if he were joking, knowing that his dad knew his college status.

"We aren't going to leave any stones unturned," said Larry Senior, realizing that he hadn't given Tui a lead-up.

Annoyed, Tui said, "I don't want to leave the island again. I was just in Anaheim. Plus, I am already committed to UH."

"You are going anyway!" Auntie Maile cut in.

Tui thought better of arguing, or storming out in a huff. He turned his head back to the kitchen table and stared at the phone until his parents left the room.

On the weekend, the flight schedule from Honolulu to Los Angeles International was open. The three of them left the family behind and took a standby flight to LA. They stayed in the Radisson Hotel, next door to USC's 10,000-seat Galen Center Arena. Tui spent that first day taking the tour of the campus, annoyed and ready for the trip to end. Running into USC Setter, Micah Christenson, and talking story with the hometown Hawaiian was the only reason Tui didn't spend his entire day silent.

Tui came back on the second day with Auntie Maile and Larry Senior to attend the morning practice before USC's match against California Baptist University. Tui was actually taken aback by how many of the USC players he already knew of, from playing against them in club, high school, and youth events. His mood improved and he decided it wouldn't hurt for him to hang out for a little while and talk story with old opponents. In the afternoon, the Tuiletas boarded a plane back to the island. With their son seated in between them, Tui's parents weighed the pros and cons of UH versus USC from the moment everyone sat down. Tui sat back in his chair and pushed his headphones into his ears. Island Jamz were going to tune them out all the way to Honolulu.

While Tui was away, Evan got confirmation that he made the USA Boys' Junior National Team, again. Micah got a notification, as well, in his first season trying out for High Performance. He was offered a position on the USA Boys' Youth National Team for the month of August.

On the Big Island, Evan was excited to have Emmett, Addie, and Avery on the court with him. The twins argued with each other constantly, but Evan was happy to play mediator at practice, as he did at home. Evan played the OH1, and Emmett the OH2. Addie and Avery shared the two Setter and Opposite positions in a 6-2 offense. Each time Addie and Avery dropped the ball in practice and started a wrestling match with one another, Evan would typically burst out in laughter watching his dad try to break them up without his paddle and slippah techniques from home. Emmett got along with Evan much better than the twins got along with one another. Regardless, the four of them on the court together were a good Hawai'i high school team, and it was special for Julie to see. It was special for Guy to see, too. Perhaps no one enjoyed it internally as much as Evan, who knew it may never happen again.

Skylan didn't flow into his first season at Moanalua as enthusiastically as Evan. Actually, he felt rather stiff about his new situation. The upside was that Moanalua wasn't in the ILH, so Skylan didn't have to worry about Tui's area-one attacks miraculously finding their way to Skylan's privates. Moanalua played in the Oahu Interscholastic Association (OIA) league, which meant Skylan set his target on a league title.

Along with Trent and Kainoa, Tui and Micah were expected to dominate the ILH, especially because Punahou Head Coach, Rick Tune, got word of what Micah did in Reno. Now he had himself another Hitter for his squad to set. And dominate, they did. No team in Hawai'i had the firepower or the ball control to keep up with Punahou during the league matches.

Signing day for all NCAA eligible athletes came before the end of the high school season. Most schools put together a ceremony for their signees to put their John Hancock to the dotted line of their National Letters of Intent. Skylan was the first to sign. He sat down between two young ladies in Moanalua's auditorium, with lei flowers from his family draped around his neck. Arlene and Dave stood behind him, and a single tear fell from Arlene's eye as her son finished signing his NLI to GCU and smiled.

Evan was next. At the end of his school day, his family met him in a back room at Kamehameha Hawai'i before volleyball practice. Julie sat down next to her son, whose neck was also covered in traditional Hawaiian lei flowers. Addie and Avery poked at Evan's neck while he read through his NLI for Stanford University.

"Can you hurry up, Evan?" Addie moaned.

"Yeah, don't you know we have places to be?" added Avery.

"Would you two shut up?" Emmett demanded. "That's not helping anything."

Julie paid her youngest boys' antics no attention. It was Evan's moment.

"Your dad and I could not be more proud of you," she reminded him as he pulled his pen from the paper.

"I know," Evan smiled at his dad, and then leaned in for a hug from his mom.

The last of the three to sign was Tui. Punahou had an evening ceremony for its signees. Tui sat down at the University of Hawai'i logoed name plate that read: Larry Tuileta Jr. There was a long list of names called before they made it to Tui. As the list made it near his name in the alphabet, Tui's palms began to sweat. *Deciding this for myself was never difficult, because I have always done things for everyone else,* he thought. *But, explaining this to the public is going to be difficult.*

Coach Pono and Micah were in attendance for Tui, sitting in the back corner of the room. Auntie Maile and Larry Senior stood behind Tui and placed one bright green lei, with purple trimmings, around his neck. Tui realized that he wanted to experience being on his own. He wanted to attend college away from the island. In that moment, he wasn't sure about his decision. Wearing a grey button-up and a grey tie under his lei, Tui stood up as the presenter said his name. His right hand was still under the table.

The presenter announced, "Our next signee is — Punahou, and collegiate, two-sport athlete — Larry Tuileta Junior."

Tui pulled his hand from under the table to expose a red and gold hat with an embroidered SC on it. Tui's move boldly said to the room, he'd de-committed from the University of Hawai'i, and he was signing to attend the University of Southern California as a duel-sport athlete. His extended family burst up from the middle of the room in cheers, sporting USC Athletics gear from head to toe. In that moment, Tui relaxed, sure of his choice.

Evan, Tui, and Skylan felt a weight that had silently pulled on them for months, lift off of their shoulders and disappear. Two weeks later, the Hawai'i high school volleyball leagues ended. Punahou, Kamehameha Hawai'i, and Moanalua each made the Hawai'i High Schools State Tournament. Tui was named the MVP of the Interscholastic League of Honolulu. Evan was awarded the MVP of the Big Island Interscholastic Federation. Capturing the first MVP award of his existence was Skylan Engleman, MVP of the Oahu Interscholastic Association.

Ka Ulukoa was well represented in the Hawai'i State Tournament, and the veterans finished atop the bracket. After losing a five-set match to the Enriques family and Kamehameha Hawai'i, Skylan and Moanalua finished States in third place. Evan, the BIIF MVP, and Tui, the ILH MVP, met in the finals of States for the last time. Tui had Kainoa on his sideline, and Micah and Trent on the court with him. Evan had his three younger brothers on his side of the net. It was the last high school match that either of them would ever play.

After four long sets of volleyball, the match ended and the players slapped hands. The jerseys were soaked. The legs were fatigued. The bond was still strong. Tui and Evan were the last in their lines, walking near the net. They stopped in front of each other and shared a hug that didn't require words along with it. Even after winning his third straight Hawai'i State Championship and the award for Hawai'i State Player of the Year, it was tough for Tui to enjoy it with his teammates. He knew, for him to win, his friend had to lose. Tui didn't say it, but with Evan, he'd never talk about that victory again.

There was only one week until graduation after States. Evan was granted a consolation during his last week of high school on the Big Island. Recognized for his influence on his peers, his abstinence from smoking and drinking, and his high-achieving academic standard, he was given the distinction, as Kamehameha Hawai'i's Male of the Year.

Graduation ceremonies ended across the island. The Ka Ulukoa guys had one last mission before the high school graduates released their minds to college. The players met their coaches at the Ka Ulukoa facility in street clothes. Coach Pono congratulated the 12th graders on completing the greatest accomplishment of their lives. Lee Lamb stopped by to tell the boys' teams that they'd be holding their trainings at Klum Gym until their departure to JOs.

"Are you guys okay with that?" Lee asked, respectfully.

Coach Pono glanced at his guys, as well as Coach Charlie, and then said, "Back to where we began? We wouldn't want it any other way."

Training was focused. No one needed direction. No one needed reminders. The coaches weren't making drastic changes to the system. The guys noticed that Coach Pono mellowed out a bunch in his coaching style at the qualifier. He didn't yell as much. In fact, he didn't yell at all. Whatever he felt the need to say, he said in a mildly toned voice. Coach Charlie gave minor technical adjustments, but most of his time was spent in the trainings showing the guys the three symbols:

He held his hands above his head in a circle when they ran defensive drills — *Big Circle.*

His index fingers and thumbs made the shape of a triangle during partner drills — *The Focus Triangle.*

His hands illustrated a small box shape during competition — *The Precious Present.*

Throughout the training, things were serious. After the training, things were loose.

"Hey, I have an idea," Tui said.

"What? Leave Evan at home when we cruise beach tomorrow?" Micah answered, jokingly.

"You're super funny, Ficus. Sleep with one eye open. Da Kine is coming," Evan jabbed back.

"No, but close," Tui said with a half-smile. "We should wear red jerseys at JOs this year."

"What are you, crazy?" Skylan added in, overhearing from across the gym.

"Yeah, not going to happen," Evan said.

"These guys are scared. I'm down for it, Tui," Micah chimed in bravely.

Tui scratched his ponytail-less scalp.

"On second thought, yeah, we aren't going to do that."

Evan caught the bus with Micah every morning to the beach, so they could practice surfing together. Evan got dropped off at the University of Hawai'i, Manoa in the afternoons to take collegiate-level summer school classes, helping to prepare him for Stanford in the fall. When Evan bailed to UH, Micah called Tui over to the Kaneohe house to talk story and plan pranks on Evan. Micah's time was limited with his guys, so he made sure to ask his mom and dad, in front of Tui, if he could take the trip to Evan's graduation party on the Big Island. With Lisa's blessing, Pono agreed and Evan, Tui, and Micah set off to Evan's home in Punalu'u.

The return trip was quiet. The guys had loads of fun running around Evan's yard and stuffing their faces with enough food to last their bodies a three-month hibernation. But as they sat together on the short plane-flight back to Honolulu, they all realized that their dream of playing together the next season in college wasn't going to come to fruition. It felt like all of these ceremonies and parties and celebrations were preparing them for separation.

Tui picked his head up from the window and said, "Hey, Evan, Micah."

"What's up, Tui?"

"Sup, Tui?"

"Let's make this a good one, yeah?" Tui said, intensely.

Evan and Micah knew what he'd meant. They tightened their lips and nodded to Tui. The three of them touched fists and fell back into their arm rests.

The last time that Pono and Charlie didn't have to leave the boys before Junior Olympics was 14 & Under in Austin. JOs was just two weeks away for the 18 & Under teams who always began the enormous tournament. Coach Pono was thankful to be around. In order to better simulate the tournament format of continuous days, the last six trainings on Oahu were held on Thursday nights, Friday nights, and Saturday mornings.

Considering his team's level of play through early June, Coach Pono decided to conduct scrimmages a week sooner than normal. Thursday's training produced the group of University of Hawai'i starters with a few All-Americans mixed in — the same group that gave the Ka Ulukoa boys lickings over the Christmas holiday break. The younger Ka Ulukoa teams caught a glimpse of the UH players coming into Klum Gym as they were exiting. Intrigued by the arrival of their favorite players to watch during UH matches in the Stan Sheriff Center, the younger teams hung around Klum Gym after their trainings to watch the UH players take on the 18-Mizuno team.

On the last Friday training before JOs, Tui rode over to the Ma'as' house with Micah and Evan.

Sitting on the Ma'as' couch with Micah and Tui, Evan asked excitedly, "Can you believe we finally took a set off those guys?"

"I know! Beating the UH players? That was so sweet," Micah said, equally excitedly.

"We were up and up with them the last couple scrimmages. It was bound to happen eventually," Tui said, proudly. Then he smiled, "But yeah, that was totally sweet!"

Micah's face suddenly turned sad.

"You look like someone killed your dog," Misty said, passing through the kitchen.

"You okay, Ficus?" Evan asked, genuinely.

Micah ignored his sister, and Evan's question.

Instead, he asked, "What do you think we are going to do at our last training on Sunday?"

"Probably the same thing we've done the past six years," Evan said half-sarcastically, unsure why Micah didn't answer his question.

"I don't think it will be that big of a deal," Tui said. "Maybe we will feel it more after JOs is over."

Micah was quiet. He urged his mind to stay in the present, although he couldn't help but think about the coming months. Yes, he was happy for his teammates; they were moving onto bigger places. Micah, however, was going to be facing the same journey, but differently. It was without them.

Sunday training had only the Ka Ulukoa guys and their coaches. Auntie Maile stopped through Klum Gym to confirm backpacks and all their contents. She reminded the guys to bring their Breakfast of Champions additions for her to collect at the airport. The thought of Auntie Maile's cooking brought a smile, accompanied by no words, to her team's faces. Micah wrapped his arms around her first and his teammates followed to drown Auntie Maile in a group hug. Pono and Charlie smiled from a distance.

One last time in Klum Gym, the guys flowed through their training routine. The coaches said nothing. Coach Pono initiated a ball into the drills. Coach Charlie stood back with his arms folded and watched the poetry that was his team managing themselves, focused. The guys each gave a handshake and a hug to one another, and then left Klum Gym. Coach Pono drew a long gaze at the glossy floor of the University of Hawai'i's Klum Gym, where he used to play. He bent down and swiped his finger across it. After picking up his brown clipboard, Pono walked over to Micah, who was waiting at the door, and placed his arm around his son's shoulder.

"Micah."

"Yeah, Dad?"

"Let's go eat."

"Shoots!"

CHAPTER 29 - LAST DANCE

Day one was a breeze for the 3rd-overall-seeded, Ka Ulukoa. All three of their pool-play matches finished in straight set wins. Day two wasn't as smooth. Ka Ulukoa went to three sets twice, with Tampa Bay Lightning 18s and Mountain View Volleyball Club 18s. Yet still, the Hawaiians made it out of their pool, dropping into the 10th seed. Pushed into a Power Pool with Balboa Bay 18s, ranked 2nd overall, and Ultimate 18-Blue (the club's second team), ranked 8th overall, day three was the hot ticket for the families and fans filling the arena. Ka Ulukoa rose to the occasion, impressively beating Balboa Bay in three sets and Ultimate in two. The Hawaiians fled the arena with the 2nd-overall seed and a place in the quarterfinals.

The seeds of the Junior Olympics 18 Open Division Gold Bracket were decided:
1 - Sports Performance Volleyball 18s
2 - Ka Ulukoa 18-Mizuno
3 - Spiral 18-Under Armor
4 - Ultimate 18-Gold
5 - Southern California Volleyball Club 18-QS
6 - Milwaukee Volleyball Club 18s
7 - The HBC 17-Black-Smack
8 - Balboa Bay 18-Asics

The team had a tough road, but they'd made it to the day four Gold Bracket. Everyone, except Coach Charlie, sat eating their bowl of pasta at the dinner table of their house in the forest, resting on the outskirts of Houston, Texas. Half of the room was laughing about the deer they'd seen outside of the house and named *Bambi*, that evening. The other half of the room was laughing about Auntie Maile racing her van down the block to follow a man, who had been obnoxiously honking behind her in the drive-thru window, before catching up to him and getting out of the van to curse him.

"Not one of my finer moments," she laughed along with her guys.
Coach Pono cut through the noise in the room.
"Individual meetings after dinner," he said. "One at a time."

The guys took turns walking into Coach Pono's room, planning to talk about what they wanted to share from the third day. Instead, Coach Pono gave each of his players the same message.

"Have fun and enjoy this last JOs." The meetings were short, that way. Less than 15 minutes had passed and everyone was done.

Evan came from his meeting last and walked down the stairs to Tui sitting on the bed next to Micah, who was flipping his Kendama up and down.

"How'd it go? Fast?" Tui asked.

Evan said, "Yeah, super fast. Er — ugh — why do we have to play The HBC guys first tomorrow? They started as the number one seed."

"Going to have to play them eventually," Tui added, "Might as well be first."

"Yeah. It's stupid they lost their seed and we gotta play them first. But, whatever," Micah said carelessly, staring at his Kendama ball landing on the mallet.

"You gonna wear those pajama pants into the arena tomorrow, Ficus?" Evan asked.

That pulled a chuckle out of Tui, and he looked over at Micah for an answer.

Micah looked at Evan sideways and said, "When have I ever not worn them? Swag!"

Tui and Evan burst into a loud cackling laugh.

"Frickin' rascal, this guy," Tui managed to spill out in between laughs.

The Houston Convention Center was gorgeous. Inside of a well-lit arena was an open space of bright red and shiny white walls. The arena was filled with booths colored red, white, and blue, making it look like an oversized 4th of July party. An escalator near the convention center entrance led to a second story, that was home to an excluded Court 1. The court was designed similarly to the Court 1 in Reno. The outline was bright blue with white lines defining the boundaries. The court tiles took on the look of real beige wood. It was all surrounded by grandstand bleachers, which seated thousands. The Hawaiians hadn't seen it since stopping by the convention center to pick up their tournament passes on their first day in town. Coach Pono took his guys up the escalator at 8:30am to see Court 1, before their 10am match. They stayed a few minutes, taking a long look at the court they hoped and planned to be playing on for the finals that afternoon. One hour away from their match, the time came to go.

The guys cruised down the escalator to Court 3 and took a seat near the waiting Coach Charlie to slip on their shoes. The HBC strode up just behind them, with emotionless gazes on the big electronic scoreboard overhead, which read each club's name and 0-0. The Hawaiians cut their eyes over at The HBC 17s. The Californians' eyes cut back. The sound of whistles that normally held the largest presence at 9am began to sound muffled, as the fans' whispers became loud conversing and the eyes around the arena shifted to Court 3.

Evan and Tui chose to hit true swings in *Quick Hitter Timing*, and honed in at the service line before their team's four minutes was done. The HBC took the second four minutes, and the audience really started to build after the first two, "OOOHHH's," of the crowd immediately after TJ DeFalco's warm-up swings bounced up near the ceiling. Both teams slapped hands and formed their huddles.

The HBC followed routine and took the attention of the gym, screaming repeatedly, "THE – H – B – C! WHAT? THE – H – B – C! WHAT?"

Micah finished his prayer and gave each one of his guys a handshake and a hug. Playoffs were on.

The HBC started receiving in rotation five, with Tuaniga at middle-front and DeFalco at left-front. DeFalco was always either their first server (since he was their best point scorer) or first attacker (so that he could start off with three full rotations in the front row). There was only one new addition to their starting lineup, a blonde-haired, and skinny, 6'5" M2 named Shane Holdaway. To no surprise, Skylan served first for Ka Ulukoa. Evan stood nervously in the back row, more nervous than usual. No, it was anxiety. He felt anxious about being in the last day of his club volleyball career. Either way, the feeling went away soon, after Tuaniga set Kimball the first ball and Kainoa, along with Tui, blocked his Front-1-attack straight down, 1-0.

Tuaniga set Kimball again, and he power-tipped the ball past Kainoa, down to the 10-foot line, 1-1.

The Libero, Blake Diamond, served his jump-float in place for Kimball. Tui passed it well, and Skylan stood straight legged to return the favor, setting Kainoa the Front-1 for a kill, 2-1.

Tui jump-floated and DeFalco approached inside for a Lob-set. The crowd pushed to the edges of their seats for the first highlight-reel swing of the match. He got the set, but Skylan's block slowed it down, enough for Tui to dig it with his hands. Skylan set Micah overhead in the back row. DeFalco swing-blocked and stuffed Micah's D-attack straight down, 2-2.

Neither team pulled in front until the lefty Opposite, Vaught, made two consecutive hitting errors in rotation one, after perfect passes from Diamond, turning the score to 5-3. The HBC gave up one more hitting error in a long rally before siding-out. DeFalco coolly walked back to serve, down 6-4.

Micah received DeFalco's tough topspin-serve on his arms. Skylan set the Go out to Evan, who killed it to the five-box. The Hawaiians found a nice rhythm.

Micah followed DeFalco with his own tough topspin-serve, and it was handled well by Diamond. The OH2, Blake Markland, took a nice swing over the top of Skylan to area-five for a kill, 7-5.

Like in Anaheim, the crowd was unusually quiet for an HBC 17s match. It was like the audience was watching professional tennis. Both teams sided-out so well, because they passed so well, and if they didn't kill the first swing then their defense was good enough to get the ball back in transition.

Ahead 11-8, Tui threw up his topspin-jump-serve. Ben Vaught's 5'7"serving and defensive sub, Jordan Molina, rubbed his hand across his nearly bald buzz-cut and then passed the serve well. Markland crushed the Bic, so hard that Tui shanked it into the crowd. But, Markland stepped on the 10-foot line, back row attack violation, 12-8. Tui missed his next topspin-serve and Tuaniga took over serving.

His laser-like jump-float sped over the net, near Tui's hands. Skylan Go-set Tui's hand-pass out to Evan. Evan cracked it to the one-box — Tuaniga got his chest in front — DeFalco stepped in and Pipe-set Markland — Tui dug — Evan chopped the Go-set — Markland dug it away from the net — Tuaniga Go-set — DeFalco ripped it to the line and got stuffed by Micah and Kainoa, 13-9.

Both teams kept siding-out. Molina subbed in for Vaught and served a standing-float, which Tui passed easily with his hands. Skylan set a flat-footed Front-1 to Kainoa. Molina dug Kainoa's cross-body attack, tight to the net. DeFalco jumped up backwards and flipped the dig behind his head, over the net, for a kill, 19-17. The HBC fans screamed their praises. Ka Ulukoa sided-out.

Tui reverted back to his jump-float-serve. Markland passed it on a dime. DeFalco stepped inside for a Lob-attack and bounced it off the 10-foot line and over the spectators' chairs. The HBC crowd really came alive. Tuaniga served his laser jump-float, again, near Tui. Kainoa approached hard for the Front-1-attack, but Skylan's set drifted high over Kainoa's shoulder. Micah, who The HBC didn't see wrap around on an X-play, popped up behind Kainoa and blasted the ball off the hands of The HBC blockers for a tool, 21-18.

Back and forth they went. Though, with the lead in hand, the

Hawaiians only had to worry about siding-out consistently. Casey Takahashi trotted on to serve. The HBC scored on a Front-1-kill. Coach Pono held the Big Circle above his head.

DeFalco ripped his intimidating topspin-serve, which clipped the tape. Kahiau dove and popped it up near Skylan's hands. Go-set — Evan smoothly tapped it off the block for a kill, 22-19.

Micah fired his topspin-serve. The pass shot out low from Diamond's arms, forcing Tuaniga to bump-set.

"Wait! Wait!" Coach Pono yelled to his blockers.

Markland approached hard and smacked it to area-six. Tui cushioned the hard-driven ball with his platform and took the transition Pipe-set from Skylan. Cross-body swing to the one-box — Tuaniga couldn't control it — kill, 23-19. The HBC's timeout didn't change the outcome. Coach Charlie held up The Focus Triangle for his guys to see. Ka Ulukoa closed the first set with a 25-22 win.

Coach Pono took a knee and spoke quietly as his guys drank from their jugs.

"Good so far. Nice job. Stay patient in transition and trust our defense. That's all from me." He pointed at Coach Charlie, "Anything, Coach?"

With his hands stationed on his hips, Coach Charlie shook his head, no.

Again, The HBC lined up with DeFalco at left-front. Ka Ulukoa started in rotation one. After the sideout, Tui would be the first server. Tui passed Markland's standing-float, too tight to the net for Skylan to touch. Kimball passed the overpass — Tuaniga Go-set to DeFalco — and he killed it cross-court off of Kahiau's arms, 0-1. Tui corrected himself on the next serve and passed it well. Skylan Go-set out to Micah and he chopped it off Tuaniga's arm for the tool.

Tied at 1-1, Kimball's 10-foot line cross-body bounce of Tuaniga's Front-1-set pulled The HBC fans from their seats early.

Diamond served his jump-float. Evan took a high and flat swing on the Go, toward the one-box. The ball hit the hands of the block and sailed deep beyond The HBC end line. Markland turned from area-six to chase it down, and dove to dig the ball back over his head. Transition Go-set to DeFalco — punishing line swing — tool off Micah. At 1-3, Diamond float-served, again. Kahiau took the serve with his platform — Go-set — Evan blocked by Tuaniga and Holdaway — Evan covered himself, but shanked it out of bounds. Kahiau passed the next ball. Skylan wrapped Micah around on the X-play. Micah tipped the ball over

DeFalco, Diamond shot in and dug it up, nicely. Tuaniga flicked it over on two, Dump-kill, 1-5. The HBC bench made their presence felt.

Auntie Maile took a nervous nibble at her nails and yelled out from the crowd, "Get it going, guys!"

Diamond's fourth serve hung in the air a while. Skylan Red-set from the pass, and one-on-one with DeFalco, Micah took a rip at the one-box. Markland stepped in and dug it up. Transition Go-set to DeFalco — he leaned back and smacked it sharp angle — three inches out! Finally, the Hawaiians sided-out, 2-5.

After DeFalco smashed a bump-set-Red down the line for a kill in rotation one, he pulled up his left sleeve, and walked back to serve, ahead 4-8.

Ka Ulukoa held off a serving run from DeFalco with a decent pass by Tui, and a Pipe-kill to complement.

The HBC responded to Evan's jump-float with a decent pass by DeFalco, and a Bic-kill from their superstar, 5-9.

Wellington Afusia subbed in off The HBC bench for Holdaway and happily trotted back to the service line. It was interesting that the two most skilled ball-control teams in the tournament had multiple players serving standing-floats. Afusia popped his over the net and ran into defense. Red-set from Skylan to Micah, who aimed for the five-box and hit the ball out wide, 5-10. Coach Pono stood on the sideline, shocked, but more concerned. He called the earliest timeout of his coaching career. Solutions of what he could say were scarce in his mind. It wasn't the right occasion to stay silent, though.

"Keep passing. Stay aggressive when we get good sets and go to finish. We are okay, right now. Be patient."

Micah passed Afusia's next standing-float, up to the net. Skylan jumped for the tight pass and pulled his hands to let the ball sail over the net. The ball dropped out of the air and fell, on Skylan's side. The HBC laughed and threw their hands in the air for the free point, 5-11. Tui passed the next standing-float, no higher than the bottom of the net. Skylan popped it up for Evan, but too far away from the net to hit. Evan set the ball over, The HBC passed the freeball — Tuaniga Go-set — DeFalco smashed it sharp cross-court for another point. Tui's next pass was better. Skylan brought Micah around on the X-play, over Kainoa's left shoulder, and Micah spatched the ball out deep, 5-13. The HBC crowd was in full throttle. Their bench was chanting, their fans were cheering, and their coaches were shouting.

Afusia served his fifth. A good pass from Tui — Red-set

to Micah — soft-blocked by DeFalco and Holdaway — easy dig for Diamond — transition Front-1 to Holdaway — tool off the block, 5-14. The Hawaiians were sliding deep into a second-set hole. It was like watching quick sand take someone slowly underground, except the look of struggle wasn't present on anyone's face. Evan passed Afusia's sixth serve with his hands, but 10 feet away from the net. Skylan gave Evan the ball back and he connected hard on the Go-set toward the five-box. His swing was soft-blocked, scooped up near the net by DeFalco, who shuffled to his left and whistled for an inside Lob-set from Tuaniga, before bouncing it down the line past Micah's solo-block.

"AAAYYY!" The HBC cheered.

Evan hung out near the net for a moment after the play, curious where the rhythm and comfort had gone. It wasn't until 5-15 that Ka Ulukoa finally sided-out, when Micah passed the standing-float perfectly and then wrapped around to finished the X-play with a clean kill to the one-box.

The HBC stayed ahead up to 14-22. As Preston dropped back to serve his standing-float, Trent Thompson come cruising up the sideline to sub in to block and hit for Skylan. Diamond passed it medium with his hands. Tuaniga flipped a long-way backset to Vaught. Vaught tipped the Red to the top of Tui and Preston's two-person block. All six Ka Ulukoa players stood and watched the soft-block fall to their court, 14-23.

After coming in for Vaught, The HBC scored again on Molina's serve. Ka Ulukoa was struggling to sideout. Molina served his standing-float for the first game point in set two. Kahiau passed it medium — D-set to Micah — DeFalco dug it up from area-six — transition Bic-set — DeFalco crushed it home, wrist-away, to even the match at one set apiece, 14-25 The HBC.

The HBC fans were elated, and screamed approval for their team as the coaching staff held their arms in the air to welcome their giddy players to the sideline. Coach Pono and Coach Charlie were stunned on their sideline. Neither had ever seen their team beat that badly in a set to 25. Though, how much did that matter? They were the champions, and Hawaiian warriors in third sets. Had it been *The Black Death* that was coined by their peers as an appropriate nickname? Regardless, Coach Pono and Coach Charlie didn't say anything unusual.

"Drink and rest. Everybody be ready to pass. Everybody be ready to sideout."

Coach Charlie looked in Skylan's eyes, watching him drink and process how he'd run his offense in the third set. Inside, Coach Charlie Jenkins felt a strong belief that he already knew what was coming.

The HBC was across the net on the opposite sideline, in a huddle, chanting, and swishing their arms like shovels, to and fro. Tui and DeFalco met at the referee stand for the coin flip. DeFalco finished pulling up the left sleeve of his shirt to expose his bicep, his signature uniform adjustment. Just then, Tui was tugging his right sleeve up off of his own bicep. DeFalco won the flip for The HBC and chose for his team to receive. The two star Outside Hitters shook hands and returned to their benches.

After the match I remember sitting in that convention center next to my long time friend, John Xie, in my own moment of silence, and thinking about what those guys had provided for me from a distance. I thought about what they'd given me that day back in January 2011, that they may never even realize had been passed on: years of curiosity; they put me through trial and error. For me, the experience was a time capsule of learning from a group that would not have a duplicate.

It was four years later and I was in Houston, Texas, just hours away from my birthplace. I knew the scene all too well. In a convention center that was heating up, I had the opportunity to watch Ka Ulukoa in their final playoff match. Call it a rivalry match if you would like. It had been a battle of two extremes and it was worth the price of admission that Tuesday in July 2014. That morning had a routine similar to the mornings before it. It had a build similar to the playoff matches before it. One could have only hoped for a result that was similar. The result proved itself to be similar, yet not identical. When it was over, the world did not stop rotating, the sun did not stop shining, but there was a moment of silence for a good match and better group of young men.

Epilogue - Dawn Patrol

That summer, Coach Pono sat with Coach Charlie in the backyard of Kaneohe.

Charlie said, "Did you read what Kahiau left in his yearbook?"

"I haven't seen it," Pono said.

Charlie pulled a sheet of paper from his pocket and straightened his mustache before reading:

Words of Wisdom
*In order to be a great volleyball player you must believe in yourself. Don't compare yourself to others and instead focus on working hard every practice. Make sure that every drill you do in practice you do with a purpose. By doing this, you get good technique down and become more consistent, and that's what volleyball is all about: being consistent. And just realize that making mistakes is a part of the game so you shouldn't get discouraged whenever you make an error. But learning from those mistakes, now that's what makes you a great player. And when you're playing a game, make sure that you focus on your side of the court. Always be ready and expect the ball on each contact regardless of which side of the court the ball is on. Don't get too ahead of yourself, and focus on each contact, one at a time. Look at each contact as an opportunity to get better. Probably the most important lesson that I have learned from volleyball that I want to leave the younger guys with is being **present**. In volleyball, being fully present is key, just like in life. Don't focus on your past or worry about what's going to happen in the future, just allow yourself to fully experience and appreciate the **present**.*
- Kahiau Machado

"That's strong," Pono said. "It's going to be different around here, Coach. No more all-nighters for the guys. No more meetings. No more of Maile's overnight organizing. And HA!" he chuckled, "No more one-thousand-dollar dinner bills for you at Morton's Steakhouse."

Charlie cracked a smile.

"You know Pono, I think there is a strong trust between you and me. I also think we trust each other's strengths and that's always transferred to our athletes. That's very rare and would be hard to duplicate."

"No doubt," Pono nodded, and felt his eyes became moist.

Charlie added, "That trust in each other has strengthened our relationship. Our relationship is family. We are family."

With the precious gift that Coach Charlie Jenkins gave them, Skylan, Tui, and Evan left home on the island for college.

Skylan flew to Phoenix, Arizona to join his best friend, Cullen, as a student-athlete for the Grand Canyon University Lobes.

Tui flew to Los Angeles. The University of Southern California was his new home as a Trojan student-athlete. As he was accustomed, his training as a USC Quarterback began immediately.

Evan flew to Northern California and finally made it to Palo Alto, home of the Stanford Cardinal. He opened the door to his dorm room and grabbed a tack to post a reminder on the wall above his bed. It read: *The More You Give, The More You Get. The More You Get, The Less You Have.*

As the others moved on into the next chapters in their lives, Micah was left with the opportunity to blossom on his own. He spent the summer with the USA Boys' Youth National Team, and then returned to Kaneohe for his senior year of high school. After verbally committing to UCLA, Micah and Pono sat together and made the decision that Micah wouldn't play club volleyball again for Ka Ulukoa and that Pono would discontinue coaching his son. The choice was not easy, though it was best for Micah's volleyball. Instead, he played his 12th-grade season of Punahou Football and Punahou Basketball. As the spring approached, Joe Worsley and Jordan Ewert, two of his teammates from the Youth National Team, invited him to play with their Northern California club team, Pacific Rim 18s. It was a nice idea, but it wasn't going to happen. Punahou Volleyball was around the corner and Pono wasn't willing to allow Micah to play another player's position without having been involved the entire season.

Pono was hesitant, but the Worsley family made the transition too easy to take a pass, after all. Plus, after Huntington Beach High School, with Torey DeFalco and Josh Tuaniga, came to Punahou to win the *Clash of the Titans* Tournament, Micah figured it could be fun to play against his other USA BYNT teammates one more time. He flew into Northern California and spent three weeks living with the Worsley's and practicing with Pac Rim 18s. They met the undefeated HBC 18s in the finals of the Junior Olympics 18 Open Division. Pac Rim beat The HBC in straight sets. Micah Ma'a was named the tournament MVP and the win made him the only player in history to win a Junior Olympic Gold Medal in the Open Division of every age group. Water.

Acknowledgments

I extend a thank you to my editor, Bonnie Kopf, for never leaving an ounce of doubt in making this book a reality. Recognition goes to my #CREW and the everlasting support of my mother, Anita Austin. Thank you to Ashanti Austin (RIP), James Austin, Jim Austin, Andrea Becker, Adam Bromberg, Jodi Cage, Tyler Carlson, Nick Castello, Ayesha Davis, Michelle Diamond, Skylan Engleman, Evan Enriques, Joshua Fisher, Tanya K Hailey, Jim Holdaway, Charlie "The Guru" Jenkins, Kristopher Johnson, Elisa Johnson, Steve Johnson, Trevor Johnson, Joe Kauliakamoa, Debbie Kauliakamoa, David Kniffin, Lee Lamb, Lisa Strand Ma'a, Micah Ma'a, Pono Ma'a, Maddison McKibbin, Alexis McPhee, Cori Mehring, Peter Mehring, Alicia Mitchell, Brock Mitchell, Noah Mitre, Jeff Nygaard, Moreen Oca, Mark "The Body" Presho, Nancy Rapp, Jay Renneker, Robert Rios, Stacy Rust, Dave Shoji, Erik Shoji, Kawika Shoji, John Speraw, Randy Totorp, Larry Tuileta Junior, Maile Tuileta, Geni Walton and many others who contributed to this effort.

GLOSSARY

Terms marked in the text by an *
First page mentioned in ( )

(Ranking System): In volleyball, the ranking system of divisions elevates from unrated or BB, which is the park and recreational level players, to the B and A level players, who have enough experience to serve, pass, set, hit, and dig a well-paced ball. Then come the AA players, who are either just surpassing the level of competitive or right on the cusp of reaching the highest level. And then the ranking system tops out with the AAA or Open level players, who are soon to be professional or recently stepping away from being professional. (Pg. 11)

GLOSSARY OF DRILLS	GLOSSARY OF ATTACKS
Start of Practice Drill:	**Quick Attacks (Middle Blockers):**
- Tennis	Front-1
- Line Footwork	Gap
- Blocking Trips	Back-1
- Base Defense	**Front Row Attacks (Outside Hitters &**
Partner Setting	**Opposites)**
Partner Passing	Go
One-Arm Digging	Red
Freeball Passing	Lob
Shoulders	X-play (X-1, X-2, and X-3)
- Throwing	**Back Row Attacks (Outside Hitters &**
- Strokes	**Opposites)**
One-Contact	Pipe
Three-Man-Pepper	D
Quick Hitter Timing	C
Partner Serving	Bic
Three-on-Three	**Dump Attacks (Setters)**
- Two contact	Dump
- Three contact	Set-over
Primary Passing	
Starting Six Transition	

10-Foot Line: one line on each side of the net, 10 feet from the net, and parallel to the net, which determines a player's back row versus front row eligibility; a back row player stepping on or in front of the line and attacking with his or her hand above the net is a violation. (Pg. 47)

5-1 Offense: a playing style in which there is one Setter for all six rotations, along with an Opposite Hitter, two Outside Hitters, two Middle Blockers, and potentially a Libero. (Pg. 74)

6-2 Offense: a playing style in which there are two Setters, who both set in the back row; both Setters may potentially attack while in the front row (as an Opposite) or have a substitute who comes into the front row to attack for them. There are still two Outside Hitters, two Middle Blockers, and potentially a Libero that go along with this playing style. (Pg. 38)

Antenna: the stick, usually red and white, attached to the net which extends the boundary of the sideline up above the height of the net; the antenna is approximately 10'4" on a 7'4" net and 11 feet high on an 8'0" net. (Pg. 50)

Back-1: a first tempo (quick), front row set to Middle Blockers in the middle of the court, just behind the Setter; it should be set just one or two feet away from the back of the Setter's head, just high enough for the Middle to extend his/her arm (Pg. 238)

Ball Control: the ability of a player to locate the ball where they want to on offense or defense. (Pg. 19)

Bic: a lower, quicker-tempo Pipe, set about seven or eight feet away from the net; intended for the back row Hitter in middle-back area-six (Pg. 257)

Blocking Trips: blocking footwork and blocking moves in the front row for Outside Hitters, Middle Blockers, Opposites, and Setters (Pg. 120)

C: a version of the "D" that is set 10 feet further into the court from the right sideline. See "D" definition; examples: C-set, C-attack. (Pg. 146)

D: a medium tempo, back row set to the Opposite Hitter, on the right side, all the way out to the antenna, set six to seven feet away from the net; intended for the back row Opposite to broad jump from behind the 10-foot-line, attack, and land in front of the 10-foot-line; examples: D-set, D-attack (Pg. 99)

Da Kine: a Pidgin word with multiple meanings; used when referring to a noun that relates to Hawai'i origin (Pg. 54)

Defensive Specialist: a player who substitutes into the back row, usually for a front row player, and plays through the back row with the purpose of improved passing or digging (Pg. 24)

Dig: using a part of the body, usually the forearm platform or hands, and popping a hit up into the air (Pg. 11)

Fifth Set: see "Set" definition.

First Set: see "Set" definition

Float Serve: a type of serve, which is intended to cross the net with no rotation at all; the effect should make the ball knuckle, move, or "float" as it crosses the plane of the net Variations: standing-float-serve, jump-float-serve. (Pg. 62)

Forearm Platform: connecting the arms with straight elbows to create a platform for the ball to contact (Pg. 30)

Fourth Set: see "Set" definition

Freeball: a type of volleyball contact, which is sent over the net with a platform or with an overhand set; a freeball is (mistakenly) commonly regarded as the easiest type of contact to handle receiving (Pg. 22)

Front-1: a first tempo (quick), front row set to Middle Blockers in the middle of the court; it should be set just one or two feet away from the Setter's forehead, just high enough for the Middle to extend his/her arm (Pg. 84)

Gap: a first tempo (quick), front row set to Middle Blockers, about ten feet into the court from the left antenna; this is generally the location where a gap is found between the middle blocker and right side blocker. The Gap should be set quickly to the height of the Middle's arm at full extension. (Pg. 94)

Go: a medium tempo, front row set to Outside Hitters on the left side, all the way out to the antenna (Pg. 67)

GPA (Grade Point Average): a ranking for a student's grades, usually on a 4.0 scale. (Pg. 157)

Grindz: Pidgin slang for food or eating (Pg. 90)

Hard Rubs: a difficult time or a close competition (Pg. 21)

Hitting Lines: a line of players hitting balls over the net while a Setter sets for them; frequently used as a warm up for practice or matches (Pg. 14)

Junior Varsity Team: a mid-level team, a step below the Varsity team, usually comprised of freshman and sophomores (Pg. 16)

Left Pocket: area on the left leg, just below the hip; a term used for where a right-hander's hitting-hand should finish the swing after he/she follows through (Pg. 58)

Lei: Hawaiian flower necklace (Pg. 40)

Libero: a player that wears the opposite color jersey of his or her team, and plays only in the back row positions (Pg. 38)

Lickings: a beating (Pg. 13)

Lob: a medium tempo, front row set to Outside Hitters on the left side, ten feet inside from the left antenna; designed for the Outside Hitter to be able to hit the gap between the opponent's area-two and area-three blockers (Pg. 99)

Mahalo: Hawaiian greeting for thanks and well wishes (Pg. 39)

Middle Blocker: a player the hits and blocks through the front row, and often gets to serve in boys' volleyball; the Libero sometimes substitutes into the back row for the Middle Blocker. (Pg. 10)

Musubi: a grilled piece of spam on top of a block of rice, wrapped in dried seaweed (Pg. 9)

Opposite: a player who plays on the right side of the court; the name comes from playing opposite from the Setter in the rotation. (Pg. 38)

Outside Hitter: a player who is responsible for passing (receiving) the serves, hitting the ball, blocking at the net, serving, and playing defense; they generally play on the left side in the front row and in area-six middle-back in the back row. There are usually two Outside Hitters on one team's half of the court at-a-time (Pg. 21)

Pau: Pidgin slang to say that something, usually an event, is finished (Pg. 38)

Pepper: to dig, set, and spike a volleyball back and forth, along with a partner; usually with feet on the ground (Pg. 5)

Pickle: a term used in baseball, when a player gets caught between two bases and is trying to get on one of the bases before he or she is tagged out (Pg. 13)

Pidgin: traditional Hawaiian language, a slang form of English (Pg. 10)

Pipe: a high set in the center of the court, about seven or eight feet away from the net; intended for the back row hitter in middle-back area-six (Pg. 84)

Point: a single point within a set/game; can be scored by winning the point in serve receive, and can also be scored by winning the point as the serving team (Pg. 11)

Pool Play: a round-robin for teams; usually four, sometimes three or five, teams are ranked in a block (or pool), and each team plays each other. At the end of the pool play, the teams will be reseeded and move into playoffs or a crossover match (Pg. 36)

Primary Passing: a drill when the serve receivers are receiving or passing balls to the Setter; once the drill starts, hitting may be added (Pg. 67)

Quick Attack: a fast tempo, front row hit or swing, contacted by Middle Blockers in the middle of the court; there are variations that are set slightly right or slightly left of center (Pg. 22)

Quick Hitter Timing: an offensive drill where the hitters are lined up in their positions, a coach tosses to the Setter and each hitter gets two chances in a row to attack, with a transition in between. After each hitter has taken his/her two swings, the drill repeats. (Pg. 69)

Rajah: Pidgin slang for roger that, or understanding; okay (Pg. 68)

Rascal: Pidgin slang; on the island, a rascal is someone, usually a kid, who is always finding him or herself in trouble. (Pg. 8)

Red: a medium tempo, front row set to the right side, all the way out to the antenna (Pg. 67)

Roll-Shot: an off-speed swing or attack which is meant to catch the defense off guard and score in a good situation, or keep the ball in play during a bad situation; the attacker will contact the spot behind or underneath the ball and make it topspin softly. (Pg. 171)

Second Set: see "Set" definition

Serve Receivers: also called passers; the players receiving the ball over the net from the server, attempting to pass it to the Setter (Pg. 67)

Serving Specialist: a player who substitutes into position one to serve and play defense

Set (from a Setter): a ball-control action in the middle of a rally; usually the second contact, rarely first contact, in which a player sets up another player to hit. A set is often accomplished with two hands and a ball that has been set should have minimal-to-no spin (Pg. 11)

Set (inside a match): First Set, Second Set, Third Set, Fourth Set, Fifth Set; also known as a game; a set is a first to 25 points (win by two) competition inside of a match. At the club level, two out of three sets must be won to win a match. At the high school, college, or professional level, three out of five sets must be won to win a match. In a best two of three, the third set is played to 15 points — win by two. In a best three of five, the fifth set is played to 15 points — win by two (Pg. 24)

Setter: the player who makes the second touch intending to set the ball to a hitter; somewhat of the quarterback of the volleyball court (Pg. 22)

Shoots: a Pidgin slang word with multiple meanings; it can mean okay, or goodbye, or be a greeting to show pleasure. It is most easily seen as a way to show that the message was received. (Pg. 39)

Sideout or Sided Out: when the team who is in serve receive (receiving the serve) finishes the play and wins the point; the team who sided-out then becomes the serving team and the other team will attempt to Sideout (Pg. 49)

Slippah: a Pidgin slang word for slipper or house shoe (Pg. 8)

Spatch: an uneven hand-contact when hitting or attacking a volleyball; a spatch causes the ball to knuckle with no spin and fly, usually far away. (Pg. 198)

Spike: third contact intended to be returned over the net with downward force; a spike is performed overhead with one arm and hand. Alternate names: hit, crack, crush, whip, snap, smash, bounce, stroke (Pg. 11)

Standing-Float-Serve: see "Float-Serve" definition (Pg. 93)

Starting Six Transition: a practice drill in which the six players expected to start in the tournament finish converting a serve-receive ball for a point, and then convert a transition toss from the coach, immediately after (Pg. 188)

Static Stretch: stretching for extended periods without any active movement in the stretches (Pg. 33)

Third Set: see "Set" definition

Tip: (also called tip-shot) an attack when a player taps the ball, softly, with open fingers over the block, rather than the traditional open-hand spike (Pg. 40)

Tool: (also called a tool-swing) when an attacker hits the ball off of the arms or hands of the blocker and lands out of bounds, resulting in a point scored (Pg. 33)

Topspin-Jump-Serve: a type of serve, usually tossed high and in front of the server, followed by a three- or four-step approach, intended to cross the net with a lot of topspin and dive downward; the topspin-jump-serve is commonly hit much harder than a float-serve. Variations: sidespin-jump-serve (Pg. 93)

Varsity Team: the highest level of team within the high school rankings (Pg. 8)

X-Play: a specialty play, run by the Outside Hitter and Opposite Hitter; all three variations, the X-1, X-2, and X-3 are faster tempo sets, which are meant to be located, set, and hit in the gaps of the opponent's block (Pg. 115)

Yellings: Pidgin slang word meaning to be screamed at or hollered at, loudly (Pg. 9)

KA ULUKOA: the spreading of courage; the growing warrior

Koa Practice   Evan Enriques

possible staff

- Run (laps) → line footwork, tennis, blocktrips, 6-man defense/ Base Defense
- Circle stretch
- setting ⟩ underhand toss to partner, get it on forehead, partner catches
- passing   (5 each); switch
- one hand/arm digging w/ step
- Freeball passing (platform; hands)
- Throwing ⟩ called it "shoulders", drive the ball (never bounce it),
- stroke   finish left pocket; opened up

- One contact — Diggers arms out in ready
              — Hitter down in ready after hit, be ready to set ball dug
              — Set the hitters hitting shoulder
              — Digger strokes the ball back to setter
              — (5 each); switch
- Three – Man – Pepper — setter turn quick to digger after setting ball
                        — set the hitting shoulder
- Quick hitter Timing — Hit two balls
                      — Hit 1;5 box (possibly freeball pass second ball)
                      — Shag the person hitting after you
- Serve w/ partner — Start at 10' line, middle of court, then service line
                   — Focus on hitting ball in the line of your partner
- 3v3 — Two contact / Three contact
- 3v3 /4v4 — Two contact / three contact
- Float serve passing for specific individuals during water break
- Primary's passing — Start w/ just passing
                    — passing w/ middle hitter
                    — passing w/ middle, go, bic, red, D
                    — Freeball coming after serve
- Starting 6 transition out of serve recieve; freeballs

- Scrimmages (on certain days)

Ka Ulukoa Practice Plan
(Written by Evan Enriques at Stanford University)

Ka Ulukoa 12-Mizuno: 2008 USAV 12 Open Junior Olympic Gold Medalists

The Enriques Boys
Pictured (Clockwise from ball): Addie Enriques, Avery Enriques, Guy Enriques, Evan Enriques, Emmett Enriques

Skylan, Dave, Seyj, & Arlene Engleman

Julie & Evan Enriques in
San Fransisco

Pictured (Left to Right): Lisa Strand, Misty, Micah, Pono, Maluhia, & Mehana Ma'a

Ka Ulukoa 14-Mizuno: 2010 USAV 14 Open Junior Olympic Gold Medalists
Pictured (Left to Right)   Front: Noah Hayashida, Kaehu Ka'a'a, Micah Ma'a, Skylan Engleman,
Austin Amian, Evan Enriques, Keenan Meyer   Back: Coach Charlie Jenkins, Larry "Tui" Tuileta,
Coach Pono Ma'a, Adrian Faitalia, Maile Tuileta

Ka Ulukoa 15-Mizuno: 2011 SCVA Invitational 15s First Place
Pictured (Left to Right)   Front: Evan Enriques, Austin Amian, Keenan Meyer, Skylan Engleman
Back: Adrian Faitalia, Noah Hayashida, Micah Ma'a, Larry "Tui" Tuileta

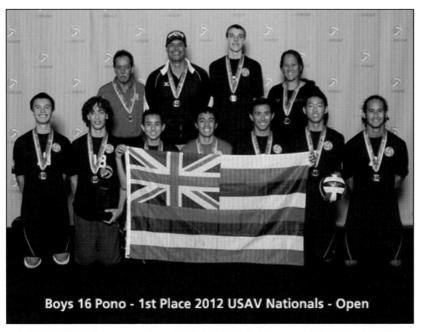

Boys 16 Pono - 1st Place 2012 USAV Nationals - Open

Pictured (Left to Right)   Front: Evan Enriques, Micah Ma'a Austin Amian, Skylan Engleman, Keenan Meyer, Noah Hayashida, Larry "Tui" Tuileta   Back: Coach Charlie Jenkins, Coach Pono Ma'a, Daniel Andrews, Maile Tuileta

Ka Ulukoa 17-Mizuno: 2013 USAV 17 Open Junior Olympic Gold Medalists
Pictured (Left to Right)   Front: Trent Thompson, Skylan Engleman, Casey Takahashi, Kahiau Machado, Kainoa Quindica, Preston Kamada   Back: Maile Tuileta, Micah Ma'a, Coach Pono Ma'a, Larry "Tui" Tuileta, Coach Charlie Jenkins

Evan Enriques passing for the USA Volleyball Boys' Junior National Team

Ka Ulukoa 18-Mizuno versus The HBC 17 Black, 2014 SCVA Invitational Semifinals

Micah Ma'a (Pictured Middle)
2015 USAV 18 Open Junior Olympic Gold Medalist & Tournament MVP
Making him the only player in history to win an Open Division Gold Medal in every age division

With Micah at his home
in Kaneohe, Hawai'i

With Tui at
University of Southern California

With Evan at Stanford University

With Skylan on top of Kamehameha Kapālama

Pictured (Left to Right):
Micah Ma'a, Maile Tuileta, Pono Ma'a, Charlie Jenkins, Skylan Englemen,
& Me (Christopher Austin)

With The Guru & Coach Pono at UCLA